BIG ROAD
BLUES

Mark Hummel

BIG ROAD BLUES

12 BARS on I-80

MOUNTAIN TOP
PUBLISHING LLC

Big Road Blues-12 Bars on I-80
All Rights Reserved.
Copyright © 2012 Mark Hummel
v4.0, r1.4

Mountain Top Publishing LLC

ISBN: 978-0-578-09767-1

PRINTED IN THE UNITED STATES OF AMERICA

Here's what the Blues World is saying about
BIG ROAD BLUES!!!

Mountain Top Publishing presents:
BIG ROAD BLUES-12 BARS ON I-80

"This book ought to be required reading for ANY aspiring blues musician. I LOVED it!"

—Huey Lewis

"Not at bad as I thought it might be. Well written! I think many will enjoy reading it."

—Charlie Musselwhite

"A great read. There haven't been too many books written about the West Coast blues scene and specifically harmonica players so Mark's story helps to fill in the gaps from a personal point of view."

—John Mayall

Like his virtuosic harmonica solos, Mark Hummel's story of travelling the highways and byways of the blues world keeps one thoroughly engaged. Mark's memoirs are a combination of precise hard hitting passages that without warning slide to tales of musical and emotional spontaneous combustion that veer off to places where this bluesman is reminded of the sources of inspiration that pointed him down this winding road in the first place.

BIG ROAD BLUES is a reminder that life really is all about "the journey".

—Peter North
CKUA Radio Network
Edmonton, Canada

Big Road Blues—With the kind of unvarnished approach that the blues demands, Hummel digs down to the core of the music and the no-holds-barred life that has gone along with it—for himself, his peers, and his mentors, alike.

—Derk Richardson
SFGate
San Francisco, California

I want to dedicate this book to my Dad
Edward J. Hummel Jr. (1928-2011)

Publisher's Note

Mark Hummel and the Blues Survivors have played their great brand of harmonica big road blues in hundreds of packed juke joints, clubs, supper clubs, nightclubs, blues festivals, playhouses, auditoriums and amphitheaters. Mark has worked with numerous producers, club owners and festival organizers throughout the USA, Canada and across the globe.

The vast majority of these hardworking folks have conducted their business with the utmost honor, respect for the blues musicians and with a real desire to keep the blues alive.

They share with Mark the love of the music, the appreciation of the great fans and the enjoyment of an exciting world wide blues scene. Some of these stories tell the sidebar tales of life on the big road and the occasional bump or flat tire a touring artist can encounter there.

They are intended for insight and reflection but the stories are not intended to be a comprehensive overview of the blues scene or the business of the blues.

They reflect on but a tiny segment of Mark's experiences in the overall three terrific decades the Blues Survivors have been touring and entertaining his fans.

Mountain Top Publishing 2012
MTPbooks.com

MOUNTAIN TOP
PUBLISHING LLC
PO 5511
San Mateo, CA 94402

Contents

Introduction

I started this book by accident while on a European tour in 2007. I wrote out the chapter just to document all the insanity that was occurring at that moment in time. When I got home Mountain Top Publishing president Charles Putris asked to read it. I forwarded the chapter from the notepad on my Palm phone and the book you're reading now is the result of his vision. My goal was to write down all the lunacy of being on the road for twenty plus years and being able to live to tell the tale. Most folks that write about their musical history are famous-but this is what it's like not to be famous and without the limos, managers, roadies, jets, beautiful models, high powered agents and big record labels. This is kind of a story of starting out over and over again-it's most musician's musical reality instead of the famous one per-centers who make it big. It's a working musician's saga or memoir. It sure doesn't mean we don't still have as good a time playing music as the rock stars do either. They're just more pampered then we are.

Many circumstances in life have changed dramatically since I started music as a teenager. Back when I began many of the Blues icons were still with us, there were record albums instead of tapes or CDs, no internet, no instructional material to learn to play harmonica other than the "On Top of Old Smokey" page that was inserted into Hohner Marine Band harmonica boxes back at the time. It was a very primitive time by comparison. Most other harp players of my generation, and there were very few, would be secretive about sharing information with other players, especially beginners.

The wonderful thing about the old timers in Blues has always been their openness towards younger players and fans. These guys were usually very approachable. I couldn't get the nerve up to approach either Lightnin' Hopkins or Big Mama Thornton though, they looked like they'd tell you where to stick it lickity split. Most of the others were easy to meet-Jimmy Reed, Muddy, Jimmy McCracklin, John Lee Hooker, Pee Wee Crayton, Roy Brown, BB King, Percy Mayfield and many others were just glad to have young white kids interested in the music that many younger African Americans had already turned their backs on by the late sixties. These performers were usually real down home regular Joe's once you got to meet them-completely unpretentious people. I loved that aspect about the musicians. That music as powerful as this could still have such humility in it's creators. I feel lucky to have been around and into Blues at this time in history. So few of these old timers are left now. To have had a chance to both see, hear and meet these icons means the world to me in retrospect. A few are still here: BB King, Jimmy McCracklin, Billy Boy Arnold, Lazy Lester, James Cotton, Matt Murphy, Buddy Guy, Jody Williams, Henry Gray and a few more that we should treasure while they're still here.

One of my other goals in writing this memoir was to document the Bay Area Blues scene in the seventies. Many of the performers I met working the blues clubs were obscure then and forgotten now and I thought writing about some of them was an important thing to do in their memory. Many of the nightspots I wrote about are long gone now, as happens in the entertainment business. It's a bit of a trip down memory lane recalling these long dormant venues and performers. Many first rate artists are never heard of outside of their little neighborhood circumference, due to lack of exposure, recordings, ambition, etc.

The other realization is that the world of van touring for Blues Bands in the United States seems to be quickly vanishing before our eyes. I always assumed if you kept your price down as an act and played good quality music you could tour like this forever. I never thought that gas prices would triple in ten years, that the nightclubs would disappear along with the audience to sustain the venues. You have to be able to work at least five to seven nights a week to tour-this seems to be no longer available to most touring acts. Blues does not seem to be being passed down to a younger audience the way it did in the Blues boom of the eighties, when Stevie Ray Vaughn, The Fabulous Thunderbirds and Robert Cray were being played in regular rotation on FM radio. This turned a new generation on to Blues at the time. Today even the major record labels can barely sustain themselves, let alone the small independent blues labels. Labels could end up being a thing of the past in the near future, thanks to internet file sharing many of the younger folks now enjoy. Bands mostly count on bandstand CD sales to make ends meet while touring nationally-without it there's no way to survive. Van tours in those days had no GPS and no cell phones for venue directions-it was all maps and phone booths.

The drawings in this memoir are done by Franck Goldwasser, my French blues guitar maestro-artist extraordinaire friend from long ago. Goldwasser and I have been friends since he first arrived in the States when he was nineteen. We did a country blues duo together for a while, even recorded some songs in the studio that were never released. Franck also accompanied me on my *Harmonica Party DVD* for Mountain Top Productions. We played acoustically, and some songs are up on Youtube from that DVD. I used Franck's drawings on my *Up & Jumpin LP* and my *Feel Like Rockin'* t-shirts that I sold for years at my gigs. I knew Franck could handle doing these drawings since it was how he started in the blues, drawing and painting his blues idols at art school in Paris. The fact that Franck had worked with many of the folks I talked about in this book helped as well, as he could vividly remember their faces. Franck lived above Eli's Mile High Club when he played in Troyce Key's house band and probably knew the place too well. When Franck recreated my t shirt illustration I asked what photo he copied the drawing from and he said he did it from memory. I was amazed!

I want to thank all the folks that have helped me make a career in music all these years. There are so many I'm probably unintentionally leaving out but I'm trying to stick to the really good tales of the road. I have to thank Charles Putris for putting this out and his contributions to the stories, Lee Hildebrand for the Forward and help in editing and Beth Grigsby for transcribing much of this from tape. I'll probably rile some feathers with these stories but I've changed a major portion of the guilty parties names for the sake of forgiveness. Obviously I don't forget.

Mark Hummel, Aug. 2011

Foreword

It was three o'clock in the morning at the Deluxe Inn Café, a tiny soul-food restaurant and juke joint nestled between warehouses and factories in industrial West Oakland. A quartet led by singer-guitarist Cool Papa played blues in the backroom, which had space for a couple dozen customers to listen and dance on the checkered linoleum floor till four or five a.m. for a cover charge of just a couple bucks.

Mark Hummel and I sat at the counter in the front room as proprietress Liz Johnson prepared our food—fried chicken for Mark, one of Liz's juicy hamburgers for me. The year probably was 1981.

Mark had begun his career as a blues musician in the Bay Area less than a decade earlier, playing with Cool Papa at the Playboy Club, a North Richmond honky tonk then owned by Papa's sister Liz. Now, Mark was leading his own popular local combo, the Blues Survivors. He'd just gotten off a gig and drove to the Deluxe to get a bite to eat, hang out with friends and soak up some of Papa's down-home blues.

"Who's your favorite harmonica player?" Mark asked me.

"Junior Parker," I replied.

"Junior Parker," he responded with an incredulous look on his face. "Why?"

"'Cause he doesn't play much, and when he does, he keeps his solos short, sometimes to just four bars," I answered.

Herman "Little Junior" Parker was a great blues singer—the greatest of them all, in my opinion—but his harmonica playing was only OK, certainly not in the same league as Little Walter, James Cotton, Junior Wells and so many others.

I was being a smart ass. Before the arrival of guys like Mark in the late '60s and early '70s, harmonica had seldom been part of the Oakland blues scene. I was something of an Oakland blues chauvinist, having been a participant in the scene as a journalist and sometimes as a drummer since the late '60s. These interlopers, as I considered them, seemed to want to blow endlessly, taking time away from the vocalists and guitarists who were the core of the Oakland sound. I was especially annoyed by hippies who brought harmonicas to blues shows and blew along from the audience, usually in the wrong key. Mark recently told me that Charlie Musselwhite's way of dealing such nuisances is to walk up to them, snatch the harp out of their mouth and send it sailing.

Soon, however, I began developing respect, indeed fondness, for Mark as an instrumentalist, vocalist, bandleader, and songwriter. I was impressed with "Gotta Make a Change," a politically pointed song he wrote and recorded later in 1981 as a 45 on his Rockinitus label. "They're givin' it to the rich, and then they're takin' it from the poor/Well, they're spendin' all our money, tryin' to start themselves a nuclear war," he sang forcefully over the Blues Survivors' Jimmy Reed-style shuffle backing. Although Mark didn't mention the Gipper by name, the lyrics were clearly aimed at the Republican administration of Ronald Reagan.

I came to realize that Mark, along with such other harp blowers as Rod Piazza in Los Angeles and Rick Estrin of Sacramento's Little Charlie and the Nightcats, had developed a new style of West Coast blues by melding classic Chicago blues of the 1950s with elements of the jump-blues sound Southern California bandleaders Joe Liggins and Roy Milton had popularized in the '40s. I dubbed this new style "California boogie blues," although the name never caught on. Mark's prowess as a singer and especially as a harmonica player continued to grow, and the quality of the musicians he hired for the Blues Survivors seemed to improve with each new edition. The fact that he was bringing such blues legends from out of town as Lowell Fulson, Eddie Taylor, Jimmy Rogers and Billy Boy Arnold to Northern California was most impressive.

I began to fantasize about one day becoming a Blues Survivor myself, if only temporarily, as I had other career obligations. I broached the idea to Mark and in 1999, after passing two auditions, was hired for a ten-day West Coast tour. Mark, guitarist Charles Wheal, bassist Steve Wolf and I traveled in Mark's van all the way from the Monterey Blues Festival to a club at a ski resort in Whistler, British Columbia. The tour ended on the 4th of July at the Waterfront Blues Festival in Portland, where we played for an outdoor audience of thousands.

The tour, thank God and Mark Hummel, came off without any of the mishaps Mark writes about in his memoirs. Although we did have to double up in the rooms—Mark stuck me with Steve, who kept me up long after the gigs ended by trying to stump me with music trivia questions—meals were provided before practically every show. We had no vehicle problems nor did we encounter inclement weather.

Mark sure took good care of his musicians, with both pay and accommodations, and showed special concern for 78-year-old Big Joe Duskin, the Cincinnati boogie-woogie pianist who was a guest artist at many of the shows. He'd had heart surgery shortly before flying in for the tour and suffered from diabetes and other health problems. Joe had Friday night off in Bellingham, Washington, while we did a show there at the Wild Buffalo. Mark phoned Joe's room repeatedly before leaving for the club, but there was never an answer. Neither did Joe respond to loud knocks on his door. Finally, as the motel manager was unlocking the door, Joe opened it and explained that he'd been on his knees praying.

On the long drives between towns, Mark, Charles, and Steve entertained each other and me with frequently hilarious, sometimes heartbreaking stories about incompetent, cheapskate club owners and promoters, crazy customers and the quirks and misadventures of former band members. Now, with the publication of *Big Road Blues*, perhaps the first book ever to chronicle the experiences of a blues band as it travels back and forth via vehicle across the United States, Canada and Europe, readers will be entertained by some of these tales about what it's like to be a survivor on the rocky blues highway.

Lee Hildebrand

CHAPTER ONE

Sitting in a Hotel

Sitting in a nondescript closet-size hotel room in the north of Holland, it's easy to reflect on one's life on the road. Far from whatever glory there is that comes from a life on stage, it's the boredom and tedium that takes up the bulk of your time away from home. It's one day after another of getting up in a strange hotel, having a quick breakfast, if there is time, and then piling into the van for another long drive. Along the way, there's a lunch break, a bathroom stop while fueling up and rushing to the gig in time to do a sound check. Then you rush from the club to find and register at the hotel or motel, grab a quick shower and go back to the club to eat a quick dinner before the show. You play the show and then hopefully have time to sleep a few hours before repeating all these things the next day and the next day and the next day, for as long as the tour lasts.

Truth be told, there are always exceptions to the "typical" day, including bad weather, faulty vehicles, crazy band members, crazy venue owners and crazy audience members. Any of these varia-tions contribute to the myriad of stories that become staples of a traveling musician's life.

As I sat there in Holland reminiscing, I couldn't help but think of a woeful tale that went into shaping an ill-fated 2007 European tour. We started in Italy and did two and a half weeks of fast-paced touring, playing daily gigs of all kinds. There were coffee shops, or cafés as the European's call them, all the way up to concerts with three to four hundred people in attendance. The Italian part of the trip went wonderfully, and we were treated like gold. There is nothing better than a tour in Italy if it goes well, so we were coming off a very positive high. We were pumped up and ready to go for the second part of the European tour.

When we got off the plane in Amsterdam, though, things took a big-time turn for the worse. We met our agent/road manager, Vulture, at the airport. In some cases, a book can be judged by its cover. My lack of confidence in Vulture came with my first sight of the man and was borne out by events that followed. His appearance was that of a silly ostrich in baggy black-leather biker pants. His small head, topped by a crop of orange hair, bobbed on a long, thin neck with a huge Adam's apple. His blue eyes were almost crossed, and his wide, thin body with longish arms gave him a gangly impression when he moved or spoke. At the same time, Vulture could be stubborn and obnoxious, especially about finances. One look at him and I thought his persona screamed, "I want to be in rock 'n' roll, but I don't have a clue how to get there. I guess I'll screw up some blues guy's life while I'm trying to figure it out!"

Vulture drove us to our hotel from the airport. After we sat down to eat breakfast, he informed us that he had purchased our food with his own money and that the cost of the food would come off the top of our pay. There was enough food on the table to feed breakfast to an orchestra for a week. There was nothing to do but eat, since Vulture claimed he had already paid for the breakfast. The guys ate their usual portions, and I figured there would be plenty left over for later in the day, but Vulture had an amazing appetite. He polished off all the food on the table, including the toast and jam.

After Vulture's unpleasant announcement that the food expenses for the tour were on us, we tried to be more careful. The next time we decided to go for pizza, since we were paying, but Vulture said, "No way. I know a good Chinese place. We can eat there." We followed his advice. The Chinese dinner was very good, but Vulture hadn't bothered to ask if we minded him smoking. He lit up and blew smoke in our faces while we ate. My guitarist Rusty Zinn was getting progressively pissed at this lack of manners and asked him to cease and desist, but that didn't stop Vulture. "You mean you guys don't smoke and you're bluesmen?" he said. The bill ended up costing over eighty bucks. The eighty bills was twice the amount I had planned for our meal budget. As Vulture finished off each of the Chinese dishes, leaving nothing for us to take back to the hotel in doggie bags, I drummed my fingers on the table. The guy wasn't quite right. He was eating everything in sight and having us pay, but what could I do? I was stuck with him as the manager for the rest of the tour. I wasn't ready to let a couple of large food bills cause a rupture with the Vulture, at least not yet.

"Man, that was really good," Vulture said as he finished off the last spoonful of fried rice.

The next day, Vulture had his wife do our laundry and fix us a wonderful meal. I was glad I hadn't yelled at him the night before. This was our one good day with Vulture, and I don't want to suggest he was premeditated in his incompetence. He was trying his best as he understood things, but music is a tough business. He'd never booked a tour before, and this was his first venture with music, money, dealing with performers and scheduling gigs. I had made a loose agreement about the money the band was to be paid on Vulture's gigs, but he didn't have any firm numbers for me to work with. We had added this Dutch tour to the tail end of our successful Italian tour, and Vulture could only provide estimates on our earnings for the gigs we were going to play for him. Unfortunately, his estimates changed greatly between our early discussions and our arrival in Holland. He was flying by the seat of his pants. What's worse, in his earlier planning, he had demanded I have my label send three hundred CDs, which was over three times the amount I would normally try to bring with me on a European tour. I could tell from the first gig with Doug Jay and Keith Dunn, our harp guests on the German portion of the tour, that I would be hauling CDs back home in large quantities. On top of that, he stuck my label with the postage for the very expensive shipment of CDs to Europe. He never reimbursed the label, as he had promised he would.

The equipment trailer that Vulture rented was twice as tall as the car that he had pulling it. It had room for a full rock band's gear with props and costumes! Our equipment, suited for a four-piece blues band, only used about one quarter of the floor of the trailer. The jumbo size of the rental would definitely add twice as much to the cost of gas, which he was deducting from our dough, along with our food. I felt like I was losing money every time I looked at the damned trailer.

After the very first gig, I could see Vulture was trying to lower our pay even more, citing extra expenses to be passed on to me that we'd never discussed. I had placed myself in a vulnerable position with him by not being guaranteed upfront an ironclad amount per show. The other harpists had signed for set payments per show that could not be disputed. Vulture was trying to cut my pay so he could pay the other harp men. He was passing their cost on to me, rather than to himself. In Vulture's earlier estimates for the costs to put the tour together, he'd left out important expenses, such as the guest harpists' daily fees and the airfare I'd paid in advance for them. When I discovered the errors and pointed them out, Vulture told me not to worry.

"You'll get your money," he said. "What's wrong? Don't you trust me?"

"Look, man, I'm six thousand miles away from home," I responded. "I don't have a solid contract, and I'm out airfare for two guys that you're supposed to have already reimbursed me for. I've never put myself in such a trusting position before in my life. I need you to start paying for some of these expenses."

"I heard you were a professional complainer," Vulture said in a tone that was meant to cut the conversation. "You have to be flexible on the costs."

"I'm a professional," I said, ignoring his insult. "I don't complain.

I just make sure and get paid, so I don't understand what you mean by 'flexible.'"

"Oh, I know, Mark, you're right," he said as he put his talon—I mean his hand—on my shoulder. "We'll talk about it later when we have all the numbers in front of us. Let's just get through this gig first, and then we'll see where we stand. I'm sure we can work something out. I just don't have all the numbers in my head right now."

This is not good leverage when working on trust with someone you barely know.

After the opening gig, I confronted Vulture again about the discrepancies in the early estimates and the payments I was now seeing. I also explained to him that we would need a dollar guarantee per gig that was closer to the estimates he had given me four or five months prior or else I would have to pull my band. I would just as soon go home if we weren't making any money and so would the guys. The romantic notion of touring Europe, just playing music and getting by, was long gone from my repertoire.

I knew Vulture would freak out and cry about it, but I suspected he would come back with a price I could live with. As I spoke to him, I could see his eyes twirling in his skull, his jaw muscles tensing and steam coming out both ears. I was going to do to him what he had planned to do to me. I had all the leverage in the negotiation. I had the band, and I had the relationships with the guest harpists. I put the shows together for him, got the players and brought the band. I made it clear, and Vulture was finally able to see it, that if he continued his big score for himself mentality, at my expense, the tour was out of the window. I almost felt bad for him, as he had to adjust his hefty promoter profit margins. I let him stew on it a bit. I wanted to be more than fair and wanted him to make some profit, but I couldn't let him cheat me.

Half an hour later, Vulture came back to my room with a lower number than I had demanded. It was, however, a much more acceptable proposition, so I readily took it. I thought we'd finally gotten back to win/win, but was I wrong/wrong.

We had the next day off from any organized gigs, but we had been invited to take part in a jam session in Utrecht. The local blues society had paid for an extra night of rooms for us. After the jam, as Rusty and I walked back to the hotel, we had to listen to Vulture's the drunken meanderings.

"I am a king—a king of the blues!" he shouted at the moon. "They all know in the Netherlands what I can do. They know in the fatherland what Vulture can do. Vulture is king!"

"More like 'King of the Road,'" I said, recalling the old Roger Miller song.

"Careful big fella," Rusty said as Vulture tripped over a cobblestone and almost fell on his face.

On the way to the gig the next day, Vulture's GPS went

completely out. He was hung over from his drinking, and we discovered, despite him having done many Mapquest searches, the poor guy had no sense of direction. He was barely capable of getting out of the parking lot in the proper direction. He didn't seem to know his own country very well. This can turn a ten-day tour into an eternity, which this tour felt like every day. There really is no lost like being lost in Europe!

"Hey, King," Rusty said at one point, as we were driving around and around in circles, "maybe you ought to study your country a little bit, you know, so you can find your way around."

"To your own ass," I said under my breath.

The next couple of gigs went smoothly until we ended up in the far northwest of Germany near the coast. It was a scenic little place, the Fair Café—or Unfair Café, as it became known after the gig. I found out, as we were attempting to check into a slipshod Chinese hotel, that Vulture was not very clear about who was paying for rooms. Was it him or the bar owner? Every time I'd ask, I'd get a different non-answer from Vulture

"Is there a contract for the gig?" I inquired.

"Yes," he said.

"Is there a guarantee?" I asked next.

"No. Well, sort of. Yes, there's a verbal guarantee of sorts," he sort of answered.

"A verbal guarantee of sorts? What the hell is that? "I shouted nervously.

"Well, you see, another visiting blues musician skipped out on the hotel payment after the club owner paid him only $150 for the whole band," Vulture told me.

"You knew the club owner doesn't keep his word, and you set up a gig in his club anyway, without a signed contract for the band?" I responded. "What were you thinking?"

"I'm sure he'll pay us," Vulture said. "I trust the club owner. I just couldn't get him to sign a contract."

I became really nervous.

It was a mid-sized venue with a one-hundred-fifty-person capacity showroom and lots of glass, wood and hanging plants. The room's acoustics sounded good at sound check. That night, the puffed-up club owner and his bossy wife held off on serving our dinner for two hours after sound check. The owner took forever pretending to be setting up the mikes and fussing with the stage. I could tell this pompous German and his Frau were used to giving orders—and used to having them followed. They enjoyed making us wait for our dinner, *essen Essen(s)zeit*. The room began filling up after dinner, and Vulture and I started to relax a little. At that point, Vulture confessed that the owner was not very trustworthy and would not be to sticking to his end of the deal if we didn't have a good turnout. Vulture thought it would all go well if we packed the club. Furthermore, he admitted he only had a loose verbal agreement with the owner about the guarantee of payment for our night's work.

After the gig, we were all thinking everything was hunky-dory. We had packed the place and rocked the house. I heard the bar had done well, and I was feeling OK until a terrified and rattled-looking Vulture came running back to the dressing room and asked for me and Keith Dunn for assistance in getting Herr Club Owner to cough up the Euros.

"Oh shit!" said Keith, an American who lives in Europe and speaks good German. "What will we do? I don't know what to say to the guy."

"You've got to help me, Mark," Vulture whined. "He won't pay us!"

"So now you want a professional complainer?" I said flatly, giving Vulture a sideways glance.

We went to the nasty little German's office to convince him that he needed to stick to the deal and not arbitrarily change the band's payment on a whim. We did our best to explain to him that his verbal word is his word, and that word is what touring acts ultimately rely on from their employers. We explained that trust is very important and all the members of the band were expecting him to keep his word about their pay. I was hoping he would listen to reason, since it is next to impossible to sue someone in Europe from overseas. Our discussion went on for twenty minutes with Vulture proclaiming his side and the club owner proclaiming that Vulture had misunderstood the deal. At one point, the owner said he was also deducting drum-rental money because we used drums that were already on the stage. After that, it seemed Vulture would throttle the guy. It was getting ready to turn into a Euro-physical confrontation. The club owner's spouse threatened to call the police, and he ordered her to do just that, to which band members shouted, "Go ahead. Call the police! We're not leaving until we get all our dough!"

The cops separated us. Two stayed with the owner, and two took us outside. Our two patiently listened to our side of the story, but once we were finished, one officer told us that this was a common problem they had with musicians playing the club. He explained that the club owner made it a practice of underpaying the bands that passed through his club, and unless we had a contract, there wasn't anything we could do. The cop added that even if we had a contract, it was more a matter for the courts than for the cops, so we would be best off to take what we could get and call it a day. The cops warned us they didn't want us to make any trouble either.

"Thanks for your help," I said to the cops.

I knew it was over. The club owner had us by our balls. This was his little game—robbing bands that played his crummy club. We had to take what the German gave us and leave it at that.

Still, the fact that it was hopeless didn't stop the Hummel-inator from going into action. I hiked up my pants, spit in my palms, rubbed them together and went back into the little German's bratwurst-smelling office. I hammered Herr Cheapskate on the drum-rental fee and got it waived. I continued to pound away on the pay and got another hundred out of him. Vulture looked like he was ready to pass out. The club owner's wife fanned herself with a menu as her husband and I went back and forth. Once I knew I had squeezed the last shekel out of him, I let up and left his office. The German was handing Euros to Vulture as I walked out.

"Thanks, Mark!" Vulture called after me.

Before we left the next morning, Vulture knocked on my door. He didn't want to pay for his mistake with the club owner. I knew that his favored option would be to take it out of the hide of the guys who'd flown six thousand miles to play for him and who were dependent on him for their transportation. I didn't want to ruin my whole day with a bitter argument. I told him we'd talk about it when we got to the next town.

As I rode in the car that morning, I enjoyed taking in the sites and smelling the coffee. After all, we were in a beautiful part of Germany with a castle on every ridge. When we got to the next gig's city limits, we stopped for petrol and a restroom break. By that point, nobody wanted to ride with Vulture. He was in a terribly bad mood about the money, driving poorly and getting lost at every exit. Also, he was as square as a pool table and twice as green, as we road warriors say about rookies. In other words, the Vulture was a total drag to be with, and we were all vying to ride with Keith in his Mercedes.

As we hung out at the petrol station, I figured it was as good a place as any to confront Vulture.

"You need to pay us for last night," I told him.

"Yeah, sure," he said. "I'm going to give you everything the club owner gave me, less the expenses for gas and some phone bills for your band."

"I'm sorry, Vulture," I said, "but you're going to have to pay us what we agreed on. That's how it works."

"The owner didn't pay me what he said he would," he insisted, "and I'm going to have to pass that loss on to you. What else can I do?"

"Look, dude," I told him, "you didn't get a contract from the owner. That's on you, not me. You didn't get a firm amount confirmed with him, yet, you promised the band, my players, a firm amount. It's unethical for you to pay us any less. That's how it works. I've had to do it many times. I feel bad, but that's just how it works out sometimes."

"I'm just going to give you what the owner gave me, less some expenses," he stated. "I know you'll understand in time."

"What I understand," I told him firmly, "is that we aren't going to do the show this evening until we get paid in full for last night's gig. I have an obligation to the guys, and I'm not going back on that. You can make your decision and let me know."

I walked away and got into Keith's Mercedes.

I figured Vulture wouldn't pay us, based on the sour look on his face after we finished talking. I thought I'd be forced to pay the band their fair pay because I knew I would not renege on them for their pay. I planned to come out of pocket to make it work for them because I told them I would. When you make an agreement on the road, you have to stick to it, otherwise nobody can trust anybody and it all goes to hell.

To my surprise, Vulture paid me in full at our next stop.

"Let's forget about last night and finish off the tour with a bang," Vulture said, but that sour face was staring at me. He was not happy.

Our next two gigs were quite fun despite the long drives, last-minute meals and the excruciating sound checks as we tried to get it right for our European audiences.

After the second-to-last gig of the tour, on a Friday night, Vulture pulled down the street in the van, away from the club and had to be reminded by the guys that he'd left the trailer full of musical gear and amps back at the club. It was a complete first for me. I'd never seen anybody do that before.

On the drive to the last gig, Vulture got lost for twenty-five minutes. When we finally arrived at the club, we had only thirty minutes left before show time. We had to run to take the stage just as we were being announced.

The morning after that last gig, I wanted to leave on a friendly note.

"You're still here," I told Vulture. "You made it. You survived the tour!"

"Goodbye and good luck," he replied curtly and walked away.

Isn't it funny, I thought to myself, the way things work out on the road? The only thing he did on the whole tour that really made him a standup guy was paying what he said he would pay on the UnFair Café, the thing that he was most pissed about.

On the European tour, we made some friends, saw some old buddies like Doug and Keith and played the hell out of some great Italian, Dutch and German venues. The time had come to make our way Paris. We almost left one of our suitcases at the railroad station in Holland. It was the one that was filled with all the CDs I did not sell on the tour. The last vestige of Vulture's mistake-ridden tour was the suitcase of CDs I had to lug with me back to the States.

Marty Dodson, our drummer, also left his stick bag in Vulture's trailer. Vulture had already dumped us off at the train station and was long gone, on his way back home. Marty's didn't know he left the stick bag behind. Suddenly, realizing it was gone, he set about looking for it at the station. We became so completely preoccupied with trying to retrace our footsteps all over the station that we almost missed our train. Keith had to pry the doors of the train open and throw the last suitcase, the one with my unsold CDs, on the train.

Marty later found out his drumsticks were still in Vulture's van. It was a relief of sorts. Vulture was notified and gave the bag to Doug Jay for safekeeping. Marty had to pay two-hundred fifty dollars, in American cash money, to have Doug overnight the bag to Paris for our gig there. It would have been cheaper for Marty to have just bought new sticks and a bag for them. At least he didn't get an antique snare drum stolen like Jim Overton had in an Amsterdam railroad station at the end of a European tour sixteen years earlier.

CHAPTER TWO

How I Got into the Blues

Traveling must be in my blood because my beginnings were
in New Haven, Connecticut, but we moved to Los Angeles
when I was one year old after my parents, Ed and Joann got
their first church appointment in California. My father was a
Methodist minister in a section of Los Angeles called Aliso
Village, a predominantly black project. The apartments were in
square cinderblock buildings with clothes lines strung alongside
the lawns out front. With just the three of us it must not have
been not too crowded in the small apartment, but I'm sure many
families in the projects lived in more crowded circumstances.
My parents became very involved with the civil rights movement
from its inception. I found out recently that my father almost
went to the sit-ins at lunch counters down south but decided
against it because of his growing family. When I was four we
moved to a house on Fresno Street right off Whittier Boulevard
in East L.A., a Hispanic community. I was always in the minor-
ity wherever I lived, went to school and attended church. I had
a somewhat unusual upbringing, but when you're a child, you
don't focus on those kinds of things. I never noticed what color
my skin was or what somebody else's was. We were all just kids.
Everyone else was an adult.

My two younger brothers, Kirk and Peter and I had either
African-American or Hispanic babysitters watching us at night
when our parents went out. The babysitters loved to play R&B and
soul music on the radio. Later on, we had a stocky young babysitter
with a blond bee-hive hairdo and layered mascara named Stella.

She had a little turntable in her car, and she'd play Motown and soul records on the record player and car radio. Stevie Wonder, the Supremes, Wilson Pickett, Smokey and the Miracles, The Midnighters, Sam the Sham and the Pharaohs, Marvin Gaye, Curtis Mayfield and the Impressions and Little Anthony were just a few of the sounds I'd hear in her souped-up Ford Fairlane. The first blues songs I ever heard, even though I wasn't aware they were was blues at the time, were Jimmy Reed's "Honest I Do" and Slim Harpo's "Baby Scratch My Back." I figured that they were part of the same black music genre I had been listening to in Stella's car. I was probably about nine or ten years old. I didn't differentiate between blues and R&B in my thinking yet. To me, it was all part of the black music that was being played around me.

I was in high school when I became more aware of blues and really got into it. The psychedelic rock bands I was listening to as a teenager were playing blues music, and I was gravitating towards it. I didn't know why at the time, but bands like Big Brother and the Holding Company, Cream, Jimi Hendrix, Blue Cheer and the Doors were all playing blues songs, and they were rocking them up. Those songs were the ones that grabbed me the most, even though I hadn't figured out why just yet. Maybe it was my youthful attempt to drive my parents from my room.

In 1968, at age thirteen, I persuaded my mother to let me go to a giant rock festival at the Rose Bowl. She let me go only because our young babysitter, Sarah, wanted to go and said she would have me back at ten that night. The show started at noon and went till one a.m., so I missed the act I most wanted to see, Big Brother and the Holding Company with Janis Joplin. The festival lineup was mind-boggling: Country Joe and the Fish, Mothers of Invention, Buddy Guy and Junior Wells, Albert King, the Byrds, Joan Baez, Buffy St. Marie and others I'm sure I've forgotten. The cover charge was only three dollars, but the Bowl was half empty due to poor promotion. Years later, both my friend Country Joe McDonald and his guitarist Barry Melton told me they didn't get paid for the gig. Joe almost started a riot. The police thought he was encouraging the hippies to run around the field rather than stay in their seats; they chased everyone back up to the stands. I remember Buddy and Junior were very slick dressers in sharkskin suits, and my little hippie mind couldn't deal with the horns they had or Junior's James Brown-like dance moves. It sure wasn't psychedelic blues, but, in retrospect, they were probably killer. I missed Albert King and Janis because the show ran so late.

I kept seeing Willie Dixon's name as the writer on many songs I liked, such as "Backdoor Man," Led Zeppelin's version of "I Can't Quit You" and "Spoonful" by Cream. I'd see Chester Burnett's (aka Howlin' Wolf) name on a Jimi Hendrix cover of "Killin' Floor" or the name McKinley Morganfield (aka Muddy Waters) on Cream's recording of "Rollin' and Tumblin'" and wonder who those authors might be? At that time, like many others who were gravitating to this music, I didn't put the two and two together of where the blues music was coming from. It wasn't until I started playing the harmonica, trying to copy licks by Jack Bruce on harmonica with Cream or John Mayall that I began to figure it out. I bought a Willie Dixon album, *I Am the Blues,* because it had several of the same songs I had been listening to on the Cream and John Mayall albums. Big Walter Horton was playing harp on it, and Willie was singing.

I borrowed a Sonny Terry-Brownie McGhee album titled *The Story of the Blues* from high school buddy Pat Murray. Sonny Terry was a blind harmonica player who worked with guitarist Brownie McGhee. They started playing together when they first met as young men, and they performed, usually as an acoustic duo, from the early 1940s through the 1970s. When I saw Brownie and Sonny at the Ash Grove in 1972, the place was packed for two weeks running.

Ash Grove was a funky, homey folk-blues coffeehouse with couches for seating that Ed Pearl started in the late 1950s on Melrose Avenue in L.A., near Hollywood. Many famous traveling blues performers from the Deep South and Chicago played there. At the time I first saw Sonny and Brownie, they were still getting along. Eventually, they started bickering on stage and it got to the point where they got along so badly that they stopped working together. They were in their prime in the '50s and '60s when they were so connected with each other's styles that they sounded like a full band when they played. Who would have guessed on that day in 1972, when I went to see Brownie and Sonny at Ash Grove, that later in life I would become Brownie McGhee's harmonica player and partner on many gigs and several recordings?

Another early blues influence was the John Brim/Elmore James album *Whose Muddy Shoes*. Little Walter played harmonica on it with Brim. I tried to learn all the Little Walter harmonica riffs off that album. I attempted to get his variety of sounds with my one harmonica, not knowing that he was using several differently keyed harmonicas to get them. I didn't know yet that harmonicas come in a variety of keys and that harmonica players switch harmonicas and keys to get different sounds. I learned such harmonica lessons very slowly in those days because nobody was talking about the diatonic or chromatic harmonica and how to play blues on them, especially about Little Walter, who was part of the tradition of blues players who didn't reveal their secret techniques. The kind of detailed instruction we have today about blues harmonica didn't exist back then. No David Barrett, Bluesharmonica.com or Harmonica Party DVDs back then to show musicians the ropes. It was all hidden tricks of the trade shared only among a few pros.

Something about the amplification of cheap diatonic harmonicas through equally cheap amps and old radio mic's formed a distorted sound that made it similar to a saxophone on steroids. The sound of Chicago amplified harmonica was my new siren song, and I thirsted for it as much as getting high on drugs and alcohol. Looking back I can see how black blues from Chicago spoke to me in a way rock music did not. Feeling like an outsider at school and home, I thought I could relate to the older blues singer's call of "I'm a stranger here in your town" and many of the other old tunes about alienation. I never felt like I fit in with the social set, the jocks, cholos, brainiacs or any of the accepted students. The only group I somewhat fit in with were the druggie-hippie types.

I remember the very first time I got new harmonicas for myself. My best friend Mike Anaradian, who I'd known since sixth grade and always got into trouble with, went into a music store, picked a few out of the harmonica case and left without paying. I kept those first harmonicas for years. I also got a chromatic harmonica from Mike, and later I traded it for a Green Bullet microphone. Thus began my lifelong interest in blues harmonica mic's, the kind the old masters were playing through.

There were a few people in my high school fooling around with harmonica then. Most of the kids in those days were more serious about the guitar. There were several good longhaired dope-smoking guitar players in high school who were friends: Mike Albert and Bobby Robles still play guitar but are doing different types of music now. Back then, though, they were really into the blues. The Delgado Brothers, a group of talented siblings, were another band that came out of my high school. They went on to record for HighTone Records and still play to this day. My classmates Bob Robles and Bobby Delgado had a blues band together with a real good harmonica player named Mike Butore. Mike took me under his wing and turned me on to several different blues records and players. That's how we learned in those days—from each other.

Mike had an incredible record collection. He turned me on to some really obscure guys at the time, like the harmonica player Kid Thomas, who Mike used to go see in L.A. Kid died a tragic death at age thirty-six. He had accidentally run over a kid and, after being found not guilty, was murdered by the grieving father following the trial. Mike learned everything he could about Little Walter and Sonny Boy and taught himself how to play like them. He helped me figure out which records to buy, who to listen to and stuff like that. I also checked out records from a public library down the street that had all kinds of LPs. I remember borrowing a *Best of the Blues* record that had Little Walter doing "Juke" and Muddy Waters doing "Got My Mojo Working" from the Newport Jazz Festival. Man, was I hooked when I heard "Juke." It really sounded like something I wanted to be able to play, and I couldn't stop playing it over and over!

My guitar-playing friend Carlos De La Paz and I used to hitch-hike up to Pasadena to hang out at J and F Records while I was in high school. John Harmer and Frank Scott, two English gents, owned the store, which was almost entirely devoted to blues re-cords. John turned me on to many of the blues classics on Chess and other labels that became my bibles for studying the genre. I was even able to acquire a couple reel-to-reel tapes of Little Walter outtakes from John that didn't come out on CD until 2009. I also met Big Al Blake and Fred Kaplan of the Hollywood Fats Band at the store. John was the first guy to tell me about Kim Wilson when he was known Goleta Slim in Santa Barbara. "He plays a splendid version of Walter's 'Roller Coaster,'" John said of Wilson.

Another high school friend of mine, Mark Dawson, gave me my first harmonica lessons in trade for a six-pack of beer. He taught me to how bend and warble notes, do hand wah-wahs, vibrato and many other harp secrets. I'll always be indebted to Mark for that. He ended up playing in Hoyt Axton's band, was Hoyt's constant sidekick on stage for many years and learned the art of songwriting from him.

Mark lent me James Cotton's *Pure Cotton*, which became pivotal in my blues harmonica development. On that album I first heard "The Creeper," Cotton's instrumental masterpiece. Knocked out by that tune, I went to see Cotton play at the Ash Grove. I introduced myself to him. He was really friendly to me, even though I was kind of a dumb, punk kid at the time.

Learning to play was now the most important facet of my life. I was completely given over to it and would eat, sleep and drink blues. I would record myself on reel-to-reel tape as I practiced along to records, so I could tell if I was approximating the licks correctly. I would play along with Little Walter's LPs, slowing them down from 33 rpm to 16 rpm to fully hear the licks that seemed over my head. I would repeat this method until I had the solos down. I wore out my copies of Walter's *Hate to See You Go* and *Confessin' the Blues* till they were nothing but scratched shellac. I own them to this day. Most nights I would play those records with the spindle up so they played over and over; that way, the next morning the sounds were thoroughly absorbed in my teenage brain.

I was in blues-rock bands my last two years of high school. I would try to get them to do more blues stuff when I played with them. Back in those days, a harp player often was considered a pain to be around, and many musicians would barely tolerate me. Luckily, enough of them did tolerate me so that I was able to stay on my path. I vividly remember not being able to sleep the nights before a high school concert and, later on, a show in the local park band shell with a couple different bands.

Before I graduated from high school at seventeen, I'd hitchhike up to Northern California quite a bit to meet other players. I remember meeting and jamming in the early 1970s in Santa Cruz at the Union Bar with Delta blues guitarist Robert Lowery and harp man Virgil Thrasher.

There was enough interest in the Bay Area that folks were aware of Muddy and Cotton, whereas in L.A., those artists had difficulty playing at larger halls. L.A. was always a Top 40 radio city compared to the Bay Area, where early FM rock radio was being pioneered. Back then, the only harmonica players you would hear on the air in L.A. were Lee Oskar of War and Magic Dick of the J. Giels Band. You had to learn their songs if you wanted to play with L.A. musicians. Those were the songs a bandleader would call if you were allowed to jam or play in their band. I learned it all, backwards and forwards. Anything with a harmonica I would learn: Stevie Wonder, John Mayall, Junior Parker, Junior Wells, George

Smith, Charlie McCoy, Lee Oskar, Rod Piazza, Little Walter, Paul Butterfield, Charlie Musselwhite, Magic Dick, Big Walter Horton, Blind Owl Wilson, Sonny Terry, Sonny Boy Williamson and Jimmy Reed. If a record had a harp on it, I'd copy it note for note. I became a student of the harmonica, as well as of the blues.

The more I played the harp, the deeper into blues I got. Eventually, I stopped listening to Butterfield because I found Little Walter's versions of his originals more to my liking. Listening to Mayall, I could tell he got his style from Sonny Boy. I wanted to study the creators of the music, not the imitators. I couldn't see why guitarists would copy Clapton's version of "Hideaway" when they could learn Freddie King's. I became a purist in blues music. If it didn't have harp, I'd barely pay it any mind. If it didn't have slide guitar, who cared about it? If it had horns and organ, it was too modern. I changed my opinion about horns and organ upon witnessing two life-changing concerts by B.B. King and Bobby Bland in the early '70s.

B.B. played a show in 1971 with Canned Heat (right after Blind Owl Wilson died) at the Pasadena Civic when I was still in high school. It was a revelation. When the Heat played, it was nothing but wall-to-wall hippies. When they finished their set, with Sam the Sham sitting in, all the hippies filed out. Older black folks came in and took their seats for B.B.'s show. His band played some warm-up numbers and introduced B.B. The place went nuts. Women were screaming out song titles and yelling, "Do it to me, B." It was complete pandemonium. It was a definite study in contrasts, especially the way B.B. took his time vocally and while soloing on the guitar. The Heat was frenetic in comparison.

Same with Bobby Bland at the Whisky a Go Go in 1973. The audience was mainly African-American and primarily female. Bobby had just put out his California LP on ABC and was doing well. He'd really rev things up with the women when he'd ask in the middle of a slow number, "Can you handle it?" to which the largest black women would holler, "I can handle it, Bobby!" He would taunt them again with, "Are you sure you can handle it?" Then the whole place would erupt with high-pitched females testifying! It was like Beatlemania, without the squeals but with just as much fervor.

Most of the local L.A. blues musicians mainly played venues in South Central or occasional gigs at the Ash Grove, Rick's Blues Bar, Topanga Corral and the Golden Bear in Huntington Beach or jazz rooms such as the Lighthouse in Hermosa Beach. These were clubs where you'd see "Harmonica" Smith, Lowell Fulson, Pee Wee Crayton, Big Joe Turner, Jimmy Witherspoon, Eddie "Cleanhead" Vinson, the Johnny Otis Orchestra, Joe Houston, Roy Brown, Joe Liggins, Roy Milton and T-Bone Walker. Luckily I got to see most of these SoCal performers at different venues over the years, but my teenage heart was with the Chicago blues stars.

I saw a blues show at the Whisky that drew more of a hippie crowd. I'd been waiting to see these guys since discovering the music. Chicago guitarist and vocalist Jimmy Rogers and his former boss Muddy Waters did a double bill, each with his own band. I was disappointed that Rogers didn't have a harp man. The only band member I recognized in Jimmy's band was drummer Hubcap Robinson. Muddy had Mojo Buford on harp, along with Sammy Lawhorn and Pee Wee Madison on guitars, Pinetop Perkins on piano, Willie "Big Eyes" Smith on drums and Fuzz Jones on bass. I didn't meet Muddy, Pinetop, Willie or Fuzz till a few years later in the Bay Area. This was an eye-opener for me, the first of many to come.

CHAPTER THREE

Beginnings: Teen Years, 1970-74

While still in high school I started out hitchhiking with my friend Dory Collier to New Orleans for Mardi Gras. We got into a heated argument in Arizona about something, and I ended up hitchhiking the rest of the way by myself. I hung out in New Orleans for about two weeks, meeting up again with Dory shortly after I arrived. I jammed there with a somewhat legendary guy named Babe Stovall. An old wino by that time, Babe had learned to play guitar from blues icon Tommy Johnson and other old-timers. I followed him around and played with him in the park where he hung out, as well as in clubs. He was a bad drunk and would pee in his pants while sitting on a park bench. He was in rough shape, but he could still play the guitar and sing. He did all these old songs like "Big Road Blues" and "Canned Heat Blues" that he had learned from directly from Johnson, which I found to be very deep. I'd travelled to the Big Easy with forty bucks in my pocket, with five to cover my way back to California. I lived on red beans and rice for a dollar a plate and stayed in a youth hostel, really just a hallway in a house, with folks sleeping on the floor, couples sometimes doing it in sleeping bags next to me. During Mardi Gras, the cops accosted hippies regularly and were throwing them in jail for merely sitting on the sidewalk.

After high school, I traveled to Buffalo and Chicago. I hitchhiked part of the way and then took a bus part of the way, switching off, depending on the amount of money I had or didn't have. I stayed outside of Buffalo with a friend I knew from high school named Mike Johnson and his friends, just relaxing by the lake since I'd just gotten out of school. A girlfriend of mine turned me on to some friends of hers in Chicago, and I stayed at their house. At the time, too scared to go on my own to the Southside or the Westside, I stayed in their apartment and didn't get to really see Chicago or hear much music. I ended up calling Bob Riedy, a piano player in Chicago who worked with old-timers like Jimmy Rogers and Carey Bell, and asked him about gigs I could go to. He gave me a long list. I was rather wet behind the ears at the time and afraid to take the El to places I didn't know. I did go to Ann Arbor, Michigan, and sat in at the Blind Pig with Boogie Woogie Red, one of the old Detroit musicians who had worked with John Lee Hooker. He played real heavy left-handed, Big Maceo-style piano. I sat in with him, and he told me, "Yeah, you kind of remind me of a boy named John Nicholas." I assumed he was referring to my sound or my love for real blues, since we bore no resemblance otherwise. Nicholas is a multi-instrumentalist who lived in Ann Arbor and Boston and has been in Texas now for many years.

I went to Boston next and found a club in Cambridge Square, the name of which I don't recall. Former Muddy Waters guitarist Luther "Snake" Johnson held the gig the night I showed up. Snake was a rough-looking character with scars on his face from where a woman had burned him with acid. He had moved to Boston and was playing with guitarist Bob Margolin sitting in and a harmonica player named Chris Stovall Brown, who let me sit in. John Nicholas came in the club with a woman on each arm and looked like a big star. I tried to get around and jam at other clubs in the Boston area, but it was hard to meet people. Like Chicago and Ann Arbor, where blues had some clout, everything was cliquish in Boston.

I gravitated back to the Bay Area because I loved the weather and I really liked that women said hello to you on the street without knowing you. I had saved enough money in Los Angeles by working different jobs and staying at my parents' house. I got jobs through Manpower, built smoke alarms and in a mattress factory. I ended up saving about nineteen dollars and moved up to Berkeley in my little VW Bug. I met a girl named Jan Patterson and moved into her house on Ashby Avenue. Through her I met Mike Lorenz, and we used to jam on the street. There was also a conga drummer named Willie King who used to be the driver for Muddy Waters back in the '50s. That impressed me no end. Willie would tell me stories from his days with Muddy, like how he would pretend he was Muddy while sitting in Mud's new Cadillac with the band name on the side to score points with female fans.

With the Fillmore Auditorium and the Carousel and Avalon ballrooms, plus other places where promoters like Bill Graham brought in all kinds of touring blues people, blues had a home in the Bay Area. When I was first living in Berkeley, a place in San Francisco called the Green Earth Café booked many blues folks on local and national levels. Muddy often played at Keystone Berkeley. There was quite a bit of blues in comparison to Los Angeles, where there were really only a couple blues venues. North Beach in San Francisco had the Coffee Gallery, Mooney's Irish Pub and a few other joints featuring blues. Later, Keystone Palo Alto, the Catalyst in Santa Cruz and Inn Of The Beginning in Cotati were presenting a good deal of blues. Another club that's still around, after closing and reopening, is Rancho Nacasio in Marin County, which used to bring in Son Seals, James Cotton and others. That made it a lot more appealing to me than living in Los Angeles, where blues was so dismissed and the atmosphere not near as conducive.

The Bay Area blues scene that featured local musicians was still on a very underground level and relegated to small bars. Nationally known bluesmen who lived in the Bay Area at the time included Charlie Musselwhite, Elvin Bishop, Nick Gravenites, Luther Tucker and Mike Bloomfield, all Chicago transplants. John Lee Hooker had moved to the Bay from Detroit and would play sometimes at the Savoy Tivoli in San Francisco, where I later saw Jimmy Reed a couple days before he died in 1976.

I ended up playing in the black clubs, because there were more of them in which to play. I wasn't famous enough to get up on stage at the Fillmore. I couldn't even get on the bandstand at the Green Earth Café till 1976. I could go to the ghetto clubs and sit in with guys there, and that's how I started playing with blues musicians at Eli's Mile High Club in Oakland and the Playboy Club in North Richmond. There were other funky blues clubs where I'd play. Minnie Lou's in North Richmond was right next to the old Club Savoy, where Jimmy McCracklin had played and immortalized the club's name in song. The Savoy was a legendary place, but by the time I played there, it had different name. Ruthie's Inn in Berkeley was a famous club where I saw Bobby Bland, with Wayne Bennett on guitar, and a few different people over the years. I was in the house band there for a minute.

When I first got to Berkeley, Mike Lorenz and I tried to get into the Berkeley Blues Festival, which was held on the U.C. campus. It had an incredible lineup that included Bukka White, Big Mama Thornton, Clifton Chenier and George Smith. It sold out. We tried sneaking in but weren't successful. I later heard several hundred hippies had managed to sneak in.

I would perform on the street for tips, with Mike on guitar. We used to play a soup kitchen right across from the Café Med for tips and a cup of soup. I'd jam with the conga players in the drum circle on the Berkeley campus. I'd sit in anywhere I could. I was checking out the blues bars and seeking out the musicians to jam with. It was new, exciting and a big deal to me. It's rewarding when years later there'll be an occasional person who will come up and say they remember me from those early days and used to jam with me. It's amazing to have folks still remember me from way back then.

CHAPTER FOUR

Old Blues Dudes

Cool Papa was the first blues guy I worked with in the Bay Area. Papa, an older, friendly, balding African American gentleman with a fun sense of humor, expressive eyes behind big glasses, plus an engaging smile, played guitar, sang and wrote incredible songs. His real name was Haskell Sadler. He was originally from Denver but came to the Bay Area in the fifties. I found out about Papa through multi-instrumentalist Ron Thompson.

I met Ron sitting at the foot of Sproul Plaza on the U.C. Berkeley campus, playing the hell out of an old National Dobro guitar. His playing grabbed my attention, as I hadn't heard anyone around at his level yet.

I got my nerve up and walked up to him and said, "Hey, man, do you ever let anybody jam?"

"What cha got, man?" he asked.

"I got a harmonica," I answered.

"Yeah, man, go ahead, man. Key of E," he responded.

After we started playing together, he asked if I knew "Rollercoaster." I tried to play it.

We became pals, and I asked him about the local blues scene.

"Where would be a good place to go to jam?" I inquired.

"There's a cool place, man, in Richmond called the Playboy Club, man," he said. "Check it out. A dude named Cool Papa runs a jam session out there"

When I got back home, I called directory assistance and asked, "Do you have a listing for Hugh Hefner's Playboy Club in Richmond?"

"We have no listing, sir," the operator answered.

"Well, do you have just the Playboy Club?" I then asked.

"Oh, yes, we have the Playboy Club," she responded.

It turned out it to be just a neighborhood bar in the ghetto. It definitely wasn't Hugh Hefner's Playboy Club. I drove out to the club in my little VW bug. It happened to be in an unincorporated, rather rural part of Richmond. Some people had chickens, goats and pigs in their yards.

The Playboy Club was a little roadhouse-type place and definitely a blues room. It had crumbling old concrete walls outside and very simple furnishings inside—just a few old tables and chairs. No doubt about it. It felt like being in the middle of Louisiana or something, and people were friendly and down home. I may have been the only pale face in there besides the bass player. Cool Papa was playing, and a guy named Charles Houff was doing the singing. I waited till the break and went up to the bass player and asked, "Do you guys ever let anybody sit in?"

"Just talk to Cool Papa," he said.

I asked Papa, leader of the house band at the Sunday night jam session, if I could sit in. He said sure and asked what harps I had.

"What are you doing next week?" he asked when I finished playing. "My harmonica player's going on vacation. You sounded really good. I'll hire you for the next five weeks."

I jumped on the gig, which happened every Friday, Saturday and Sunday, temporarily filling in for Dr. Blues, a full-time medical student who played harmonica part-time. Papa told me he'd pay me forty or fifty bucks for three nights a week. After playing with him five weeks, we stayed in touch. Years later he eventually had both legs amputated due to diabetes, which finally killed him. Papa had an unusual guitar style, kind of a cross between Pee Wee Crayton and Lightnin' Hopkins. Either humor or pathos filled his songwriting, depending on what the tune called for. He was a wonderful guy and always cool to his musicians. I remember him telling me about some of the now-famous people who used to play with him in the sixties, like Boz Scaggs, Steve Miller and Tracy Nelson.

I knew Charles Houff—a great blues singer, real friendly guy and kind of a tragic figure—from the same period, until he passed away. When one of his kids was murdered, he kept it to himself when he came by the club that night. Nothing but skin and bones, he put every fiber of his being into his vocals. Charles hollered the blues, in an interesting style that was sort of a mix of Howlin' Wolf meeting Little Johnny Taylor. Sonny Lane told me that Wolf once caught Charlie's act and wanted to take him to Chicago.

Bass player Reggie Scanlon (later of the popular New Orleans band, the Radiators) and I played in Texas guitarist and vocalist Sonny Rhodes' band at the Playboy Club for about two weeks. A handsome middle-aged man who usually wore a turban ALA Chuck Willis, Sonny had long sideburns and a balding pate when he left the turban home. The money was never what Sonny said it would be, which resulted in our short stay. He would come up to us at the end of the gig and say, "It's only five dollars tonight, but next week I can guarantee it's gonna be at least twenty."

I remember playing at the Playboy Club with Sonny when he got so drunk he passed out on the lap steel guitar L.C. Robinson had willed to him, right in the middle of a song. The drummer poked him with a drumstick, and Sonny came right back in on the beat and finished his solo.

I also did a gig with Sonny at the Savoy Tivoli in San Francisco. When I arrived, I realized I had left my harmonicas all the way back in Berkeley. I had to drive across the bridge to get them and showed up an hour late for the gig.

Once, I ran into Sonny at a Jimmy Dawkins gig at the Green Earth Café in San Francisco. Sonny showed up to intimidate the Chicago bluesman.

"I came to tell Jimmy Dawkins he's got no business coming to Sonny Rhodes' town and taking Sonny Rhodes' gigs," he told me. "I'm gonna go tell him right now."

Sonny went up to Dawkins and said, "What do you think you're doing coming to my town and taking all my gigs? I don't come to Chicago and steal your gigs. What you coming to San Francisco and taking Sonny Rhodes' gigs for? That's some fucked-up shit. You'd better play somethin' serious tonight."

When Dawkins came on after Sonny gave him his spiel, he looked visibly nervous, seemed kind of shaken and never really recovered the whole night while Sonny stared him down from the crowd. It was classic Sonny.

Sonny would make some amazing statements, like the time he phoned me and said, "Mark Hummel, a promoter from France told me he's gonna start a blues festival. He gonna hire nothing but white blues bands. Gonna leave them black blues musicians at home. He gonna have Little Charlie and the Nightcats, Ron Thompson and the Resistors, Mark Hummel and the Blues Survivors, Rod Piazza and the Mighty Flyers." Sonny went on to name about fifty other white blues bands. Sonny interrupted the promoter and said," Hold up. You fixing to FUCK UP and leave the BAD MOTHERFUCKER AT HOME! Sonny Rhodes is supposed to be over there!"Unfortunately, it's become somewhat prophetic in the blues world.

One time, when I ran into Sonny at the San Francisco Blues Festival, he told me, "Mark Hummel, you one of the biggest assholes I know. I'm telling you this because Sonny Rhodes an asshole. Sonny Rhodes such a big asshole that he can pick out another asshole when he see him. That's why I know you an asshole, 'cause Sonny Rhodes a big asshole. So asshole to asshole, I'm gonna tell you, you all right."

Sonny has always been quite the character. I last saw him over in Luxembourg at a festival we did for Tano Ro. When we saw each other, he flipped me two birds. I flipped him right back, and we had a good old time. He's one of the all-time greats in my book.

Sonny had his own Rhodes-Way label for a while, and I played on a record by Robert Kelton on which Lex Silva, Gary Hines and I backed him up. Kelton had written a song that Junior Parker recorded called "Man or Mouse." He played guitar on many of blues legend Jimmy McCracklin's early sides. By the time I recorded with Kelton, he had gotten up there in years. I also did a record with Johnny Waters on that label.

Playing a New Year's gig with Sonny at the Playboy Club could be quite an experience. Instead of popping champagne corks, people would fire their guns outside in back of the club. I thought at first that firecrackers were exploding, but the owner, Liz Johnson, told me, "No, they're firing off their guns out back, honey."

One time, while we were on break at the Playboy, a guy held a knife to another fellow's throat and threatened to cut him. Time froze completely, like you just knew it was going to go one way or the other within a second or two. I watched Liz talk him out of it.

Liz later owned the Deluxe Inn Café in West Oakland. I remember her evicting Gary Hines' girlfriend, Ruby, a black woman about ten years older than Gary, a white guy and the drummer in the Blues Survivors. She used to get into barroom brawls with him on a regular basis. If we were playing a gig, many times she would start dancing with some guy in the audience. They'd start grinding on each other as Gary would get so worked up he'd jump out from behind the drums and start to tussle with either her or the guy she was dancing with.

One time we were playing a gig at Eli's where Johnny Waters stopped in the middle of a song because Gary had gotten into a fistfight after jumping out from behind the drums. He rolled around on the floor with this guy, and they rolled right onto stage during the song Johnny was trying to sing, all thanks to Ruby dancing with the guy to make Gary jealous.

"Hold it. Hold it. Hold it!" Johnny demanded after stopping the song. "You guys are going to quit that fighting so I can finish this goddamn song. Stop it, now!"

They looked up at him at the same time, kind of embarrassed, as if they didn't realize what they had gotten themselves into. Johnny launched back into the song. What a comical scene!

One time Gary had bought a new truck and pulled it up to the front of the club. While we were inside playing, Ruby got mad at Gary, took a full bottle of beer, walked outside and threw the bottle, smashing out the entire windshield of the truck.

"Ruby, you get outta here and don't you come back!" Liz demanded.

After Ruby left, Gary came out and looked at his brand-new truck with the windshield gone. A look of complete and utter shock crossed his face as he saw what his beloved girlfriend had accomplished.

Another time, we were at a party at harpman Dave Earl's house. He had a new recording studio in his garage and a new control booth in the back of the garage. Ruby and Gary got into a fight in the control booth. She took off her high-heeled shoe and beat him over the head with it. I couldn't hear a thing through the plate glass window, but I could see her pummeling the hell out of him with her shoe.

The ballad of Ruby and Gary went on for quite a while.

I first met Lowell Fulson back in those early days. Middle-aged at the time I was introduced to him, Lowell still had a full head of red hair, just as his nickname "Tulsa Red" implied. His smile showed off a big gold tooth, and he knew how to dress to impress, never looking the "Tramp" he sang about in his hit. Lowell was originally from Oklahoma, a half-black freedman on his father's side and Choctaw on his mother's. I first worked with him at Letha's Safari Room in Richmond. Letha, Lowell's cousin, was a shake dancer. Shake dancers did something similar to lap dancing. They would "shake it" for the customers, wiggling their butt cheeks in all kinds of wild, rhythmic movements. Sometimes they'd do the same thing with the band. Letha would shake her ass in front of the band and simulate which of the guys were getting erections by holding up her two fingers indicate how big they were.

Letha hired me to play with Lowell in the late-'70s. At rehearsal the bass player could play all the funky stuff and slaps, but he'd never played an actual shuffle. Lowell had to show him how to walk on the bass. We also had horns in the band. I believe Lowell was a little bit lit by show time, but he still played a good set. The audience really dug into what he was doing. During the break, Lowell told me, "I like your harmonica playing. You sound like a soprano sax." That made my day.

About five years later, around 1981, I started hiring Lowell for several dates in the Bay Area. I booked anywhere from five to ten dates with him each time he came up from L.A., and we did many successful shows, with plenty of press, and good turnouts. I would usually get Earl "Good Rockin'" Brown, the alto sax player who played on several of his recordings on the Swing Time label back in the late 40's and early 50's. He's also on some of Lowell's Checker sides and played in Muddy's band for a tour. Earl was an awesome foil to what Lowell did, playing Louis Jordan-type lines on the alto. We got to be real good at playing behind Lowell. We even did a gig outside at Jack London Square in Oakland with Lowell, Earl and their old Swing Time band mate Lloyd Glenn on piano. The gig sounded killer till Lowell broke a string and never got his guitar back in tune during the set.

I think what Lowell liked about me is that I would book the gigs, and I wouldn't get in his way with my harmonica. One time Kim Wilson came down and wanted to sit in. Lowell said to me, "I haven't played with Kim in a long time. Why don't you just stay up here with me?" Kim was high and badgered me to let him play, and, finally, I did. Then I saw what was happening. Kim played Chicago blues over what Lowell was doing, and Lowell wasn't really a Chicago blues kind of guitar player.

Lowell could play everything from Lightnin' Hopkins-style country blues guitar, which he'd learned from working behind Texas Alexander, to the modern T-Bone Walker-influenced style he would become famous for. In In the 60's, Fulson cut records like "Tramp" with a boogaloo funk beat. He covered all these different genres in the blues, and his guitar playing was funky and great. When I started hiring him in 1981, he played some very fiery, wicked guitar and sang his ass off. I always loved Lowell's voice and his songwriting. Lowell was the George Jones of blues in the sense that his vocal phrasing is uniquely his own. One of the all-time great blues songwriters, Lowell composed such classics as "Reconsider Baby," "Black Nights,"

"Three O'clock Blues," "Honey Hush," "Hung Down Head" and "Tramp." He also recorded "Blue Shadows," "Too Many Drivers" and "Everyday I Have the Blues," songs he didn't write but made major hits out of.

I used to try to get Lowell to do different songs of his that were favorites of mine, and many times he would oblige me with, "Hung Down Head," or the old Tampa Red number "You Don't Know My Mind." I also remember that on one of the earliest gigs I did with him, he requested I do "Juke." He played one of the worst versions of "Juke" I've ever heard on the guitar, but I think he did it just to say, "I like the harmonica stuff, too." I always played more like a horn when with him, and I think he appreciated that. Lowell was one of the greats and was revered by all, from B.B. King to all the Chicago blues musicians.

I played with Brownie McGhee back then too. I got to meet him through my friend Carroll Peery. Carroll was a little guy who looked a bit like a chain-smoking Yoda and talked in a soft voice that drew all the young girls to him. I don't think he often took advantage of all the female attention, which drew them in even more so. Carroll also happened to be one of the most amazing astrologists I've ever met, and I saw him meet people for the first time and guess their birthdates and birth times. I met him back in the late 70's, when he hung out at a place called the Café Mediterranean. It was the most famous coffeehouse on Telegraph Avenue in Berkeley, and everybody hung out there, from Country Joe McDonald to Mario Savio and Patty Hearst. Carroll was always there, and I also would see him at all the blues shows. If I went to a Charlie Musselwhite gig or to see John Lee Hooker, Brownie and Sonny or whomever, he'd be there.

I kept wondering, who is this guy? One day I read an article in the paper about people who had changed vocations, and there was a picture of Carroll with an article about how he had been a booking agent for various blues people like Lightnin' Hopkins, Big Mama Thornton, Brownie and Sonny, Big Joe Williams and the

Chambers Brothers. It went on to describe how Carroll became an astrologer. He worked with handicapped and mentally retarded people, among other things. When I saw that article, I worked up the courage to approach him and say, "Man, what's your story? I heard you used to work with all these blues people." He started telling me all about working at the Ash Grove and the Cabale in Berkeley and how he had met all these different folks there. He later introduced me to some of them, including Brownie McGhee, Barbara Dane, Mose Allison, Taj Mahal, Charlie Musselwhite and John Lee Hooker.

Over time Carroll and I became best friends and started writing songs together. We hung out almost every day at the Café Med. I'd hear all about how he used to book the Chambers Brothers and how he used to hang out with Brownie and Sonny. I learned important insights about songwriting from him. I also learned stuff about being careful what you wish for, because when you get it, you'd better be happy with it. In other words, if you ever get a hit song, it had better be something you like. His most pointed story was about the Chambers Brothers, who had been a gospel and blues group before they wrote, "Time Has Come Today." From then on, they had to do "Time Has Come Today" at every show, even though they really weren't too crazy about the song. If you do have a hit, you better like it, because you will be obligated to do it night after night. That was good advice for me, even if I've never had to worry about having a hit record.

Carroll knew Brownie from L.A. but had talked Brownie into moving to Oakland in the early '70s. One night while visiting my friend Sonny Lane in Oakland, Brownie dropped by. I watched Brownie put away about a fifth of Johnny Walker Scotch whiskey and still be coherent. He was a feisty guy, and a little scary if you didn't know him. He had very strong opinions, and he could be taken for a racist if you didn't know him well. Brownie would speak his mind in a heartbeat. At the time I met him, he and Sonny Terry were on the outs and breaking up as a duo.

Sonny and Brownie had not been getting along for a long time, and Carroll convinced Brownie that I could get him some work as a solo artist. I booked gigs for him with the Blues Survivors backing him up. It was an experience getting to know and work with Brownie. Brownie could be a heavy drinker but was very professional at the same time. He would never mess up a show due to his drinking, although he'd sometimes get a little sloppy.

Brownie had polio when he was a child, and as a result, one shoe had a thicker heel than the other and he walked with a marked limp. Brownie had been quite handsome in his youth, had many girlfriends and held an air of confidence about himself, despite the limp. A masterful entertainer, he could talk to an audience better than anybody I think I've ever worked with. Sonny Lane always said, "Brownie could have been a politician 'cause he can talk so pretty!" Brownie would tell stories while he was playing guitar. He also played fine blues piano and said he played left hand for Big Maceo after the pianist's stroke. Brownie played both acoustic and electric guitars. Tim Kaihatsu, a guitar player who played with Charlie Musselwhite and Robert Cray , told me that Brownie reminded him of Louis Myers when he was playing electric guitar. He had that urban-country blues approach on the guitar.

My favorite gigs with Brownie were when we performed as a duo. I wouldn't try to play like Sonny at all. I would play more in the Chicago blues, John Lee Williamson or Big Walter style when working with Brownie, and I think he appreciated that. Brownie and Sonny toured on the American Folk Blues Festival with Little Walter in the mid-'60s. Brownie talked crap about Sonny Terry. So did Walter, according to Brownie. I think in his heart he really loved Sonny's playing, but when I would ask him about it, he would always dis him and say things like, "Sonny couldn't play!" I'd ask him, "What are you talking about? Sure he could." When Sonny passed away in 1986, it hit Brownie hard. After Sonny died, Brownie talked a lot more reverently about him and his playing. Sonny and Brownie were such a powerful duo when they were in their prime, but before their breakup they were more like Neil Simon's *Sunshine Boys*. They were one of the top acts in blues and folk and appeared in movies like *The Jerk.* Brownie appeared in both *Angel Heart* and *Face in the Crowd.* Sonny Lane told me that Muddy Waters said he hated to follow Brownie and Sonny onstage because those two guys could make so much sound and were so revered by audiences.

I spent time at Brownie's house, and he had scrapbooks of places he'd played all over the world, for royal families in England, India and different parts of Africa. He'd played in nearly every country imaginable and did several State Department tours. He also played with just about every musician, in every different format—jazz, folk, blues and rock.

When Sonny and Brownie did their A&M album, they had many famous musicians on it, from John Mayall to Randy Newman. Brownie had wanted to hire a band to tour behind that record, but Sonny refused to change to a band format for reasons either monetary or musical. This split in ideas lead to their demise as a partnership.

I was lucky enough to get Brownie to play on my first Flying Fish CD, on a song I wrote called "Learned My Lesson (Changed My Ways)" about my getting sober. He backed me up on vocals and guitar. I had quit drinking about six months before he did. It was amazing to me that Brownie sobered up and quit drinking that late in life, because he was probably in his seventies when he quit.

I helped get Brownie a recording for Pat Ford's Blue Rock'it label. I played with guitarist Robben Ford, pianist Clay Cotton, bassist Steve Ehrmann and different musicians behind Brownie on the album, titled *Facts Of Life*. I'm still thrilled that Brownie honored me by recording two of my songs, "Let Me Go," and "Ease My Mind," which were somewhat patterned after songs he had written many years before.

Back in the early 80's, I opened a show for guitarist Albert King at a club in San Rafael. Albert being a huge guy with a very intimidating presence, it never crossed my mind to introduce myself, or talk to him. After our opening set, I went backstage, and Albert grabbed my hand and said, "Man, you the harmonica player. You blowin' your ass off, man. You playin' my kind of blues." That made my night! My guitar player at the time was Pat Chase, and Albert wouldn't even shake his hand or speak to him, though he was a lefty like Albert. It didn't stop Pat from trying to start a conversation though. Albert was intimidating to guitar players. He was mean to the sound man as well and balled him out that night. I'm glad he was pleased with me. Albert King was one hell of a guitar player. At the San Francisco Blues Festival, I remember standing three feet away from the back of his amp and his tone was just one of the hairiest guitar sounds I've ever heard anybody get out of an amplifier, like a redwood in a forest of spruces.

I got to know Dave Myers in Chicago in the early nineties. I first met him when I went to B.L.U.E.S. and sat in with Sunnyland Slim and Steve Freund in 1989. I met Dave again through Rusty Zinn, who had become really good friends with him. We would all get together and go eat at Veloy's in Hyde Park, a place where all the old blues guys hung out. Billy Boy Arnold would eat there, and I met Jimmy Lee Robinson there. Rusty and I would usually call Dave every time we'd come to town and get together at Veloy's. Dave played in the Aces when they backed Little Walter. He played both guitar and bass with that band, and his brother Louis played lead guitar. I was lucky enough to get Dave to play on my *Heart of Chicago* CD a few years later, along with Willie "Big Eyes" Smith, Bob Stroger, Billy Flynn and Barrelhouse Chuck. Dave was a wonderful guy and told great stories. He could really mangle the English language when he wanted to, like talking about Robert Junior Lockwood being a really "extinguished" gentleman or saying, "I de-swear I wouldn't lie." Dave played guitar in the early '90s like Jimmy Rogers played in the 50's. His stuff sounded beautiful. I stayed in touch with Dave every time we'd play Chicago. He'd usually come to the gig and hang out or sit in. I stayed in touch even after Dave's legs were amputated due to diabetes until he passed in September 2001. It seemed odd not to see Dave at the clubs when he took sick and died. He was such a presence on the scene. It was a heartbreaking way to go, as it is for many of the older bluesmen who didn't have the kind of resources or savings more known musicians sometimes had.

I met Dave's brother, guitarist Louis Myers, in 1990 and went to his house with my former guitarist Curtis Smith. I was shocked to see Louis living in such a dangerous part of South Side Chicago, with ten or fifteen locks on his apartment door. Louis was very good to us, gracious as can be, showing us a snapshot of himself and B.B. King from the '50s on his mantel. It was depressing to see someone with the recording history this man had just barely eking out a living. Louis was in his late fifties by then and had already had a stroke. He came down to our gig that night and sat in, playing some fabulous harmonica for the audience. Louis learned harp from Little Walter when he was playing behind him in the '50s and could emulate his sound closer than anyone.

I met Charles Brown in the eighties when he was living in Berkeley. He was one of the most famous singing piano players of the 1940s, along with Nat King Cole. Charles greatly influenced Ray Charles, Otis Spann, Eddie Boyd, Willie Mabon, Floyd Dixon, Mose Allison, Dr. John and just about every other piano player worth his salt in rhythm and blues.

Charles had lived briefly in Berkeley in the mid-'40s before moving to Los Angeles. When he moved back in the eighties, he didn't have much work. Few people even knew he was still alive. He'd been wasting away in L.A., not working very much. I heard from somebody that he was back in the Bay Area. I was doing a blues series in San Francisco and called him and offered him a gig. Charles said, "If you could learn my songs, I'd be glad to try to do something with you. I'll give you a tape of some of my songs, and maybe you guys can learn them and we'll go ahead and do the gig and see how it comes out." We worked on some of his material and rehearsed with him. The gig came off well. Charles had a good time and so did we. Gradually, his name got back out there a little more.

At one point in the early eighties, my friend Scott Tolmie was getting married and asked me about hiring pianist Katie Webster, who had been living in Oakland. I said, "I don't think she lives around here anymore. She moved back to Louisiana, but Charles Brown lives here. Maybe Charles will do it." I called Charles and told him about it, and he put together a trio with a bass player and guitar player and played my friend's wedding. I had gotten him some halfway decent money for the gig, and he was very thankful. He told me, "If there's ever anything I can do for you, any recordings, anything like that, I'd love to do them." So I invited him to do some recording with me in about 1987. He came in and did two beautiful numbers with me: an instrumental version of "Summertime" on which he overdubbed his piano part, and "When I'm Not with You," a duet by just me and him. He wrote that one, and I used it later in the early nineties on my first Flying Fish album.

Charles also played on my *Low Down to Uptown* CD, right before he died. He did a version of "In a Sentimental Mood," and we also recorded "Angel Eyes" and "Tenderly." After the session I payed him in cash, and he had me drop him off in his wheelchair at the racetrack, where everyone there knew him by name. Charles practically lived at the track. I played him the mixes at a nursing home when he was on his deathbed. His saxophonist Clifford Soloman was saying his last goodbyes to Charles when I arrived. It was very sad, but Charles seemed very pleased with the songs. I ended up using only "Sentimental Mood" on the CD. I introduced my daughter to him when she was a baby. He had several great stories about his friend Amos Milburn and other celebrities of the day. He'd had a "Hollywood wedding" with the glamorous singer Mabel Scott, who he described as the "Diana Ross of the 1940s." He used to say, "I was the Michael Jackson of the 1940s." Charles was a superstar back then, and, lucky for us, he had a second successful career.

I met Eddie Boyd in the early 80's on a trip to Helsinki, Finland. A deejay brought me to Eddie's house, and I hung out for a couple hours. Eddie was a very intelligent guy and had a bevy of good stories about his early days in Chicago. Eddie told about the time in the early '60s, after returning to Chicago from a tour of Europe, he saw Otis Spann standing in from of a club, pulled over, rolled down his window, said hello and told the pianist he'd be right back after he parked his car. After returning from parking, Eddie approached an extremely inebriated Spann, who said, "Man, I ain't seen you in three months, since you left for Europe," not remembering he has just spoken to Eddie moments before he parked his car. Eddie called the English blues guitarist Peter Green a "white man with a black man's soul." He was bitter about the way Leonard and Phil Chess had handled his career and about the workings of the recording industry. I figure he moved to Helsinki because he felt like he got a lot more respect in Europe than he did in the United States. The second time I went to Finland, I spent the afternoon at Eddie's, just talking with him and listening to him tell great stories about his experiences with Leonard Chess (whom he despised) and Little Walter playing with Robert Jr. Lockwood (he loved Lockwood, hated Walter). Dave Myers told me a few years later that Walter's band had given Eddie a run for his money on a southern tour in the '50s, which may have figured heavily on his opinion of Walter.

I also met Muddy Waters and the guys in his band. Because I lived right around the corner from where they stayed whenever they came to town, the Flamingo Motel in Berkeley, I would go over and just hang out with them and catch a ride to the gig with them. That way I could get into the gig without having to pay. One of the coolest things I ever saw was at a show they played at the Old Waldorf in San Francisco. The club owner was glad-handing Muddy, and Muddy just kind of let it roll right off of him. The owner and staff would tell him how great he was, and Muddy would say, "Thank you very much. Thank you very much," and walk right by them and on into the dressing room. Muddy knew he was regal talent.

I would be back in the dressing room sometimes, hanging out with them. I drank up all of Muddy's Courvoisier once. It was embarrassing, because he looked over at me and said, "Where all my Courvoisier?" He saw I was really drunk and went, "Oh," but he let it roll off his back. Worse yet, Musselwhite, who opened for Muddy that night, said to me, "I can always tell when you're drunk 'cause you slur your words." Charlie was such a serious drunk at that time that it really worried me to hear him say those words. By the end of the night Muddy gave us a ride home after Willie "Big Eyes" Smith got pissed at Muddy for giving him backseat driving instructions. Willie hopped out of the van before we even left the parking garage, and Muddy ended up driving. I had wondered if Willie was going to show up the next day, but he did. Muddy was especially deferential to Willie that night because Willie was playing his ass off.

"This boy been back here for twenty years giving me a hard time, but he sure is playing tonight," Muddy said.

When Johnny Waters asked Muddy at the Flamingo Motel about using his last name, Muddy just said, "As long as you give me my copyright on songs, I'm fine with that."

I met Gatemouth Brown when I was playing with the Sue Foley Band back in the 80's. He came to our gig at Blues Harbor in Atlanta two nights in a row, and we hung out with him. We asked him about different bluesmen he'd known, and he put all of them down—T-Bone, B.B., Albert and Freddie King, none of them could play, according to Gate. When I asked him about Snooks Eaglin, who was his Louisiana neighbor, Gate just said, "I heard of the boy." Snooks was the only guitarist he didn't put down.

Gate gave Sue a hard time about wearing blue jeans on stage. "Girl, you gonna have a hard enough time in this industry, being a girl," he said. "You'd better start dressing up on stage." Sue took his advice and she did.

In 2004, the first time I had Willie Smith on one of my blow-outs as a drummer, he also did a few songs on harmonica. He played drums behind just about everybody on the show, including Carey Bell and Lazy Lester. I started having some run-ins with John Cephus at one point on that gig. I found out later that it was mainly due to a big misunderstanding, but at the time it seemed like he was just giving me grief. He started drinking while we were playing in Santa Cruz. He apparently couldn't hold his liquor and got in my face right after Carey had played. Steve Freund was playing on the show with Carey, and Cephus said, "Why you got that white boy on the guitar?"

"Because they know each other from Chicago," I said, adding, "What business is it of yours? It's not your gig."

"He was up there messing it all up," Cephus responded.

I went up to Carey and asked, "Did you feel like he was messing you up?"

"No, he's fine," Carey answered. "I've known Steve forever, man. Steve did fine."

I took Cephus' aside and asked, "Why are you giving me so much shit?"

"I don't need your shit," he responded.

"You know what?" I told him. "You can go home tomorrow. I'll take you to the airport right now if you're going to continue giving me grief like that."

"You think you some kind of white king or something, don't you?" Cephus retorted. "You think you the white slave master."

"You know, I've had just about enough out of you," I countered. "I'm going to take you to the airport tomorrow."

"Them boys is ripping me off for my CD money," he suddenly charged.

I took him back to the hotel at the end of the gig. Later that night, I talked to Willie Smith, and he ran down exactly what had happened. Apparently, there had been a misunderstanding about the money that Cephus wanted for his CDs and what the guys who were selling them were charging. Cephus thought they were selling them for more than they were giving him. I knew the people who were selling the CDs and that they were honest and weren't trying to rip anybody off. There had been a definite misunderstanding. Then Willie told me that he had seen something go down where one guy had taken a twenty and given Cephus fifteen dollars for a CD. When I heard that, I knew that that's where the misunderstanding came from.

After that, I tossed and turned, unable to sleep. I also found out later that Cephus wasn't supposed to drink because of his diabetes and that when he drank he got kind of crazy. The next morning I went by his room and told him that Willie had explained to me what had happened and that I hadn't known about it the night before. I told him, "I'm sorry for raising my voice to you." Cephus apologized to me, too. We shook hands and did the rest of the gigs together and everything was all right, but it had been a bad scene. I really appreciated the fact that Willie took me aside and explained exactly what had happened. I have Willie Smith's big eyes to thank for that. Willie is the greatest, period!

CHAPTER FIVE
Boogie Jake

I met Boogie Jake in about 1975. I was really interested in playing with him because he was harp icon Little Walter's cousin. His real name was Matthew Jacobs, and he was originally from Marksville, Louisiana. He recorded a song called "My Starter Won't Start This Morning" and several others in 1959 and '60.

By 1975, Jake was living in Berkeley. I was playing with Reggie Scanlon. Reggie had played several gigs with Professor Longhair and is currently the Radiators' bass player. He was older than me and a little more hip. He also played with Boogie Bill Webb, Snooks Eaglin and James Booker in New Orleans, his hometown.

Reggie had been around quite a few of the older bluesmen and knew the life. I had been with my girlfriend Houston for a year or two when I met him. She had put me through all kinds of paces. One time I did a nine p.m. to two a.m. gig at the Playboy Club in Richmond and then a two to six in the morning gig. Reggie was playing bass, Jerry Robinson was playing drums and Ron Thompson was on guitar. While we were in the middle of a song at three a.m., a guy came in with a sawed-off shotgun and threatened some woman. Midway through my solo, I turned around and saw Jerry hiding behind his drums and Ron Thompson throwing his guitar up in the air and running out the door. I heard Jerry say, "Get down, Mark," so I dove behind my speaker cabinet. Everyone was hiding under chairs and tables. The cops showed up, but the guy with the shotgun had gone.

That night, I got stopped by the cops on my way home. They said, "We don't see too many white faces around here at six in the morning in North Richmond. We just want to know what the hell you're doing around here." I said I'd just finished playing a gig.

I told Houston I was coming over after the gig, but when I got to her house, the door was locked. I rang the doorbell, and she didn't answer. Normally, she would leave the key in the mailbox. I went around back and looked in the window. There were two bodies in her bed, and I could see both her feet and a guy's feet sticking out. I was tempted to open the window and just urinate all over their feet, which were right up by the window. Instead, I huffed off and drove back home in my car. About a half hour later, she called and said, "You were here, weren't you?" I answered, "Yes, I was." I think we broke up for a day or two or maybe a week. In sixteen years, we broke up about two hundred times.

Reggie used to give me relationship advice in his Brooklyn-sounding New Orleans accent, "You're taking it too seriously. Don't take it so seriously. It's no big deal, you know. People do it all the time. She does it. Why don't you do it?" After a while I started taking his advice seriously. She'd mess around; I'd mess around on her. She'd get jealous of me. We'd go back and forth. We were a very volatile couple at the time. Reggie was at least giving me a little bit of counseling on not taking it so seriously and just letting it go.

I eventually located Boogie Jake. Reggie, Jerry, a guitar player from Louisiana named Eddie Ray and I went over to Jake's house and rehearsed with him. He sang and played "Early Morning Blues," "My Starter Won't Start This Morning" and other songs he had recorded. He did a few Little Walter numbers, like "Last Night" and "Blues with a Feeling," and he also would try to do B.B. King tunes and stuff he thought was a little more hip, although he was basically a country blues artist who electrified his guitar.

Jake could really play in that Lightnin' Hopkins style or Lightnin' Slim style of guitar. He excelled at that and that type of singing, but when he would try to do B.B. King, he would get completely lost and it usually would result in a fiasco. I knew it was going to be just a solid mess, but he could handle the more down-home stuff.

We started doing some shows with Jake and even did a 45 on the Blues Connoisseur label with "Automobile Blues" on one side and "Boogie Train" on the other. I remember being on a great show that San Francisco Blues Festival organizer Tom Mazzolini put together, probably the first and only really big show that we did with that group. We even had our picture in *Living Blues* magazine; I was in the photo, but it was kind of blurred and you couldn't tell who I was. The caption read, "Mark Holman on harmonica," and I remember how disappointed I was that my name wasn't correct.

Mazzolini's show featured Floyd Dixon, Sonny Rhodes, L.C. Robinson with saxophonist Wild Willie Moore and us. Floyd had just come out of semi-retirement and was sounding really good. His bass player and a drummer were primarily jazz guys and sounded great. L.C., on the other hand, was precarious. He recently had done a couple albums on ABC Bluesway and Arhoolie Records. He claimed to have played for Bonnie and Clyde at a picnic in Texas, so he went back quite a long way, to the 1930s.

L.C. tried to hire Reggie and Jerry. He asked, "How much you boys want?" They told him, "We got to get fifteen dollars." L.C. said, "I'll give you ten." They told him to forget it, so he came back to them with the fifteen and they ended up playing the gig with him. The show was in a high school gymnasium. It was Boogie Jake and the band, Floyd in the middle and Sonny after that. L.C. closed with Reggie and Jerry in the rhythm section. The best part of L.C.'s set was between songs when he changed suits behind a curtain, which was only about a foot from the back of the wall. Every time he changed behind the curtain, you'd see the curtain flailing around and then he came out in another special outfit, like a gold lamé suit. He then did a couple numbers, went back behind the curtain with more flailing around and came out in a lime-green jumpsuit. He did a couple more tunes, went behind the curtain, flailed around a little more and came out in some kind of red-sparkle suit. It helped that he worked for a dry-cleaning business, but he ended up dying from inhaling those horrible fumes that dry cleaners used back then. It was definitely one of the most entertaining shows I ever saw, for entirely different reasons of course. L.C. was funky on the lap-steel guitar. Sonny Rhodes ended up inheriting the lap steel after L.C. died because they had become pals.

Jake took requests from the audience. Someone asked for B.B. King's "Whole Lotta Lovin'," and Jake said, "Ladies and gentlemen, I'm going to do a song. I don't know it. The band don't know it, but we gonna do it for you anyway." He then launched into a catastrophic rendition of B.B.'s song. It was hilarious only in retrospect.

Jake's band lasted maybe a year, before I hooked up with Johnny Waters. Many a good time was had playing in my early years on the front lines of the East Bay blues scene. I miss it now, especially the camaraderie among the blues players back then.

CHAPTER SIX

Johnny Waters and Sonny Lane

I'd been around the Bay Area for about two or three years play-ing with different blues groups and working in the different blues clubs. Ron Thompson had told me about the Playboy Club. I then heard about Eli's Mile High Club in Oakland, and I ended up giving Troyce Key, the guitar player in the house band, a har-monica lesson. Troyce, a sharp-dressed cat was the first rock 'n' roll artist on Warner Bros. Records; Eddie Cochran played gui-tar on his first session for the company. Troyce even appeared on "American Bandstand." He had a group from Fresno called the Rhythm Rockers with a singer, guitarist and piano player named J.J. Malone. Troyce was a white guy originally from Louisiana, but he mostly played with black bands.

Troyce's harmonica lesson wasn't much of a lesson. We just hung out all day and talked about blues. I played him different blues records, and he told me stories about people he'd played with over the years. I went over to a place called Minnie's Can-do on Haight Street in San Francisco and met J.J. Malone with Charlie Banks on bass. Troyce played guitar and some harmonica at the time. We talked about trading harmonica lessons for guitar lessons because I'd always fooled around on guitar, but we never got around to the guitar lessons.

I first met Sonny Rhodes at Eli's. Sonny, another sharp dresser, originally from Smithville, Texas, always wore a turban, Chuck Willis-style, and was very well-respected in Texas and on the Bay Area scene. He'd been Junior Parker's valet in the 1960s and played bass with Freddie King. Sonny began calling himself the "Sheik of East Oakland" and the "Disciple of the Blues." He had recorded several singles locally for the Galaxy label and an LP with Gary Smith on a Swedish label.

I walked up to Sonny at Eli's and said, "Do you think I could jam with you?

"What do you play?" he asked.

"Harmonica," I replied.

"You know Gary Smith?" he then asked.

"Yeah, I know Gary Smith," I said. "He's really great."

"Gary Smith played with me," Sonny said, adding, "You know Charlie Musselwhite?"

"Yeah, Charlie Musselwhite's great," I answered.

"Charlie Musselwhite played with me," Sonny said. "You know Rick Estrin?"

"Yeah, Rick Estrin's great," I said.

"Rick Estrin played with me," Sonny commented before asking, "so you wanna play harmonica with me, huh?"

"Yeah, that'd be great," I responded.

I was stoked to be meeting Sonny and then getting to do some gigs with him. It was 1976. I'd play gigs at Eli's, as well as attend the club's jam sessions. At one session, a tall handsome older black gentleman got up and started singing a Muddy Waters song—I think he sang "Country Boy"—and I was really knocked out.

"Could I play behind you?" I asked him.

"Yeah, go ahead," he answered.

I really had a good time playing with him.

"What's your name?" I asked.

"Johnny Sandifer," he said.

"Wow, you sound really great, man," I told him. "You're the only guy I've heard around here that plays Chicago blues."

"We ought to get together sometime," he suggested.

I found out later that Johnny was from Jackson, Mississippi and had grown up with the blues as a teenager before moving to Oakland. His neighbor in Jackson was country blues guitarist Bubba Brown, session guitarist Mel Brown's father.

A month or two later, I got a phone call from another older guy working at Eli's, J.J. Jones, a singer and guitar player who played more in the Albert King/B.B. King style. He bore a striking resemblance to his late cousin Eddie Jones, better known as Guitar Slim. J.J. was short and thin and always smiling.

"Hey, Mark," he said over the phone, "we want to start a band."

"Who's we?" I inquired.

"Me and a guy named Johnny Sandifer," J.J. answered. "He's starting to call himself Johnny Waters."

"Really," I said. "I know Johnny. Johnny's great."

"We want to start a band with you, and we want you to come down and jam with us," J.J. said, adding, "Can you find a rhythm section?"

I 'm thinking, hum, they don't have a rhythm section, but they want to start a band. I thought, OK, I'll give this a whirl. I lined up a drummer and a bass player I'd heard about, and we all got together. We played at Johnny's house or J.J.'s house—can't remember which—and it sounded good. J.J. didn't fit into the Chicago blues thing as well as Johnny did, but we made it work anyway.

Not long after that, a few weeks later, we ended up with the house gig at Eli's. By this time, in 1976, Eli's had become the main blues club in Oakland. It was owned by Eli Thornton and his wife Alberta. Eli had a girlfriend on the side, a singer named Frankie Williams. Eli was constantly hitting on women at the club. Alberta put up with it, but I don't know if she knew. Eventually, Frankie shot Eli to death at the club.

After we did the Eli's house gig for a month or two, J.J. came to Johnny and me and told us he's got to leave the band to go back to driving a truck. We had just started getting the band off the ground when J.J. up and quit.

A week or two later, we found out that J.J. had hired an all-new band and kept the house gig at Eli's. Johnny and I put our heads together and decided, to hell with this, we'll go ahead and find somebody else. Sonny Lane, a guitar player who was a long-time friend of Johnny's, could be the perfect replacement, so we called him. I was twenty-two, and these guys were both in their forties.

I had heard about Sonny because he used to play rhythm guitar in a band with Hi-Tide Harris and Rick Estrin, and he'd also played rhythm guitar with Charlie Musselwhite for a minute.

Sonny was as much into Chicago blues as Johnny, so he made a better fit than J.J. Jones had.

We started getting together and jamming some with drummer Gary Hine and a bass player named Mike. Mike didn't last long, and we ended up with Lex Silva. Lex used to play with John Lee Hooker, and I'd heard about him from Ron Thompson, whom he'd done gigs with, and Ken Swank, who played drums in Hooker's band.

Lex had been around. He'd done some recordings and road-work with Hooker and had played many gigs with Luther Tucker. Lex also had played on L.C. Robinson's ABC-BluesWay album. Lex had plenty of experience, but I'd also heard that he liked to pop pills and drink like a fish.

By the time Lex joined us, he had stopped the pills but still drank. Little did I know how much? I found that out down the road. We did have a good group, because Lex was a solid bass player and could do it in his sleep, literally! Gary was probably the weakest link in the band at the time because his meter wasn't quite up to the standard I think Lex was used to.

Johnny and Sonny were definitely old-school, Chicago blues-type players, but they had a real problem keeping their guitars in tune, especially Sonny. It was quite disconcerting to hear him tune his guitar when I would give him an E; he would bend the string so far out of tune that there would be no clue as to where it was going or how to get it back in tune. Eventually, I talked Sonny into getting a strobe tuner, a brand-new contraption at the time. Strobe tuners were huge boxes that sat on top of amplifiers and had strobe lights that you could tune the strings to. They cost about three hundred dollars back then. This became an elaborate ritual that we would go through every night with Sonny and the strobe tuner, but it was the only way to keep the guitars in tune.

Johnny had to be one of the soulful Chicago-style blues sing-ers on the West Coast. He could sing Otis Rush, Muddy Waters, Little Walter and Jimmy Rogers's songs, and he sang Muddy and

Otis's songs especially well. He could phrase like Muddy and had a very powerful voice. I saw Johnny as somebody who had great potential.

Johnny, from Mississippi, and Sonny, from Arkansas, provided my introduction to hanging out with older, Southern blues musicians, both from the standpoint of the culture and the history. I was just a young, white kid and thought I knew it all, but nonetheless, I was totally intrigued with the stories these guys told, particularly those about hanging out with Muddy Waters' band in the 1960s, which Sonny had done. Sonny had even dated Little Walter's sister Silvia and met Muddy through her. Sonny claimed that Muddy wrote his song "She's Nineteen Years Old" about Silvia. Johnny and Sonny both claimed to have met and heard Mississippi bluesman Boyd Gilmore when he hoboed through Oakland in the '60s.

We had a straight-ahead Chicago blues band and called our-selves Mississippi Johnny Waters and the Blues Survivors. We played at a place in Berkeley called Michael's Den, which used to be a blues club called the Tenth Street Inn. At the time, my girl-friend Houston worked there as a bartender. Charlie Musselwhite and Hi-Tide Harris had played there when it was the Tenth Street Inn, and when Michael bought it, he really wanted to keep it a blues club.

Like the entrepreneur I found myself becoming, I would help people try to create a scene. I helped Michael hook up with dif-ferent bluesmen like Cool Papa, Ron Thompson, Sonny Rhodes, J.J. Malone and Troyce Key. Eventually, he had a club that booked blues five or six nights a week. Johnny, Sonny and I held down the Monday night spot. On the nights we were playing, there could be anywhere from five people to fifty people. Being a small club, we were playing for a very small amount of money, ten or fifteen dol-lars a night, but it was a good place to get our chops together and tighten up our act. This was 1978.

When you're playing clubs and there are hardly any custom-ers, the musicians start drinking a little more than usual, taking advantage of the bar because they're not getting paid very well. Johnny would get sloshed and not do a very good show some nights. Same with Lex. Sonny and I tended to drink less but do more drugs. Cocaine being very popular at the time, we would level it off with alcohol.

Sonny and I became very good pals, and we used to talk on the phone every day. Lane's one of the funniest people I ever got to know on the blues scene. He had a wicked sense of humor and a skewed way of looking at things. He'd have one voice when you called him in the morning. "What's happenin'?" he'd say slowly in low tones. When you'd call him at night, he'd say, "Hey, man, what's goin' on?" in a real high pitch.

Sonny would say stuff like, "The blues men nowadays are more likely to come in on a 747 than behind a mule." He'd say, "Those

Europeans, they just want a blues man that wears some overalls and is plowing with his mule, but nowadays he might drive up in a Lincoln Continental wearing a three-piece suit. They can't handle that." Sonny would make fun of young white players copying blues licks off records and holding such reverence for them. "Fuck a lick," was Sonny's response. Sonny made his living as a postal worker but loved blues as I did.

Sonny's greatest responses were reserved for musicians we knew. Of harmonica man Rod Piazza, who Sonny thought was the greatest, he would say, "Rod don't give a fuck about following nobody; he follow Little Walter if he wanna!" Sonny claimed he saw George Smith in 1968 with Muddy's band and George would wear an overcoat indoors when it was eighty-plus degrees indoors and onstage. "George Smith crazy," Sonny would swear. When Sonny first saw the Fabulous Thunderbirds in 1978, he turned to me and said,"Them dudes out front is good, but the baddest dude in the band that bass player. He bad!" (He was referring to Keith Ferguson.) Very perceptive, I realized later on. Of Oakland guitarist Hi-Tide Harris, Sonny would just say, "Tide crazy, man" or "Tide scared of Rick"(Estrin).

Sonny was fascinated with country singer Loretta Lynn. She was his favorite. "Man, Loretta Lynn, man, she know how to sing," he'd say. "Like Muddy Waters sing blues, she can sing country." He also loved going to Egypt. He'd go on Mideast tours where he would ride on camels and take pictures with people, and he used to always make fun of what he called "the big, fat, Southern white tourists that would come there and expect to be in America, even though they were in Egypt, honking their car horns at camel riders and looking for McDonalds." Or,"What if Andre Segovia (famed Spanish classical guitarist) walked into one of Muddy's gigs? What do you think he'd say? He'd say, "What kind of ignint shit is this? This is not music." He had a very hilarious take on things.

Houston sold cocaine during those years. Sonny and another friend of mine, Mike Ryan, got so into cocaine that they let their cars stop running and stopped paying their bills and everything else. I broke up with Houston at one point and told her that since she wouldn't stop selling cocaine, we wouldn't be able to see each other because my friends were using up all their money buying drugs from her and were not able to sustain themselves because they were so hooked on drugs. To her credit, she did stop selling cocaine, but the guys had gotten too deep into it.

Tragically, Sonny ended up dying of Lou Gehrig's disease at a very young age, in his late forties, in 1987. Johnny got lung cancer, around the same time, from smoking and working in a steel mill for many years. Carroll Peery and I put together a benefit for them at a large club in Oakland called the Omni, which was owned by John and Toby Nady. About 1,200 people showed up that Monday night for the all-star show. We had John Lee Hooker, Brownie McGhee, Jimmy McCracklin, Charlie Musselwhite, Troyce Key, Little Charlie and the Nightcats, Ron Thompson, J.J. Malone, the Blues Survivors and Sonny Rhodes.

Ron went off on Sonny Rhodes backstage during the benefit. Sonny used to like to mess with people, and on that particular day, he was messing with Ron and me. Sonny said, "Mark Hummel here is one of the biggest assholes I know. Why, look, here come another asshole, Ron Thompson." Ron blew up and said in a very fast radio drag racing hyped-up voice, "Hey, man, what do you mean, calling me an asshole, man? Hey, man, you're an asshole. Fuck you, Sonny. Hey, man, don't talk that shit." He then threw down his guitar and stormed out of the room. Jay Peterson, Little Charlie's bass player at the time, had a little nephew who had tagged along. The kid, a twelve-year-old pre-gang banger type, mumbled,"Hey, what's with the midget?" Everyone cracked up at that, due to Ron's short height.

Sonny Lane and Johnny Waters passed away within weeks of each other in 1987. It was a very sad time when those guys died. We had played together for four years, from about 1977 to '81. I think about them a lot and really miss them. I wrote two songs that were inspired by them: "Rollin' from Side to Side" on my *Heart of Chicago* CD and "Bluesman" on *Married to the Blues.*

I issued some tunes on Johnny from when we played with Eddie Taylor, from a gig we did with Luther Tucker and a song from the 1980 San Francisco Blues Festival. They appear on the Mountain Top CD *Mark Hummel's Chicago Blues Party.* I played two San Francisco Blues Festivals with Johnny and Sonny, in 1977 and in 1980. We headlined the second one, with Francis Clay sitting in on drums at the end of the show.

Hanging around Johnny and Lex caused me to start thinking about not drinking so heavily. One time, while on a trip to
San Luis Obispo with Walter Shufflesworth from the Dynatones
on drums, Lex went into the liquor store and came out with a
twelve-pack of beer. Walter was behind him, mumbling, "Plasma,"
under his breath. The next morning, at about seven, Johnny and
Lex were drinking beers and watching cartoons at the motel.

Boy, I'm glad I'm not like that, I thought. To me, drinking in the
morning signified being an alcoholic. I realized later on that if you
stay up all night drinking, you're as much of an alcoholic as the guy
that pops his beer at seven a.m. I learned a lot about drinking from
both Lex and Johnny, as well as from J.J. Malone, a fabulously talented
musician that used to play with Troyce in the Over the Hill Gang, for-
mally known as the Rhythm Rockers, at Eli's Mile High Club.

J.J. happened to be one of the most gifted musicians I knew
around in the Bay Area. He had a hit on Galaxy Records called "It's a

Shame" in the early '70s. It got played heavily on KDIA in Oakland, and J.J. opened for the Jackson Five, Al Green and other R&B head-liners because of his hit. I think it charted in the Bay Area, New Orleans, Atlanta, Chicago and Detroit. It was one of those records that, because J.J. didn't go out and tour behind it, soon sank like a stone, but it was a big hit for a minute. J.J. could play guitar and piano equally well. He sang real soulfully and was a stone bluesman.

We used to have little jam sessions at J.J.'s house in Oakland. He would run his reel-to-reel recorder and make tapes of our jams. Sonny Rhodes, Sonny Lane and I would hang out there. I met Curtis Salgado there before he was with Robert Cray. He had a band called the Nighthawks in Eugene, Oregon. We were both in our early twenties at that point. Sonny Rhodes called me up, told me to get over to J.J.'s and introduced me to him.

Curt and I were both way into Little Walter and Sonny Boy Williamson and all the old guys. I remember his harmonica play-ing more than anything, but later on, when I saw Curt with Cray, I realized he also was a great singer. He's indirectly responsible for the Blues Brothers, thanks to John Belushi kindling a friend-ship with Curt in Eugene while filming *Animal House*. Belushi and Curt would hang out at on nights after Cray gigs, and Belushi would pick Curt's brain about musicians to hire for Curt's dream band. Curtis said he'd get Steve Cropper, Duck Dunn and Matt "Guitar" Murphy. Imagine Curt's surprise when months later he was watching *Saturday Night Live* and Belushi introduced a blues song, dedicated it to "Curtis and the Cray Band" and was playing with Curt's dream band? Cab Calloway's character in *The Blues Brothers* movie is named Curtis, and the *Briefcase Full of Blues* CD is dedicated to Salgado. Curtis is a huge star in the Pacific north-west and is always a welcome performer on my Blues Harmonica Blowouts. He is another miracle of sobriety, and I know he thanks his lucky stars for it. He could have died long ago if he had main-tained his old lifestyle from the days when he was working with Cray and Roomful of Blues.

JOHNNY WATERS AND SONNY LANE

J.J. Malone had a hell of a drinking problem right from the get-go. One time I did a gig with Sonny Lane and J.J. where J.J got drunk even before we started the gig. Sonny had to give him a ride back home before the gig. He told me that J.J. crawled out of the front seat of the car onto the grass and couldn't even walk. He was crying. It was sad to hear such stories, but they were really warnings to me of what I didn't want to become drinking-wise. J.J. and Charlie Musselwhite, in particular, both had developed such reputations for drinking that people were scared to hire them because they didn't know if they would be reliable enough once they got to gigs to be able to finish their shows.

I became very aware of the perils of alcohol at that point. At the same time, I was into drugs and would do cocaine and drink all night long. If I did coke, I could stay up drinking longer. I would have a drink, do lines of coke and then I would be able to drink into the early morning hours. I was learning about the pitfalls of drink and drugs, but I wasn't ready to quit. It seemed as if blues, alcohol and drugs were so tied together that I didn't know how to separate the three. I thought doing coke made you feel like a successful star. I thought you had to drink to be a bluesman. I didn't quit back when I was playing with Johnny and Sonny. I just got worse and worse.

Part of the problem was that in comparing myself to Johnny Waters, Charlie Musselwhite, J.J. Malone or Lex Silva—guys who obviously had alcohol problems—I could see that I wasn't near as bad as they were and, because of that, figured I didn't have a problem. I learned the things not to do from them, but I certainly didn't learn how to avoid hangovers or how to avoid excess. I tended to put off the heavy drinking until after the gig was over.

It got to a point later on, after I'd stopped playing with Johnny and Sonny, where I found I was drinking in excess during gigs. I tried not to drink before a gig, but once it started, I felt like I had to have at least a drink or a toot before we went on stage.

Many times, especially at low-paying gigs, club owners would offer us unlimited free drinks. If I felt like I wasn't getting paid enough, I would go to extremes with the alcohol. There was a club in Lafayette, California, called the Round-Up Saloon where the pay was minimal, but I always felt like I could make up for it by drinking more. I must have driven back from that gig in a blackout more than once. One night I was so hammered I drove the twenty or so miles home without my lights because a fuse had gone out. I'm still amazed that I made it home on many nights.

My hangovers would be worse after a night of doing cocaine and alcohol together; they'd last between twelve and twenty-four hours. It got to the point where I would swear off booze and drugs the next day, but a day or two later, if someone offered me a drink or a toot, I was right there doing it. That went on for a solid year before I finally stopped imbibing. I hated myself all the more because I couldn't quit and kept lying to myself.

I saw Johnny on stage one time and thought he was wearing two-tone pants until I noticed a puddle around his foot. Not that I didn't ruin a couple mattresses not making it to the bathroom in time. Lex would get so drunk that he would pass out in the middle of a song; the drummer would poke him with a drum stick, and he'd come right back in on the beat. I thought, wow, that takes talent to be able to come right back in on the beat after passing out. I became almost envious that those guys could do this kind of stuff. I wondered why I couldn't get hammered like that. I realized, however, that I had too much responsibility as bandleader and no one to take up the slack.

Lex had a girlfriend named Debbie who would drive him to gigs, unload all his equipment and pack it back up for him. One time, when he had to drive himself to a gig at the Saloon in San Francisco, he parked in the alley after the gig. Lex was one of those drunks with an angel looking out for him. He had forgotten to put the parking brake on, and the car literally rolled onto Grant Avenue and down the street to the middle of Columbus and Broadway. Lex chased it while carrying his bass guitar. It rolled into the middle of the intersection and, miraculously, didn't get nailed by any cars or run anybody over. It just came to a dead stop in one of the busiest intersections in San Francisco at two in the morning. That's what I would call drunkard's luck!

I once got busted for drunk driving while I was driving Lex's station wagon back from the gig because he was too hammered. The cop said, "If he would have been driving, you'd be dead right now, but because you were driving, you're going to jail for drunk driving," because we had a twelve-pack in the front seat. Lex was mad because the station wagon got impounded, but I was the one who spent the night in jail in my dressy stage outfit. Because it was my first offense, I went to court and I was able to get out of it, even though I had been right at the legal limit of .10.

Lex eventually sobered up but died about a year later. He was only about forty-one. He died of a heart attack at the wheel of his car while stopped at a red light. As much damage as he did to himself, it's amazing that he was able to live as long as he did. I guess Lex's luck did run out.

With people like Lex around me, I always figured I didn't have a problem. Down the road though, by the time I was twenty-seven, I had quit drinking and drugs, mainly because I'd had enough during the last year of my drinking and drugging. It wasn't fun anymore. Several people I knew stopped drinking around the same time. Both Rick Estrin and Robert Cray keyboardist Jim Pugh stopped drinking and doing drugs, in part because I had told them I was sober. They didn't think I had a problem, so I guess that gave them pause for self-reflection.

At the same time, Rick was the one who told me a story about me wanting to follow him back to my house in my car because I was too drunk to drive. He had said, "You got to be crazy if you think I'm going to get in front of you while you're too drunk to drive." I thought at the time it was a brilliant idea.

I was a little envious of guys like Charlie and Lex, who could get up on stage and function like they weren't too wasted to play, although I would usually be hammered myself by the last set and thinking that I was really smoking until I'd listen to a tape of it later on and realize I was playing sloppy. There's that edge you're able to get—or so I thought—from drinking and drugs. If I hit it just right, I could play my best blues. I think what most of us alcoholic bluesmen were trying to achieve was that perfect high where you're not too hammered or too sober. I think most of us were scared to play sober. There was something about playing sober that was frightening; I couldn't loosen up and couldn't stretch out, just couldn't get that warm little edge that I could get when I'd had just the right amount of alcohol. The problem was that it only lasted for a very small amount of time before I went over the edge and started playing sloppy. I no longer had the kind of control that I'd had when I got that warm feeling going with just the right amount of booze and drugs together.

Eventually, between my cocaine-dealing girlfriend and all the people that were giving me blow on breaks during gigs, I got to a point where every time I would do a line of cocaine, my nose would start bleeding immediately. That really scared me because I realized there was no way I could play harmonica if I had a deviated septum. I wouldn't be able to get the kind of wind I needed to blow the harmonica. In between the nosebleeds, the hangovers and having ulcers that hurt bad, I knew there was a limited amount of time I could sustain that lifestyle.

There's a certain point where I had a cutoff line. I mean, Musselwhite had a big enough name that he could always get gigs. I never had the kind of name where I could just get gigs on my reputation. I had to really be able to put out and play a good show if I was going to be able to keep working. I knew if I messed up with drugs and alcohol that eventually people would just stop hiring me.

All those things together made me realize that I would eventually have to give up alcohol and drugs if I was going to make a career in music. It had gotten to the point where I'd be looking forward more to the drinking and the drugging on breaks than going back on stage and playing the next set. That really scared me. I'm lucky to have stopped at a young age. Both Charlie and J.J. gave it a few more years before sobering up, but thank God they did.

CHAPTER SEVEN

Charlie Musselwhite

Charlie Musselwhite is considered by most blues harp players of my generation to be one of the most important figures in the '60s blues revival. He remains a very important artist on the blues scene. Charlie was one of the earliest young southern-born white musicians to pick up old African-American musical styles from originators like Will Shade, Johnny Young, Walter Horton, Big Joe Williams, Otis Spann and others he befriended in Memphis and later in Chicago, where he moved in 1962. He and such other young Chicago players as Paul Butterfield, Mike Bloomfield, Elvin Bishop and Nick Gravenites formed close friendships with the older icons and spearheaded the white blues boom in the '60s that brought blues into the mainstream where it would become one of America's most celebrated worldwide exports.

This boom also boosted the careers of veterans like Muddy Waters, B.B. King and Otis Rush. Their young Chicago musician fans' enthusiasm helped get them work in rock venues across the U.S.A. Before this, the older blues musicians were playing for smaller and smaller crowds, due to changing music styles, which meant that black folks were increasingly turning their backs on blues music. Charlie was at the forefront of this movement and was one the first blues harmonica players I listened to on records and went to see in person.

During this era there were not many harp players known enough to tour the country and make records that sounded authentic. The only touring ones I remember were Charlie, Junior Wells, James Cotton, Sonny Terry and Paul Butterfield. They all had a huge impact on me and my contemporaries. All of them played the hippie ballroom, rock festival and nightclub circuits of the day and turned many youngsters on to the blues harp. Charlie and Cotton are still extremely active, both touring and recording. Charlie has become the preeminent harp master on today's scene and retains the largest following. Two recent film soundtracks featured his harmonica prominently: *Into the Wild* and *Black Snake Moan*. Charlie has recently toured and recorded with Cindy Lauper and Hot Tuna. In the world of blues and trendsetting harmonica, Musselwhite has definitely earned his rightful place.

Charlie quit drinking in the mid-'80s, and since that time, thanks to his wife and manager Henrietta and to Rosebud Agency, his career has been on an uphill trajectory. Charlie now looks younger and healthier than he did thirty years ago. I have some colorful stories, however, about our days as drinkers.

I was a teenager when I first saw Musselwhite perform at the Ash Grove in L.A. My mother dropped me off and picked me up there after his performance. I already had a few of his albums then, so I was looking forward to seeing him live. Charlie looked like a cross between Robert Mitchum and Johnny Cash in those days, except Musselwhite sported a mustache. He slicked back his hair with Royal Crown gel, which gave him a '50s look. In the band were a big, burly biker-looking fellow named Alberto Gianquinto on piano, Robben Ford's brother Pat on drums and a bass player whose name I can't remember. Curiously, there was no guitar player. Charlie played a number of Little Walter tunes and "Christo Redemptor," the Duke Pearson jazz ballad that became Charlie's signature. This left quite an impact on me as a young wanna-be harp player.

Back in 1980, I was doing a project called the Blues Workshop Series, something an old girlfriend, Rosie Menninger, had dreamed up. She knew how to write grants and had gotten me one from the California Arts Council, which she was a part of, along with Peter Coyote and some other famous people. It was for a series of workshops over a six-month period.

The workshops were held at different venues around California, mainly in Northern California. I only did one a month, the first one with Charlie at the Sleeping Lady Café in Marin County. The Sleeping Lady was a club where ex-Paul Butterfield piano player Mark Naftalin booked a Blue Monday series and did a live radio broadcast.

I told Naftalin I would bring Charlie in to do a thirty-minute interview and then he would play with the band. It was a hell of a band: Francis Clay on drums, Luther Tucker and Ron Thompson on guitars and Naftalin on piano. This workshop would be the kickoff. I sent out press releases to the *San Francisco Chronicle* and other newspapers.

About two weeks before the show, Charlie called me up and told me in his thick Southern drawl, "Hey, I think I got a good one for you." I wondered what he was talking about.

Charlie phoned me up the day of the show and said, "It's my birthday. What are you going to get me?"

"Happy birthday, Charlie," I answered. "What would you like?"

"How 'bout a fifth of Old Grand-Dad?" he said.

I beat it down to the supermarket and grabbed a bottle. While I was standing in line holding the fifth, people were looking at me, probably thinking I was going to drink it. I was self-conscious about my drinking at that point. I thought that everyone was going to think I'm drinking in the middle of the day.

When I got to Charlie's house, he said, "Thank you. You want some?" I had him pour me an inch or so of the Old Grand-Dad, and he finished off the rest in about an hour. I started to get a little nervous. I was giving him a ride to the gig, and on the way there, he looked over at me and said, "Hey, let's stop by the liquor store so I can get a half-pint." I was thinking he was going to be hammered by the time we got the gig. He kind of stumbled into the club. The place was packed to the rafters, with all the seats taken and people sitting on the floor.

We got on stage, and Naftalin introduced each of us. Then I asked Charlie my first question: "Charlie, how long have you been playing?"

Charlie hesitated for a bit. "How long have *you* been playing?" he responded.

I tried again, asking, "Who did you listen to when you were growing up?"

"Oh, let's see," he responded, scratching his head. "Peg Leg Howell, Birmingham Jones."

"How about Little Walter?" I asked, knowing Charlie had hung out with Walter.

"Yeah, I've heard of him," Charlie replied even though they had been friends.

At this point I knew I wasn't going to get help from Charlie. My face was beet red. Naftalin saw that I was in trouble and jumped in and said, "Charlie, I hear you can play fifteen positions on the harmonica. Let's hear them all."

Charlie answered, "Well . . ."

Naftalin and the band then started playing, and Charlie pulled off the gig just fine playing with the band. The next day, in the in the entertainment section of the *San Francisco Chronicle*, the review said, "The Blues. Some things are better played and not talked about."

The only good things regarding the *Chronicle* article were that it never mentioned my name and didn't have a picture of me. It may have named the workshop series, but I can't be sure. The rest of the workshops went well, compared to the kickoff with Charlie.

I booked Charlie with my band for a handful of gigs after he had stopped drinking hard liquor and was just drinking beer and wine. I was impressed when I first heard he'd dropped the hard booze. I had just stopped drinking myself, and I was expecting that he'd be sober on the gigs with me. On the way to the first one, after I'd picked him up at his house, he said, "Let's stop at a liquor store. I want to get myself a little wine." Charlie bought a gallon of cheap red wine, sat in the van and drank half of it on the way to Sacramento. He drank the other half on the way back. I don't think I've seen anybody drink quite so much wine.

Another incident happened about four or five years later while I was booking Charlie on a few dates. One, at JJ's in San Jose, was quite a fiasco. Charlie rode with me in my van. On the way there, Charlie was steadily putting away a half gallon of wine.

JJ's was jam-packed when we got there and the crowd was impatient for us start the show

I went up to June Stanley, a dour-looking, heavily made-up woman who co-owned the club with her brother Max, and informed her that Charlie had arrived with me.

It was a three-set night. I would do the first one, and Charlie would do the last two. The place was about as full as I'd ever seen it. When I finished my set, I told Charlie, "You can use my mike and my amp if you want, or you can play through the PA, whichever you want to do."

I gave Charlie a big introduction for his first set. He had decided to go through the PA. With the band playing behind him, he grabbed a microphone, blew a couple notes into it and then threw it on the ground. The sound guy looked up in shock. Then he took another PA mike off one of the stands, blew through it and threw it on the ground. Then he picked up my mike.

"Oh, no, don't do it, Charlie," I murmured.

He didn't. He put it back on my amp and finally picked up a third PA mike. He dealt with it but didn't seem real happy with that one either.

As Charlie played the first song, a group of people were talking loudly at one of the front tables. "Are you people going to talk or are you gonna shut the fuck up," he said off mike, though rather loudly. They looked up at him in horror and didn't say another word. After that, things got relatively calm, and Charlie seemed to be digging the way the set was going. He finished the first set without a hitch and started the second. Before we knew it, the night was over and Charlie said goodnight to the crowd. People clapped louder and louder as he walking off the stage.

I was outside while Charlie was finishing out the show. A guy with a framed black-and-white photo of Charlie from 1968 asked me, "Do you think Mr. Musselwhite could sign this for me?" I told him that I didn't know but would ask Charlie. "

Back inside JJ's, people were demanding an encore. I figured Charlie would do one more song. I was standing right next to Max, June's brother. Charlie lumbered up to the stage, went up to the mike and said, "Now, look." I was thinking he was going to say, "We'd love to play another number for you." Instead Charlie told the fans, "Now, look, you people are the biggest bunch of assholes that I've ever played for in my life and I'll take any one of you right now and stick it where the sun don't shine." Jaws dropped. Charlie had the balls to say what most of us have wanted to say, at one time or another, to a rude crowd.

"I guess that means Charlie's not gonna do another one, huh?" Max whispered in my ear.

"I guess not," I said, imitating Charlie's dead pan southern drawl.

Everyone walked away in shock. The poor guy who wanted his picture signed? It never happened. I gave Charlie a ride home to Richmond, and we talked about what a lame club it was and how he'd never go back and what assholes those people were. It was an interesting evening, to say the least.

Back when I was living in Berkeley, Charlie and Henrietta sometimes would stop by to say hello after they had gone thrift-store shopping or, as Charlie called it, "Thrifting and drifting."Charlie has always been very supportive to me when I've needed favors. Once, he gave me a very enthusiastic quote to use on a poster promoting one of my CDs. He also got me hooked up with Seydel Harmonicas, which was great for me because I was able to get a very generous sponsorship from the company. Charlie also persuaded me to buy a Sonny Jr. Super Cruncher harp amp, which remains my favorite amplifier.

When I asked Charlie if he'd play on my *Married to the Blues* CD, he never even asked what I was going to pay him. He just did it. We did an instrumental called "High-Steppin'" that he worked out a harmony part for. He overdubbed his solo on it, and then we did an acoustic blues with him on guitar and me on harmonica, which is on my *Retroactive* CD

Many harp players in my age group who know Charlie can do impressions of his distinctive Mississippi drawl out of love for him and because he's such a rascal. One time Charlie called Frank Goldwasser to hire him for a gig, and Frank told him he knew it was me trying to put one over on him. I think I do Charlie's voice with the best of them, excepting the man himself, of course.

Since these stories of twenty five plus years ago, Charlie has become a new man since sobering up in the mid-80s. Musselwhite is a miracle, a sobriety success story of epic proportions. Back then, I never thought he'd outlive his old friends Paul Butterfield and Mike Bloomfield (who both OD'd in the 80s). Musselwhite has redeemed himself to become the southern gentleman he was raised up to be, it was just obscured by alcohol back then. He's still got the wicked sense of humor, but now shows good manners when dealing with the public.

Charlie just finished a Little Walter Tribute, his sixth Blowout tour with us in 2012 and it was the most fun any of us have had on a Blowout. Charlie was the hit of the show on a star-studded line-up including his buddy Billy Boy Arnold, Curtis Salgado, Sugar Ray Norcia, myself, Billy Flynn and Little Charlie Baty. Between his top-of-his-game harmonica playing and stories about his interactions with his old friend Walter, it made for a stellar show in every respect. Musselwhite is one of the most professional musicians I've dealt with in a long time, the first one ready at check out time in the morning(he's always been prompt), always asking questions in a polite manner without being demanding, tipping the band at tour's end, even helping to carry band gear when necessary. Even the first musician to send a thank you email at tour's end! A consummate pro in other words and always fun to ride in the van with as he spins fabulous stories from the old days in Memphis and Chicago. Charlie is also a well read deep thinker with an open mind, a southerner with left wing politics that show his sense of compassion for the downtrodden(which I always saw in his love of African American blues and the older musicians' acceptance of Charlie). In the twenty first century Charlie's name has become synonymous with top flight quality blues harp playing after decades of honing his craft-he's still my mother's favorite harp player when he plays "Christo Redentor"!

CHAPTER EIGHT

James Cotton

James Cotton was one of the first Chicago blues artists I saw live, and his *Pure Cotton* was one of the first LPs I ever owned. I was about sixteen when I saw him at the Ash Grove in L.A. on a Monday night at the beginning of a week-long run. In his band were Matt "Guitar" Murphy, saxophonist Little Bo, bassist Charles Calmese and drummer Kenny Johnson. They were probably on their first tour together. They did mostly songs off *100% Cotton* and Little Walter covers. There were only a handful of patrons there, but what has always stuck with me was how Cotton still delivered to the audience with no slacking at all.

I remember talking to him outside on the break and how patient, friendly and tolerant he was, considering the things I said to him. I asked him what his favorite LP was.

"All of them," he said.

"Not me," I responded. "I like the first two best."

I asked him about Butterfield.

"I dig Paul," Cotton said, "He's my friend."

"I like you better," I told him.

He seemed amused by me and my brashness at sixteen and took it all in stride. I always try to remember how his demeanor was toward me then when I'm talking to young players and playing in front of sparse crowds. Audience look at it like the only thing that matters is your performance. There are no other variables in their eyes, only what you do on stage.

I've tried to play like Cotton, Little Walter, Big Walter, Junior Wells, Sonny Boy and many of the other greats since I started, but Cotton's influence has grown stronger in my playing as the years pass. I recorded his version of "The Creeper" in 2004 on my *Blowing My Horn* CD, and it has become one of the most requested numbers from my fans. Tongue blocking the harp while bending is something I got when I was about eighteen, a result of learning that it was the only way I was going to play "The Creeper" correctly. Bill Lupkin gave me that harp lesson when I was about eighteen, and I was blown away when he told me Cotton blocked and bent at the same time.

I met Cotton many times after that. I saw him go through many different stages, from being strung out so bad in New Orleans in the '80s that I didn't even recognize him to seeing him completely turn his life around after some serious health scares in the early part of the millennium. Cotton is a strong man. He's done things that would have killed many men several times over, from drugs and booze to getting shot five times in the chest while playing a nightclub with Muddy's band, and he's still here with us.

Cotton started performing on my Blues Harmonica Blowouts in 2001. He's done at least six tours with us, and I have always been awed, intimidated and excited about working with this man who at twelve years old, lived with and opened shows for Sonny

Boy Williamson, played with Howlin' Wolf as a teenager and got the harp chair in Muddy's band after Little Walter. Cotton is a survivor to the max and the last of the Chicago blues greats on harmonica. He's also the go-to man for lyrics and knows more blues songs than anyone out there. Long live James Cotton!

CHAPTER NINE

The Eddie Taylor Incident

I brought Chicago guitarist Eddie Taylor to Northern California in 1982 for a tour that included a set at the San Francisco Blues Festival. The tour initially was going to feature both Eddie and Sunnyland Slim, but there was a major snafu that caused Sunnyland not being able to make that dream tour. I had begun negotiations to hire Sunnyland through Barry Dalton, a promoter who used to play harmonica with Sunnyland and later booked shows at a club in San Francisco. Sunnyland was a great blues piano player who lived in Chicago and was one of the first blues musicians to start his own record label. He was born in Mississippi in 1906 and played with all the greats, Muddy Waters, Little Walter, Jimmy Rogers, Howlin' Wolf and George Smith, among them. Sunnyland was known around the world as one of the premier Chicago bluesmen and will always be associated with bringing Muddy to Leonard Chess, as well as for having recorded with Muddy and Walter. Barry brought Sunnyland to California for the first time in 1972. I remember seeing Barry playing harmonica with Sunnyland's band at the Monterey Jazz Festival that year.

Barry later became Sunnyland's manager and in that capacity brought him to California on several other occasions. At one point, I talked to Tom Mazzolini, the S.F. Blues Festival producer about the possibility of bringing Sunnyland and Eddie to Northern California for a tour. Tom said he'd like to have them on his festival, so I phoned Barry.

"What would you think about me booking Sunnyland with Eddie Taylor for some gigs in the Bay Area?" I asked him.

"Yeah," he said, "That'd be great. You know I manage Sunnyland, don't you?"

"That's why I'm calling you, to make sure that it would be all right," I answered.

"It should be fine," he said. "No problem."

I phoned Sunnyland at the number Barry had given me and began negotiating with him about gigs in California.

"I'd love to come out and play with you," he told me. "I have to get five hundred bucks a gig, and yeah, I know Eddie Taylor real well. He's worked with me many times."

When it came time to start scheduling dates, I phoned Barry and told him I wanted to book Sunnyland for the San Francisco Blues Festival and some club dates.

"Sunnyland?" Barry scoffed. "I'm Sunnyland's manager. I'm the only one that gets to book him on anything. Nobody else books Sunnyland. Do you understand? If you book him on the San Francisco Blues Festival or on any Northern California tour, I will sue you and the donkey you and Tom Mazzolini rode in on!"

When I told Tom what Barry said, he didn't know what to think.

"What do you want to do?" I asked Tom, still wondering what was up with Barry's Dr. Jekyll/Mr. Hyde personality.

"Let's see what happens to this 'donkey' we're riding on," Tom answered.

As it turned out, Tom's words were prophetic.

We soon were getting letters in the mail from Barry's lawyer threatening to sue. When I phoned Sunnyland trying to find out what was going on, he initially refused to talk to me. I suddenly had become persona non grata!

When Sunnyland finally spoke to me, he said, "I don't think I'm going to be able to make it out because I'm sick, man. I'm not feeling too good."

After receiving the threatening letters, Tom and I threw in the towel concerning Sunnyland.

I phoned Eddie and he assured me he was still game to come out, with or without Sunnyland. Eddie and I negotiated his price, one that we could both live with, and we shook hands, verbally, on the telephone. I also booked another couple of weeks of dates for him in the Bay Area, as well as at the Sacramento Blues Festival with Little Charlie and the Nightcats, since Eddie and Nightcat's harpman Rick Estrin were old friends in Chicago.

My friend Carroll Peery just happened to be visiting Chicago the day Eddie was supposed to fly to San Francisco. He went to Eddie's house to personally escort him to the airport. Carroll was shocked to find Eddie unpacked and half-dressed when he arrived. They hurriedly packed a suitcase and rushed to O'Hare, getting there with barely enough time to get Eddie on the plane. Eddie had cataract surgery about two weeks before, plus a wire from the huge brush of a street sweeper had gone into the same messed-up eye he'd just had surgery on. This threw off his depth perception considerably when he played guitar, so it's possible he may not have felt comfortable coming to California because of his eye.

Eddie's first gig in California was the San Francisco Blues Festival. John Hammond, who also was playing the festival, was blown away by meeting Eddie. They became friendly right off. As they talked, we learned that, when he was a kid, Eddie used to hide under floorboards of a juke joint in Mississippi and listen to the blues. He had seen and heard both Charley Patton and Robert Johnson when they rambled through his small town. Both John and I were in awe. John, unlike some other people Eddie met during the tour, gave him respect. It was my first time meeting John, whom I would book for my Blues Harmonica Blowouts some thirty years later.

Eddie stayed at my friend Phil Ajioka's house. Phil was a huge fan of Eddie's guitar mastery, and Eddie enjoyed staying with him instead of at a hotel or motel.

One person I had called about booking a gig with Eddie was Clark Nardella, a paste-white, sunglasses-wearing musician who looked like a vampire by day and at night had a blues radio broadcast in San Rafael.

"I already have Johnny Littlejohn booked on that date, but what can you tell me about this Eddie Taylor?" Clark asked.

"He played on all of Jimmy Reed's records and with Elmore James, John Lee Hooker and plenty of the Vee-Jay stuff," I informed him, adding, "Eddie also did some records of his own—some very great stuff."

I sent Clark one of Eddie's records.

"I really like Eddie's record," Clark said when I phoned again. "It's great! He sounds like a real blues guy, but I do have Johnny Littlejohn that very same night."

"What can you do?" I asked.

"I can give him a portion of the door," he responded. "I'll do my best to get Eddie close to what Johnny Littlejohn is getting, which is a hundred dollars."

"As long as you can get in that price range, I think Eddie will be cool with it," I told Clark.

When it came time for the gig, I showed up with Eddie and Phil in my car. We brought in an old Fender twin reverb with two twelve-inch speakers that Eddie was borrowing at the time. Eddie would crank the knobs up to full on everything except the bass knob, which he left at zero. He controlled the volume through his guitar.

"What songs are you going to do?" Clark asked Eddie before the show. "This is a live radio broadcast."

"I'm just gonna do the blues," Eddie told him. "I'm gonna do, you know, simple stuff. I want to keep it simple."

" Eddie," Clark insisted, "I need to know what songs you're going to do."

"Well, you know, man, I'll just keep it simple," Eddie said. "I'll give you the key, and I'll count them in."

"But Eddie," Clark stressed, "I need to know exactly what songs you're going to do. This is going out live on the radio with twenty-thousand people listening. I need to know the exact songs you're going to do."

"I'm gonna do a shuffle in E, and I'm gonna do a slow blues in A," Eddie answered, tuning his guitar as he spoke.

Clark stormed off the stage like a rhino in heat. Eddie got really perplexed and started packing up his guitar. He looked at me and Phil and shook his head.

"Take me home," Eddie said. "Get me outta here. I want you to take me to the damn airport right now. Fuck this guy! He don't know nothin' about the blues!"

Phil and I weren't going to try to stop Eddie Taylor. As we followed him out of the club, we passed the emcee of the show.

"Where are you guys going?" he asked us.

"Well, your boy Clark, just pissed Eddie Taylor off," I told him. "Eddie wants us to take him to the airport. He wants outta here."

"He really fucked up big time," the emcee stated flatly.

"Eddie didn't fuck up," I responded. "Eddie is a living legend, and you just aren't smart enough to know it. You and Clark fucked up, bro! Big time!"

We packed up Eddie's guitar and amp. As Phil and I were putting them in the trunk, Clark came ambling out as if nothing had happened and he hadn't just insulted one of the icons of the blues.

"Where you guys going?" he asked, seemingly surprised.

"I guess you pissed Eddie off, and he wants us to take him to the airport," I said. "He wants to leave."

"He can't do that," Clark responded. "We're having a live radio broadcast here, and we're going on in about an hour."

"You better apologize to him and figure out what the hell you're doing," I responded.

Clark walked up to Eddie to speak, but before he could say anything, Eddie held up his hand.

"Listen," Eddie said while looking at the ground. "You know, I played with John Lee Hooker. I played with Jimmy Reed. I played with Elmore James. I played with Muddy Waters. I played with all these guys and not like some sideman! I knew them, and they knew me. I don't need any kind of shit like this. I don't need to be disrespected."

"Well, Eddie, you weren't telling me the songs you were going to do," Clark said. "I've been through a lot this week. My wife left me last week, and she took my dog with her. Then my dog died while she had him, and I wasn't there, man. He died all alone in some house he didn't know, and I wasn't there. It's been a very hard week for me, Eddie. I want you to do the show. And you know what? I apologize, and if my apology's not enough, I'll get down on my knees for you right now and apologize on my knees. I need you to play the show." Clark got down on both his knees in front of us. We were all in shock at his act of contrition.

"You ain't gotta do that," Eddie told him. "I don't want none of that. You can get up. I just don't want to be treated bad. I'll do the show. If it means that much to you, I'll do the show."

Eddie did a good show for the broadcast, playing up a storm on guitar and singing the blues. Unfortunately, I could see the backup band snickering behind Eddie's back at his down south demeanor, checkered polyester suit and short height, though Eddie got a great response from the packed house of howling blues lovers. At the end of the evening, when the show was over, I went to collect Eddie's money from Clark. He handed me thirty-five dollars.

"What is this?" I asked, staring at the bills in my hand.

"That's Eddie's pay," Clark told me.

"Eddie was supposed to get close to what Johnny Littlejohn was getting," I stated forcefully. "You told me Johnny was getting one hundred dollars. I told Eddie he'd get close to a hundred. It was packed in there. Now you're making me look bad."

I squared up in front of Clark. There was no way he was going to get away with that crap!

"I'm paying him the same amount that I'm paying all the side guys, and that's how it goes," he said. "All he's going to make is what the side guys made. There's no reason for me to pay him anymore."

It was as if we'd never had our original discussion. To me, it was the same as stealing.

"That's bullshit!" I told him.

"Well, that's all he's getting," Clark said as he turned and walked away.

My friend Carroll, who was behind me, grabbed my shoulder and restrained me. I was so pissed that I wanted to go after Clark and kick the smugness out of him.

"Let's go," Carroll said. "This guy isn't worth it. You won't accomplish anything."

Eddie had watched the whole thing, and his facial expression never changed as Clark spoke. I handed Eddie the thirty-five dollars and shrugged my shoulders. I was just livid, but there was nothing I could do.

Eddie folded the bills in half, dropped them in his pocket and said, "Fuck the man! Let's just go."

As we drove away, I thought about the bullshit sad story that Clark had laid on Eddie and the rest of us about his wife leaving him and his dog dying all in the same week. It had been a sorrowful story, with Clark on his knees and all, but that's probably why Clark paid him so badly, knowing what he had to do to get Eddie to perform instead of letting Eddie walk away. It had been a real lesson for me in low-down double dealing. I think sometimes I felt as bad about it as Eddie did. I'll never forget seeing this great man being so disrespected on the blues highway.

Girlfriends of Revenge

...st guitar players to tour with me
...as very into blues at the time and
...He could wail on West Coast or
...What more could a new bandlead-
...al, as touring musicians go, but
...up with some really wild and
...at I didn't have wild and crazy
...did, but Pat always managed to
...layed with the Blues Survivors
...y and Sonny were in the band

...thin guy with a crop of brown hair and a friendly disposition. He bares a more than striking resemblance to George Thorogood, but was shorter. It was no surprise that the ladies liked him. As we traveled together, his woman friends began showing up at the gigs. We were playing a local show in either Martinez or Concord, and Pat met and went home with a woman old enough to be his grandmother. I don't think there's anything wrong with younger guys dating older women, and older guys do it all the time with younger women, but these were the days before "cougar" was a common word. No matter how politically correct you tried to be, it still looked weird as they hung out together between sets. Pat's mother-figure girlfriend followed us around for a while, from gig to gig, and I never picked up a hint what it was that Pat dug about

her. I guess it was just his thing. He and his granny flame were together a few months before she disappeared.

Next came Sweet Sue, a wild and crazy African-American
woman who loved to hang out with Pat and come to all our gigs.
Her previous boyfriend, my bass player at the time, had been with
her for months before she met Pat. Pat stole her away from him, if
you want to call it that. Pat did the bass man a big favor. Pat stayed
with Sweet Sue for over a year. She always got crushes on different
musicians and fooled around with them behind Pat's back. It was
very disconcerting for me to watch, and I never quite knew what
to do about it. Should I tell Pat? I decided not to talk to him about
it since it was really none of my business. Pat's roving eye infuri-
ated Sue though she was fooling around with other guys.

One time, when we were coming back from a Northern

California gig, we decided not to stay in a motel but to drive directly back to Oakland. We got to Pat's house at three in the morning and discovered Sue in the living room snorting cocaine with several guys. The situation was more than a little suspect to me, but I said nothing to Pat and quickly got the hell out of there. Pat stayed behind. Only he knows what happened in that house for the rest of the night. I never asked Pat if he was bothered about what Sue was doing, but he didn't appear to be jealous.

I heard an interesting story about the end of Pat's relationship with Sue. Apparently, when Pat left her, all he did was leave a sticky note on her refrigerator that read, "Bye, had to go." That was it. Pat moved all of his crap out of the house they had been sharing. One minute he was there, and the next minute he was gone. He didn't seem to react or care about things the way most people do. He seemed less engaged in the emotional side of life than most of the musicians I have known. I viewed it as a survival technique. Pat definitely had an interesting way about him.

Pat continued touring with the band all across the United States and even to foreign countries. While in Canada during the mid-'80s, he met a woman that he later married. I don't remember her name, but I definitely remember her.

We would usually play a week in each town—one at the King Eddie Hotel in Calgary and one at Blues on Whyte in Edmonton. The King Eddie Hotel was an old five-story brick building that had managed to escape the wrecking ball and became the home of the Calgary blues scene during the '80s and '90s. Blues on Whyte, the best-known blues venue in Edmonton, had a big white-and-blue marquee. It always gave me a good feeling to see the band's name up there as we drove into town. Edmonton was a great blues town that also had a few other blues clubs we liked playing at, including the Howlin' Wolf and the Media Club.

I enjoyed hanging out with a friendly woman named Emily in Calgary during my week there, although I didn't sleep with her. I knew I would be seeing a girlfriend named Anne in Edmonton, so I kept it simple with the Calgary woman. Before driving to Edmonton, I phoned Anne, whom I'd hooked up with on my previous Canadian tour and let her know I was coming.

As the days passed in Calgary, the band members and I became preoccupied with what Pat was doing with his women. It wasn't that we were nosey; it was just that Pat's relationships were spilling over into the public domain. An older woman, who knew Pat from our trip to Calgary years before, arrived around the same time. She had the hots for him big time, and he seemed to have the hots for her as well. She was definitely a granny looker with snow-white hair and probably in her middle sixties. Pat was in his late twenties, but love conquers all. He ended up digging the older woman for a while. They were all over each other in public, and I still remember the looks on the faces of the Canadians when they saw Pat making out with her. I wish I'd had a camera to capture those jaw-dropping stares.

The younger woman that Pat would later wed was friends with his older girlfriend, and he somehow managed to date both of them. He went back and forth, from the older to the younger one. We never knew which one he would be with. The two women seemed to be aware of what was happening, but we were never quite sure. I certainly never asked Pat, and he never mentioned it to me.

I used to speculate about which woman Pat would show up with on the gig. The older lady suddenly split for unknown reasons. The younger woman had taken a train from Calgary to Edmonton. Now she was always hanging around with us in Edmonton, and she got closer to Pat during our stay. I'd spent the entire week with my companion Anne, and we had a good time together. We both knew I would have to be leaving soon, but we tried to stay in the moment and avoided thinking about the inevitable.

Then, without any warning, Calgary Emily showed up at the club on our last night in Edmonton. I really didn't know how to handle the situation. Anne didn't attend the show that last night, but I was planning to see her afterwards. I definitely didn't want to mislead Calgary Emily or make her feel bad. I tried to be friendly, but at the same time we didn't talk a whole lot. I didn't want to hurt her feelings, but coming to see me unannounced had been a mistake on her part. We were just friends, but she read the relationship differently and I was stuck in an awkward situation. I did my best to be an honorable guy during the breaks and said goodnight to her at the end of the show.

I breathed a huge sigh of relief when Emily left. I thought I'd done a good job of handling a tricky situation and patted myself on the back with both hands. Mark Hummel, the nice guy harmonica player, is straight shooter. It all worked out in the end—or so I thought.

What I didn't know is that Pat's girlfriend, who had been at the club that night, told Edmonton Anne about Calgary Emily. Pat's girlfriend informed Anne that the girl had come all the way from Calgary to see me at my invitation. That crushed Anne. Pat's girlfriend had made me sound like some kind of sex-fiend manipulator who was lying to cover his ass with two different women at the same time. It took me hours to explain the whole story to her. I'm not sure she ever fully believed me. Our happy bubble had burst.

The next day, as we were preparing to return to the States via Calgary, Pat asked me if I could give his girlfriend a ride back to Calgary in the van.

"I'm not really game to do that at this point, Pat," I answered. "Your girlfriend really pissed me off yesterday."

"Really? Why?" he asked.

I told him what had happened and, of course, he told his girlfriend. She got in my face about talking to Pat before I talked to her about what had happened the night before. Can you imagine her yelling at me for having been upset about her lying and gossiping about me to my Edmonton friend? She called me a double-dealing bad guy.

"You told Anne that I had invited a girl from Calgary to our last gig, which is bullshit," I told her. "Where did you get off doing that? What's worse is that you were wrong and hurt people's feelings!"

I guess I didn't really care anymore. The damage had been done. My relationship Anne would never be the same.

Pat still expected me to give his girlfriend a ride to Calgary, even after she'd told me off. What balls! What could I do? I gave in and let her ride, although I argued with her most of the way back to Calgary and told her what I thought of her meddling in my business. She was a tough bird, though, and finally told me to shut up. She and Pat then started arguing about something else, and she wailed on him. I kind of enjoyed that. I knew I had set her off, and Pat got a beating for it.

She's the Canadian who Pat ended up marrying. They lived in Washington for many years before getting a divorce.

I've stayed in touch with Pat over the years, and the last time I heard from him was when he phoned me when we were headed toward El Paso. I was on the front end of a three-week road trip, and he lives there.

"Hey," Pat asked, "you want to go get some great Mexican food? You're my pal, Mark. I want take you to the best Mexican place that I can think of. This restaurant is the pride of El Paso."

We showed up at the place hungry and ready to eat. I had the usual gang of suspects, except for Jay Hanson, who was on the tour instead of our regular drummer, Marty Dodson. I also had guitarist Rusty Zinn, bassist R.W. Grigsby and Jim Johnson, our harmonica-playing driver and merch guy. Pat was waiting for us in the parking lot. Jay got a bad vibe right away.

Pat is kind of an odd duck for Texas. His pale white face had been burned by the blazing Texas sun. It was orange, brown, red, and white in different places. "Who is this burn victim?" Jay whispered to me when he saw Pat's multi-colored face. "I don't want to have dinner with him."

I overrode Jay's concerns, and we went inside to eat. Pat had brought along a group of old pictures of me and him together and photos of famous musicians he had played with. There were great shots of Pat with John Lee Hooker, Pee Wee Crayton, Smokey Wilson, Lowell Fulson and others, and he told us stories about some of the gigs he'd played with them. Later, when my friend Ray Varner asked Pat to bring his favorite "albums" to play on his radio program, Pat brought the same photo "albums" and described them on the air instead.

Pat mentioned in passing that he'd always wanted to put some country-and-western stuff into our shows when we played together but that I would never let him do it. I made no comment. He reiterated his claim that this was the best Mexican restaurant in town, "The true pride of El Paso." A dark haired-waitress in a festive blue-and-white dress approached our table. We all ordered food, except for Pat. Pat declined to order anything and didn't even eat the chips and salsa. I asked him how come he wasn't eating, and he said he'd just had dinner. Hot plates of lard-laden food, including heaping portions of refried beans and rice, were placed in front of all of us, except Pat. We downed our spicy meals and rounded them off with more chips, I paid for our food and left.

After driving down the highway for about three hours, all four of us were suddenly hit with horrific lower intestinal pain. The food had been terrible to begin with, but at the time I didn't want to say anything about it to Pat. How could I tell him that his restaurant not the pride of El Paso? I came to call the place El Gaso in El Paso. I had to exit the Texas highway frequently so that Jim, Rusty, Jay, R.W. and I could explode in gas-station toilets. We left a trail of gastric horror all across the panhandle!

I started to think that maybe Pat Chase's restaurant choice had been revenge on Mark Hummel and the Blues Survivors. Pat is an interesting case study in someone who wants to be something other than what he is. He had wanted to play country music most of the time he was in my blues band. He even mentioned it again that night in El Paso. I'd never given Pat's suggestions any traction. "Let's stick to the meat and potatoes," I'd tell him. "Let's stick to the blues."

I think Pat was always resentful of the fact that I demanded he play blues all night and that I was inflexible about his wanting to do country stuff. He would occasionally show me country-and-western riffs and songs, which I liked listening to but didn't want to incorporate into our repertoire. Pat was a better and more interesting blues guitar player than he was a country player. That's why all the old blues guys whose photos he carried around loved him. Lowell Fulson, Brownie McGhee and others thought of Pat as a terrific, very creative blues guitar player. He'd lived in Chicago for a period and played with the real blues folks. He'd gotten to know Albert Collins, Big Walter Horton, Sunnyland Slim (whose house he stayed at for a couple months), Big Time Sarah and many other Chicago blues greats. They schooled him in the blues. Pat knew how to play the real blues, just like the old-timers.

Pat was a son of the blues who was great at it, but all he wanted to do was play country music. Go figure!

And next time, Pat, I pick the Mexican restaurant!

CHAPTER ELEVEN

Anthony Paule

A nthony Paule was an irreplaceable band member. He's a great guy to have in any band, not only because he is a fine guitar player but also because he's a fabulous mechanic. I met Anthony in the late '70s when he used to live in Marin County. I got to know him a bit when I was playing with Mississippi Johnny Waters and Sonny Lane and visited him at his house in San Rafael. His outstanding record collection outclasses that of anyone I know, and I know a number of guys with great record collections. Anthony's is special, filled with all kinds of hard-to-find blues and other rare stuff I have never seen anywhere else.

We became good friends over time and jammed every chance we got. I liked his style and the way we worked together. After Pat Chase left the band in 1986, Anthony started playing with the Blues Survivors. At that time the configuration of the band was June Core on the drums, Anthony on guitar, and Tim Wagar on bass. After Tim, we hired Mike Judge, future creator of Beavis and Butt-head.

When he had time, Anthony worked on the van while we were in the Bay Area. He then lived in San Francisco and worked for his brother's airport shuttle company, which used the same exact Dodge vans as mine. He knew everything about how to repair them when they broke down or wouldn't start. Once, stalled at the side of the road in Colorado, he figured out a problem with my van within ten minutes, where otherwise we would have spent three hours or longer in a garage.

He played with me for about a year and a half, including the tour of misfortune I call the Hey, Harpster Tour. He also played on the infamous European trip, during which he roomed with Dave some of the time and got to see him in action. On that tour, the Blues Survivors traveled with the Roy Rogers' band on a double bill. "Hey, Harpster" Dave, who'd just left my band, was playing in Roy's band. Anthony needed a good sense of humor for that—and so did I!

CHAPTER TWELVE

Hey, Harpster

In 1987, I booked a nine-week tour of the West, Midwest and South. I had Anthony Paule on guitar, and June Core on the drums. Tim Wager, my bass player for the prior three years, had to bow out due to his dad's health problems. Through a mutual friend I found a replacement named Dave who had spent time on the road playing bass for Maria Muldaur. With his red beard and hat, Dave looked like a pot-bellied version of General George Armstrong Custer with a voice like Dr. John crossed with Wolfman Jack. The first rehearsal went great, and Dave seemed to be a solid bass player. Our first gig was in Salt Lake City.

We deadheaded out of California, stopping for a late dinner in Wendover, Nevada, at a casino that had a full buffet. As stood in line, we ran into Tommy Castro, who was out on the road with the Dynatones, long before he started his own band. Tommy is often labeled "the hardest working bluesman on the planet," giving me a strong run for the title! It's not hard to believe that title when you run into Tommy at a buffet like that one, loaded with semi-bad food and MSG, on the road a million miles from home. After a brief conversation with Tommy, I joined my guys at our table. As I sat down, I noticed Dave had heaped nothing but meat on his plate. Dave served himself huge mounds of greasy meat and gravy without a veggie on the side. As I finished my salad, Dave went back to the buffet and loaded up his plate for seconds, and again it was all meat. I didn't think about it until later that night as we were driving to the gig. The van was suddenly exploding with sounds of gastric flatus and rotten smells emanating from the bowels our new friend.

"Sorry, bro'," Dave rasped after every expulsion.

In spite of the freezing weather, I had to drive with the windows open to keep from gagging.

We were playing two weeks in Colorado, starting in Steamboat Springs, Little Bear in Evergreen and many other Colorado stops before heading down into Texas. They say human beings can adjust to anything, but that might not be true. I never got used to that bad air coming out of Dave's meat-filled gut.

I thought Dave's gas was the worst of it, but I found out he had an even more dangerous habit. While driving through Kansas, I noticed Dave had lit up a joint.

"What the hell you doing?" I demanded as I smelled the sweet stink of the weed.

"It's cool, bro'!"Dave rasped calmly. "It helps to get rid of the fart stink back here!"

I couldn't believe this guy was willing to risk us all going to jail and having the van impounded in the middle of western Kansas just to relive the stink of his farts.

"Put it out," I shouted. "Eat some goddamn vegetables if you want to get rid of that gas! You must have twenty pounds of meat down there rotting in your intestines!"

"Sure, Mark, no problem," he said without emotion. "Isn't weed a vegetable?"

The other guys laughed, and I heard the hiss of him sucking in more smoke from the joint. Dave wasn't going to listen to me, and that's a bad sign when you are trying to manage a team out on the road. Dave was a loose cannon, and the smell of weed kept coming from the back of the van. What could I do? I couldn't stop the van and scold him like he's a kid and throw his weed away. I turned up the stereo and listened to Little Walter's "Crazy Mixed Up World."

Fortunately, we didn't get stopped and made it out of Kansas. The guys told me after the tour this was the least of my worries. Dave had been having his connection back home ship him envelopes of cocaine to all the venues we played on this tour so he could stay fully loaded throughout the trip!

We played in Dallas that week to an enthusiastic audience. I met Anson Funderburgh on that visit. Born in Plano, Texas, Anson had a first rate band that included Sam Myers, the great harmonica player. I mentioned to Anson that we were heading down to Jackson, Mississippi, for our next gig. He told me to get a hold of his buddy, harp player and songwriter Greg "Fingers" Taylor, while we were there.

On our drive to the next show, Dave made a call. It turned out to be awful news. His ex-wife brutally informed him she'd decided to move lock, stock and barrel to the East Coast and was taking their eight-year-old daughter with her. Dave found he couldn't do anything to stop it. I felt bad for him, but I didn't really understand the pain he was in. I probably wasn't as sensitive as I could have been. I'd been absorbed in the tour and bringing it off the best I could. Dave's problems were secondary, and so were his feelings. I didn't spend time thinking about how he felt about her leaving

California with his daughter while he was thousands of miles away on the road.

I would have plenty of reason to think about Dave's family train wreck when I found myself in the same boat ten years later.

When we got to Jackson, we played an upstairs club called George St. Grocery in an old two-story brick building in the shadow of the capitol. During the day, the place is a restaurant that offers a full menu. We rocked the house that night, but a problem was developing. Dave's bass had been getting louder and louder as the tour went on. It soon would drive me nuts. I was thinking I might be going crazy, but June mentioned it to me as well. At least I knew it wasn't just me. That night in Jackson, as Dave blazed away way over the top at eleven decibels, I turned around and gave him the "bring it down" hand signal. Dave nodded okay but didn't change his setting.

"Turn it down," I told him again.

This time he flipped me the bird.

"Fuck you, harpster," he rasped so loud that everyone in the audience heard him."Fuck you!"

My new friend Fingers Taylor was on the bandstand with us that night. He is probably best known for the time he spent playing harmonica with Jimmy Buffet and the Coral Reefer Band.

I'd been embarrassed by Dave's behavior, but I played through it. I never asked Fingers if he heard Dave's rude comment to me, but I bet he did. I did conclude the gig without saying another word to Dave. I knew he was having some issues, but I chose to ignore it.

After we finished our gig, Fingers invited us down to a late-night session at a local blues juke joint called the Subway Lounge, deep in the Jackson 'hood. The Subway is a historical site in Jackson and was featured in the blues documentary *Last of the Mississippi Jukes*. We arrived there after two a.m. and were the only palefaces in the bar. I met Jimmy the owner for the first time that morning, and he asked us to sit in. We happily obliged. Meanwhile, Dave was getting drunker and drunker and stepping on people's feet and saying, "Sorry, bro'."

Dave had finally gotten on my last nerve, and no matter what his problems were, I decided to get rid of him. He could take his bad air, his loud bass, his booze, his weed and his obnoxious personality to some other band. I wanted to get out of a situation I could tell was going to hell in a fart basket.

I called Tim Wagar, my old bass player, to see if he could fly in, but he was unable to join us because his dad still needed him. I begged, but to no avail. Tim did the right thing by not leaving his dad.

Poor June, who roomed with Dave half the time, had to listen to him all night long, crying and screaming that he's going to kill "the harpster." Dave locked himself in the bathroom, drank whiskey while lying in the bathtub, alternately crying about his wife and daughter leaving him and how he hated "the harpster." Dave's sudden desire for privacy was a stark change from his normal behavior. June complained he had to listen to the loud burps and farts Dave's stomach set in motion when Dave got up in the morning. Dave's routine began with the daily exercise of eating a submarine sandwich or his leftover dinner scraps while on the toilet taking his morning dump. Dave performed all this without even having the decency to close the bathroom door. June had to be in shock the first time he woke up and realized what Dave was up to in the john, but then, seemingly overnight, Dave's restroom pattern changed. He began closing the door in the morning and not leaving till the night. June couldn't get in when he needed to and had to use our bathroom each day instead of his own. Although June is a live-and-let-live kind of guy, he told me he couldn't take any more of Dave's behavior.

Our tour made a stop in Birmingham, Alabama, Dave's home town. After playing our gig there the first night, we went back to the hotel. Dave asked me about the checkout time, and I told him eleven a.m. He took off to spend the night with his friends, and I didn't really think about it. June had to be happy about getting a normal night's sleep and a morning without Dave's anti-hygienic antics. At eleven the next day, no Dave. At twelve, still no Dave. I called the number he left me, but the phone just kept ringing. I wanted to leave without him, but I had a feeling that if I did I wouldn't have a bass player on the next gig. We hung out for another two hours before Dave showed up. He was drunk, hadn't showered and appeared to have been up all night. I was livid, as were June and Anthony. When I called him on it, he answered,"I call a spade a spade and *you* ain't one!"

Dave slept on the entire ride to New Orleans. We threw a moving van carpet over him to stifle his farts and general stink. I expected Dave to go over the edge in the Big Easy, but nothing major happened in New Orleans too far out of the ordinary. He turned his volume down a few decibels so I could make it through the shows, and he was closing the bathroom door for June and not staying all day.

We next hit Grand Emporium in Kansas City, Missouri, then Zoo Bar in Lincoln, Nebraska (always one of our favorite stops) and Missoula, Montana, all in a blur of mid-tour amnesia. There were other stops that I'm sure I'm forgetting. The tour ground down in a haze of bad air and bad vibes from Dave.

By the time we hit Laramie, Wyoming, the rhythm section was pulling in two different directions. Dave would always speed up while June tried to maintain a steady, mellow groove. It was toward the end of the trip, thank God, and there was some light at the end of the flatus tunnel.

After the long drive home, we dropped Dave off and I didn't see him again until about a year or so later while on a European tour double billed with Roy Rogers, in whose band Dave was playing bass. I got to see another bandleader go through everything I had experienced. Dave hadn't changed a bit and gave Roy the same fart-filled poor experience that I had suffered though on the Midwest-Southern tour.

Anthony tells a great story from that Rogers-Hummel European tour. As we were gigging though Sweden, Anthony roomed with Dave, just as June had done on our earlier trip. One night Dave brought a drunken Swede who could not speak English back to the room. Anthony visited with them for a while and then pretended to go to sleep on his bed. The Swedish girl fell asleep alongside Dave on his bed. Dave woke up in the middle of the night and tried to perform oral sex on the sleeping Swede. She began beating him on the head with her shoe, shouting at him in Swedish. Dave kept on going, trying to be amorous. Anthony said he did everything he could not to burst out laughing. The Swedish girl heard Anthony laughing while Dave was trying to do his thing and fled their room after cursing him out in Swedish. So much for Dave's art of seduction!

CHAPTER THIRTEEN

Bad Weather Blues

Catastrophic weather conditions and severe auto accidents are the two potential disasters touring musicians who drive from gig to gig must worry about. I've found in my twenty-seven years of road traveling that every year I worry more about the odds than I ever did before. It can be the odds of getting into a fender-bender or major crash, or the odds of running into some really dangerous weather, like a tornado or blizzard, that could hurt me or other band members. Either way, touring is a game against the odds. A good bandleader tries to find ways to avoid the dark side of the Big Road Blues by stacking the odds in his favor.

A large part of touring safely is surviving the weather conditions you find while cruising down the nation's highways, from coast to coast, gig to gig. Understanding the weather, as they say, is "an art, not a science," although science has quite a bit to do with it. It's the art of knowing when it's time to get the hell out of somewhere bad and the science of having the right equipment to help you get out of trouble when it comes.

One of the first bad storms we encountered was back in 1984 when we did a little trip to a ski resort in Mammoth Lakes, California. The lodge at the resort had a nightclub that would book bands for a week or even two. We left two days ahead of our opening night just so we could get acclimated to the elevation. The town sits at an elevation of over eight thousand feet, with Mammoth Mountain looming across the skyline.

We had a long day of driving ahead of us, and I had worked

it out with the booking agent to make sure we could come in a couple days early. Unfortunately, in leaving early, we got hit by one of the worst storms in the Sierras in quite a few years. The Blues Survivors didn't have the luxury of a touring van yet, and we were driving our own cars to gigs. I rode to Mammoth Lake with my guitar player, Pat Chase, in his Datsun station wagon with a little camper shell on top. Bass player Tim Wagar and drummer Norman Winkler rode in Norman's small Toyota. Such trips convinced me I needed a van.

On our way up through the Sierras on Highway 50, Pat and I got about as far as Placerville when freezing rain started pouring down in sheets. The radio news announced that there was going to be snow down to about two thousand feet, which is low for the Northern California area. By dusk, about twenty miles outside Lake Tahoe, the snow was so thick and deep that the road was closed. The snow fell in such huge flakes that we couldn't see four feet in front of us. We could go no further and pulled into a little roadside hotel. Pat and I spent the night there in the hopes the conditions would improve the next day. The weather in the Sierras didn't cooperate. Just ask the Donner party! Pat and I ended up driving out the next day in whiteout conditions. We literally couldn't see more than three or five feet ahead as we scraped along the side of the mountain on the icy roads.

It turned out to be one of the most frightful rides of my life. The view from Pat's Datsun was so white that we couldn't tell where the road ended and where the snow bank began. We couldn't tell if we were going to go off the mountain or hit a tree. We could barely see the taillights of the car or truck in front of us, but we had to try to keep up with the vehicle ahead—or else. If we lost it and didn't see any taillights, we were in even deeper scratch because we had no idea where the road was or which way to turn. We piled into a snow bank on the shoulder of the road at one point. We drove three or five miles an hour, with our noses pressed against the windshield trying to see, until we finally made it to Lake Tahoe.

There still was no improvement in the driving conditions as we continued on to Mammoth Lake.

We made it only as far as Bishop, California, the following day and still had another fifty or sixty miles to go to get to our destination. The road was closed and hadn't been plowed because the conditions were too extreme even for the snowplows. The California Highway Patrol had shut down the road for several hours. A ride that would normally have taken us six to seven hours wound up taking us closer to thirty-six hours to get to the lodge.

The Blues Survivors' tours became more organized in the mid-'80s when we got the first van. We drove through many storms during several winter tours in Colorado and Utah. We usually did between four and eight weeks in Colorado alone, a week or two at a time at different ski resorts. Playing the ski resorts, however, meant driving through snow storms, and going from one resort to another meant driving totally through the mountains. There were a few times driving in whiteout conditions on those mountain highways that weren't quite as bad as the Sierras, but they were bad enough to scare me and scare the hell out of everybody riding with me.

I used to do all-night drives through really bad, mountainous terrain in the wintertime. It didn't matter if there was a snowstorm, black ice all over the roads on nights as pitch-black as they get only in the Rocky Mountains, freezing rain or fog as thick as your grandma's ankles. I might have been scared out of my mind whether or not we were even going to make it to the next venue, but I still pushed ahead! I drove in many extreme snow blizzards in those days. I kind of liked it, but today I rarely do night drives in lousy weather. I don't venture into Canada in the winter anymore, especially western Canada.

Another hairy storm descended on us when we were coming back from an East Coast tour, mostly in Florida, in December 1990. Bassist Burt Winn, guitarist Curtis Smith and drummer Eric Mossberger were with me on a nine-week tour. It felt like we had been on the road forever, and the weeks started to wear on us.

On our way back from Florida, we drove straight across the country with only one stop in Texas and another in New Mexico. We took I-40, trying to avoid the bad weather, yet we still managed to run into an ice storm one night that made the road impassable from about two until six a.m. We sat at a dead stop on I-40 outside of Flagstaff in a line of cars miles long. The one radio station we could pick up played the same Larry King interview over and over, but we listened on, hoping to hear breaking news about the weather. Curtis got so stir-crazy that he jumped out of the van and started running around on the ice, just to blow off steam. We felt like prisoners in the van. It had been a long tour, and now there was this long wait.

"Shut up, Larry, you dumb ass!" Curtis screamed as King asked some movie star about a divorce.

We finally made it home late the next afternoon after an extremely long and tedious drive.

In 2001, the Blues Survivors were in caught in the worst ice storm we've ever experienced on the road. Marty Dodson, Steve Wolf, Charles Wheal and I were on our way down south. Marty wanted to stop and visit his ex-wife in Dallas, so figured we'd stay the night in Dallas and drive on the next day to the first gig of our tour. We hadn't bothered to check the radio for the weather and had no idea of what we were about to drive into. As we motored into Dallas, we were surprised to see overturned cars, cars and semi-truck trailers twisted sideways, passenger buses on the side of the highway and cars that had spun out into the middle of the road. It seemed as if some giant child had left his toy cars and trucks all over the road. There seemed to be no rhyme or reason to the scene, which was a truly frightening sight to behold. I had only seen a sight like this one other time, driving through Albuquerque, when no one seemed to know how to drive on snow. The cars had skidded into each other and all over the side of the road.

The next day, when we left Dallas, the ice was worse than it had been when we arrived. Driving through East Texas about an hour or two out of Dallas, the icy weather was so bad that we were literally driving about two miles an hour and could still feel the van fish-tailing. People were having accidents left and right all around us. The traffic was bumper-to-bumper because everybody had to drive so slow just to get through the slick stretch of road.

In May 2004, we were deadheading it home from Chicago. It was not at a time of year when one would think of snow, but we ended up driving into a huge snowstorm in the Sierras. Chain requirements were in effect across the summit. I had recently purchased a new van and had placed the chains from the old van in it. I had to hire a roadside chain guy to put the chains on my van, but they didn't fit. We were at the very top of the Sierras in bumper-to-bumper traffic. The drive up had taken about two hours. The chain man told me we'd have to go all the way back to Reno to get the right chains.

It was another debacle that resulted in frayed nerves all the way around. After almost completing the thirty-six-hour trip home from Chicago, we sat in traffic for hours waiting for chains to be installed. It was just a bit too much, even for a traveling bluesman. The moral of the story is that you never know when you're going to need snow chains. Nowadays, I make sure they fit before I leave my driveway. Don't leave home without them!

In 2007, while the Blues Survivors were doing an East Coast Blues Harmonica Blowout tour with Charlie Musselwhite and Kim Wilson, we found ourselves in the middle of another hairy storm. Fortunately, we didn't have to drive very far on the icy roads, but few fans in the area were willing to risk driving on the slick black ice to come to the show. A local radio station had even advised people to stay home that night, and we wound up playing for a tiny crowd. For those fans who attended, it was like an up-close-and-personal blowout. Charlie and Kim played as if we had an audience of thousands listening, and those folks who were brave enough to come out got a really great show with super performances.

After the gig, as we were trying to load the equipment into the van, the ground was so slippery we could barely walk the five feet from the door of the club to the van without falling on our asses. In fact, we did fall, more than once. It was an incredible sight watching the guys slip-sliding around with the amps and almost falling forward as we loaded the stuff into the van. Ice storms are at the top of my list of dangerous conditions to avoid while on the road and even in parking lots.

I also have been stuck in floods. One happened when I played with Sue Foley. I left the van in a parking lot in Oshkosh, Wisconsin, and went to see a movie. When I came back, three feet of standing water covered the parking lot from rain that had come down while I was in the theater. Fortunately, my van was in an elevated part of the lot, so I wasn't stuck in the water. It was rather amazing, though, to see all that water had accumulated while I attended a two-hour movie.

I've dealt with tornados over the years, too. I first experienced bad tornado weather in the '90s, when I was touring with Pacemaker, Vance and Joe Foy. Most tornadoes happen down south or in the lower part of the Midwest, in an area known as Tornado Alley, from Arkansas to the Texas Panhandle through Oklahoma and down into Alabama and the top of Louisiana.

The scariest tornado weather driving is at night because there's no way of seeing where it's coming from. All you'll see at night is horrible rain and hail, and you have no idea if there's a tornado to the side, to the front or anywhere else around your vehicle. Between the hail and the rain, there's no way of knowing where or when you'll run into a deadly tornado. There have been quite a few tours where we'd be driving with only ten-to-twenty-foot visibility while hearing tornado reports over the radio. We never hit a tornado, but we saw some of the aftereffects. Overturned Winnebagos and semi-trucks littered the highway as we drove along. It was very scary stuff.

I drove through Alabama one time with Steve Wolf, Charles Wheal and Mark Thaice, a guitarist-turned-drummer from

Belgium who'd never been near a tornado in his life. The sky was turning purple, and the clouds were revolving in a circular motion, as if they were going to form a tornado any minute. We were listening to tornado warnings on the radio, but fortunately for us, we only saw funnel clouds in the distance. None came close to us, but Thaice was terrified.

"If we see the funnel cone, get under one of these overpasses," one of the guys said. "And crawl up into the corner!"

"Really?" Thaice asked. "What if we can't find an overpass?"

"Then get under the van," another Blues Survivor said, "and hang onto the axel."

"The axel?" Thaice asked. "Under the van?"

"Yeah," he was told. "Get under the van and loop your arms around the axel. That way the tornado can't pick you up!"

"Really?" the even-more-scared musician wondered.

I had never before seen the sky such a creepy greenish-purplish color. Scary-looking clouds boiled angrily in the sky. The wind picked up for a while. Then the day became eerily still. I thought we would see a twister any minute as we kept flying down an empty highway in spite of the radio warnings. That night, we drove through more bad weather where tornadoes were being reported all around us.

In 2007, on the return trip from the ice-storm tour, we were on Highway 20 going trough East Texas, an area known as the "A-hole of the world." We were deadheading it home from the long blowout tour when we arrived at a point where the Texas Highway Patrol had closed the road due to a tornado hitting ground ahead of us. We had to sit for three hours on a highway off ramp while the roadway ahead was cleared of tornado wreckage.

It was yet another example of the Bad Weather Blues that has dogged me and the Blues Survivors on our tours across the United States.

CHAPTER FOURTEEN

No Lights or Heater in Colorado

I bought my first van in 1985. The Blues Survivors, made up at the time of drummer June Core, bassist Tim Wagar and guitarist Pat Chase, were coming back from playing a gig in New Mexico. We were going to drive straight through to our next show, pulling an all-nighter from New Mexico up to Denver. It was in the late fall, going into winter, and it was starting to get freezing cold. I didn't have anything to keep the van warm except a heater and some funky homemade insulation I'd created out of old carpet and hung on the insides of the van. Somewhere between midnight and one in the morning, the heater crapped out. It started getting really cold in the van. We could see our breath in billowy clouds when we exhaled.

"This is the kind of cold weather people die in," Pat said grimly.

The van's headlights then grew dimmer and dimmer. I didn't know it at the time, but these were sure signs that the alternator was failing. The gradual dimming of the headlights added to our trepidation in the middle of nowhere. It was freezing, and the outlook was not good.

The guys all sat huddled together, warming their cold hands by rubbing them together or blowing on them as we drove. We were all watching the lights slowly fade and wondering if we were going to make it or die out there in the Colorado wilderness. It's a strange feeling to have your welfare, and maybe even your survival, based on the random luck of whether your alternator will fail as you drive down a highway over freezing tundra. We all sat like that for a few hours, wondering if we were going to make it to our destination. We finally drove into Denver, with no lights and no heater, but still in one piece. Although we were definitely a lot colder than we wanted to be, we were still lucky that we made it. Chance had been on our side—this time.

I also remember a hailstorm in Nebraska about twelve years later. We were driving to either Lincoln or Omaha in the tour van when we started hearing reports on the radio about tornadoes in the area. The Midwest region we were driving through is known as the Tornado Belt and is the scene of countless savage storms each year. The chance of getting hit by a tornado was a real possibility. Mark Bohn, who was playing drums with us, was scared to death of tornadoes. The radio was putting out ever-more-ominous tornado warnings by the minute and finally warning the folks in our area to seek shelter. The sky was getting darker and more threatening by the second. Bohn was freaking out.

"Come on, Hummel!" he shouted. "Turn around and get the hell out of here!"

"Relax, Bohn," I said, "We're gonna be fine—I think."

We started passing by RVs with their windshields busted out, which definitely gave us good cause for panic. The fact that there were no people around added to our fear. As the sky grew even darker, the wind died completely. It was like everything hung for a few moments in total stillness, not a sound, not even a whisper. I pulled the van to a halt, afraid that I might be driving right into the tornado. Then, without any warning, all hell broke loose. Before I could figure out what was happening, it started hailing. It sounded like somebody was firing on the van with a machine gun.

"Turn around, Hummel, before it's too late!" guitarist Chris Masterson and bassist Randy Bermudes screamed simultaneously.

We made a U-turn in the middle of I-80 and went across the island in the middle of the highway. I wanted to get off at the next exit because the hail was getting so loud I panicked. It sounded like somebody was beating the roof of the van with baseball bats or crowbars. Dings from the hailstones began appearing on the inside roof of the van. Hailstones the size of lemons crashed into the windshield.

"God help us!" Bohn screamed. "We're in the tornado!"

"It's OK, Bohn," I shouted back. "It's only hail!" I only wish I believed what I'd said to him. I was scared shitless. I was sure we were going to see a funnel cloud at any moment!

We got to a gas station just in the nick of time to pull under the overhang over the gas pumps. We started seeing baseball-size hail bouncing about five feet when it hit the road and banging away like cannon fire on top of the overhang. All kinds of people were in the station's convenience store trying to get away from the hail.

"Do ya think the tornado's gonna hit us?" Bohn asked the female clerk.

"It might," she answered flatly.

He appeared ready to pass out from stress and stayed inside the store until the hail stopped and the clouds lifted.

"That was a close one," Bohn said when we were back in the van driving again.

The hail did enough damage to the van that I had to have the roof repaired and the windshield replaced when I got back home. Fortunately, my insurance company paid for it. After that I avoided touring the Tornado Belt in tornado season.

Another very close call was when the cruise control on the van went helter-skelter in the middle of Ohio. Charles Wheal, who shared driving duties on the trip with Marty Dodson, Steve Wolf and me, was behind the wheel when the cruise control stuck and wouldn't click off. He was trying to make up some time and was cruising at eighty miles an hour. He shouted to me, in his smooth, polished English accent, that the van was out of control.

"Eh, Mark, we 'alve ourselves a wee bit of a tilley up 'ere," Charles said. "The van 'as become like a runaway train 'ere." He tried desperately to tap on the cruise control buttons, with his fingers and palms. There was no response.

"We're losing it up 'ere!" Charles shouted to me. "The cruise control won't shut off!"

"Tap the brakes with your foot," I shouted back to him as the van picked up speed. "See if it doesn't engage!" It didn't work. The van was an unstoppable rocket filled with amps and instruments and the Blues Survivors!

We all started to panic at that point because none of the tricks Charles and I were trying worked. There appeared to be no way to stop the van or reengage the cruise control mechanism. If Charles put the van in neutral, it would burn up the engine in a few minutes and wreak havoc on the transmission gearing. We were going through Dayton, Ohio, a place I have never thought about living or dying in.

"Throw it in neutral! I shouted. "To hell with the engine! We've got to slow her down!"

Charles saw an off-ramp, and I yelled to him to put it in neutral just for a minute, enough time to apply the brakes and slow the van, so we could careen off the freeway without rolling over. Fortunately, there were no vehicles in front of us that day. Another inexplicable miracle of this event was that at the very bottom of this off-ramp there was an auto dealership and repair service that just happened to service Fords. We pulled our Ford van into the driveway, with Charles pressing his foot into the brake and letting the engine run in neutral until we stopped. Luckily, the mechanic was right there on site and was able to disconnect the cruise control before the engine burned up.

One of our scariest incidents happened in Colorado in 1985. I was traveling with Pat Chase, Tim Wagar and drummer Jimi Bott. We were driving over Rabbit Ears Pass, above Steamboat Springs, and climbing to ten thousand feet at the summit. The weather was cold and clear, but the roads were covered with patches of thick black ice. I was driving about ten miles an hour when I suddenly lost control of the van. We spun out of control on the slippery pavement and were doing donuts in the middle of the highway, spinning like a top. The only way to stop was to go right into the snow banks that lined the sides of the pass. We slid right into a huge snow bank. CRUNCH!

Hitting a snow bank is like hitting a tree. We all flew forward inside the van with the equipment and instruments flying around us.

"Nice driving," I heard one of the guys moan.

"Black ice," I replied.

"Dumb ass!" someone in the rear commented.

We put all the equipment back in place and secured it this time. We couldn't find any damage to the equipment and nobody had gotten hurt. The van seemed all right as well.

"No problem," I said as we got rolling again. We made if over the pass without further trouble.

I had thought everything was fine until we got to Nevada. I started hearing a strange noise. By the time we were in the Sierras, a steady shudder was growing in intensity. It had become a loud banging noise by the time we were near Vacaville, California. The snow embankment had taken out the rear end of the van, causing a break in lining and all the rear end. Differential fluid had leaked out. I thought about trying to make it the remaining sixty-five miles home with the van the way it was, but ended up having it towed to Richmond. Our respective girlfriends and/or friends had to come and pick us up from the repair shop.

"It's just one problem after another on these tours," one of the girlfriends commented. "Don't you ever get sick of this? You should quit this touring before something really bad happens."

"Don't be like that, baby," her boyfriend responded. "I can't quit this shit. It's what I do. Aren't you glad to see me?"

When I called my girlfriend to come and get me, she asked what had happened. I thought for a minute, while staring at my van up on the rack, and told her, "No worries. It's part of what I do, but that new rear end is going to cost me a fortune."

"I'm just happy you're home," she said after a long pause, "even with your blown rear end."

CHAPTER FIFTEEN

Burning Van Fest

In 1986 I still had my first touring van, the original Blues Survivors' Dodge van that I bought in 1984. It was old when I bought it, and after three years of relentless touring across the country, the engine had started to sputter and the transmission was slipping and getting shaky. I was getting ready to go to Europe for five weeks and had a Colorado tour set up for when I got back. I took the van in to have the transmission done while I was out of the country. Five weeks seemed like plenty of time for the mechanics to fix it while I was away.

"We know you brought it in for the transmission problems, but there are some other issues," the head mechanic at a transmission company in San Leandro said."The engine seems old, too. You might want to think about replacing the engine, with as many miles as you have on it."

"How much extra would that be?" I asked nervously.

"Twenty-four hundred dollars," he said. "The transmission will be twelve hundred and the engine twelve hundred."

"Twenty-four hundred total?" I inquired.

"That's right," he said.

"Okay," I agreed. "I'll go ahead and have the extra work done. I just need to make sure you have it done by the time I get back from Europe."

"No problem," he assured me. "We've got five weeks, and that's plenty of time to work on it. We'll have it done by the time you get back. No sweat."

I had no contact with the garage during my European trip.

This was long before the days of the Internet and cell phones. It was next to impossible to call the U.S. from Europe in those days.

After returning home and resting a day, I phoned the garage and asked the twenty-four hundred dollar question.

"Is the van done?" I asked.

"We haven't gotten to it yet," I was told. "We'll get to that van of yours tomorrow."

"Wait a minute!" I responded. "You guys have had it for five weeks. I don't understand."

"We've had a really busy time, and we've had quite a few other vans to fix in here," the head mechanic said. "We're going to get to it tomorrow and have it done by Friday."

I had already paid twelve hundred dollars as a deposit. There wasn't anything I could do, but I wanted him to understand my predicament.

"Look," I said. "I'm leaving in ten days for my next tour, and I have to have the van packed up and ready to go by then."

"No problem," he said.

The van was not done when I called back the next day. I was furious.

"We've got the transmission fixed, but we haven't finished the engine yet," I was told. "And," he added, "we ran into some additional problems we have to correct."

"You guys better get on it," I demanded. "I've got to get out on the road really quick here, and I'd like to get it back before the day I have to leave for the tour."

I called the following Thursday, and they stalled me again. I began giving the guy a piece of my mind.

"You can come pick it up tomorrow," he said, interrupting my tirade.

"Okay," I said, "but I'm not calling tomorrow. I'm just coming to the garage."

I picked up the van the next day. I was miffed at the garage for taking all that time but happy to be behind the wheel and ready to get going on the road. As I was driving home from the shop, the van started to jerk a bit and misfire. I called the garage to complain when I got to my house.

"It'll probably just take a little while to break in, you know," the mechanic told me. "The transmission's fine, and the engine probably will just take a little while to break in. Did you check the oil?"

"Yeah," I replied. "The oil's fine."

"Well, okay, then," he said. "Don't worry about it. It'll be fine."

I had a gig that night in Walnut Creek, California. At the time I had Anthony Paule playing guitar, June Core on drums and Mike Judge on bass. As I was driving down Highway 24 from Berkeley to the gig, I felt a twitch in the engine. I was right outside of Lafayette, about fifteen miles east of Berkeley, when I noticed the engine missing more and more. It was sputtering and lurching. Then I started seeing flames flaring out of the exhaust pipe. I kept driving for another minute, and burning pieces of something began shooting out of the pipe, leaving little piles of burning material along the highway.

"Your van's on fire!" a guy screamed as he drove alongside me, honking.

Something smelled really awful, like burning plastic. The fumes were overwhelming. Smoke poured from the dashboard as I pulled off the freeway at the Lafayette exit. I drove past a gas station, so in case the van blew up, it wouldn't blow up the gas station too. I ran into a restaurant next to the gas station and used the pay phone for an emergency call. In the meantime, I saw billows of smoke pouring out of the dashboard and steering column. The next thing I knew, a full-fledged fire was coming out of the front of the van.

I called the fire department.

"My van's on fire" I shouted into the phone. "You gotta come. I'm at the East Lafayette exit. Major car fire! Hurry!"

I hung up and ran outside to the burning vehicle. I started pulling equipment out from the back of the van like a madman.

My PA system, amplifier and harmonicas were all in the back. I was afraid the engine was going to explode with me right inside. I removed the equipment as fast as I could and put everything on the edge of a dirt lot where I had pulled over. Once I emptied the van, I kept moving my stuff further and further away as six-foot flames shot from the front of the van. Customers had walked out of the restaurant to watch the spectacle, perhaps hoping to see the van explode. The fire department came and put out the fire. The crowd went back inside the restaurant. My first show of the night was over.

I called Mike Judge, who had a little pickup truck, from the pay phone.

"You're not going to believe this," I said, "but my van just burned up in Lafayette and you're going to have to come get me."

Mike was already at the club setting up his gear by the time I called him. He was the only one at the club with a vehicle large enough to come get me and my stuff. He drove to Lafayette, and we put the PA, my amplifier and harmonicas in the back of the pickup. I left my smoking van, and we went to the club. Mike gave me a ride home after the gig, and I fell into bed. The fire had left me exhausted. I didn't know quite what to do.

I went back to Lafayette with an AAA tow truck the next day and had the burnt shell of my van towed to my girlfriend's house. It was a Saturday morning. I was supposed to be leaving for Colorado on Tuesday. I called a lawyer buddy of mine, Dennis Antenore, and told him the story about the shoddy repairs and what had happened to my new engine.

"What can I do about this?" I asked Dennis. "This garage just took twenty-four hundred dollars from me. They put in a new transmission and an engine that blew up on me in two days. Now I've got no van. I've got no way to do this next tour. These rip-off guys have just about put me out of business! I need you to help me out."

Dennis drafted a letter threatening a lawsuit if the shop didn't give me my money back and pay for a rental van for the tour. Apparently feeling bad or not wanting negative publicity, the shop coughed up money for both the low Blue Book value of the van and renting one for the tour. It cost the garage somewhere between twelve hundred or two thousand dollars for the rental. It was their bad luck that we had a three-to-four-week road tour, instead of a shorter one.

Fortunately, the shop cut me a check for my burned-out van and the rental right away, but the whole episode left me very stressed out. I just hope I don't have to go to any more burning van fests. They're not my kind of show!

CHAPTER SIXTEEN

Kirk-Dave Tour

I stopped playing with guitarist Buddy Reed in 1988 after the first Italian trip because he joined Bill Tarsha's band in Phoenix. I was looking for a band to go out on a tour of the United States. I was working at the time with Doug Rynak, who used to play piano with Anson Funderburgh, and he had a female singer named Dona McGee. I had met Doug and Dona previously, on a Colorado trip, and they were doing a kind of jazz-blues thing together. She sang in a style reminiscent of Billie Holiday, Ella Johnson and Dinah Washington. Dona was better than anybody I'd ever heard singing these jazz-blues styles. I liked Doug's piano playing because he could play both Chicago blues and the kind of swinging jazzy blues stuff I was becoming increasingly interested in.

June Core, after three and a half years of being on the road with me, decided he wanted to get off it for a while. I was changing, and the band was changing, but I wanted to keep it going. I didn't know what else to do.

I started looking around for another guitarist and drummer. There were two people I'd heard about and wanted a chance to try out. One was a drummer from Germany named Kirk, who was in the Bay Area either as a tourist or with a green card, I don't know which. Kirk had been working around with some local bands. The guitar player was a guy named Dave who had contacted me through somebody else's referral. He came to see me at Eli's Mile High Club when I had Buddy in the band and phoned me after hearing me and Buddy perform on Tom Mazzolini's long-running KPFA blues radio show, "**Blues by the Bay**."

"I heard your guitar player the other night," Dave said. "He's not shit. You should hire me because I'm way better than him."

"Really?" I responded. "What makes you think that?"

"Because I'm a guitar player and I know," he answered. "I know that he ain't shit and I'm way better. I could play all those things he was playing backwards and sideways."

The guy was way too cocky for me, and I ended the conversation. He phoned again a couple months later.

"I know you're still looking," he said.

"If you've got a place where I can hear you, I'd like to come by," I told him.

Dave was playing a gig in North Beach in San Francisco. I got up on stage, and we played a few tunes together. It was obvious he could play and that he knew his way around a blues guitar. I decided I'd try him on some gigs around town and see how it went. I did the same with Kirk, the German drummer. He was very cocky, too, thinking we Americans were all a bit slow in the head.

At that point, I didn't really have any other guys that I could take on the road. Pickings were kind of slim in the Bay Area for musicians available to leave town for a three-week tour. I had to lower my expectations.

At least I already had a bass player. Burt Winn had just started working with the Blues Survivors. For the tour, Burt traveled with his wife in his own car part for part of the trip and with us in the van the rest of the time. It was Burt's first road trip ever, and he was very excited about it. Doug and Dona followed us in had their own vehicle. The guitar player and drummer—and Burt, for a period—traveled in the van with me.

We did gigs in the Southwest and Midwest and throughout the South. At that time, we could go down through the southern part of the country and play a solid two to three weeks. Those were good times for the blues, but blues bands can't really do that anymore. You're lucky if you can get five dates in the South nowadays on a two-week stretch. Back then we could play three to four dates in Texas alone, five or six dates in Louisiana and Mississippi, and even more in Arkansas and Tennessee. We kept busy down south on those tours, but times have certainly changed.

We played a place called Froggy Bottom's in Dallas on our way across Texas. I'd played there a couple years before with "Hey, Harpster" Dave on bass, Anthony Paule on guitar and June Core on drums. The first time had been really successful, but when we returned, it was not nearly as good. The club cut out one of our nights, and we were stranded in Dallas for two nights without work.

The club was on its last legs of supporting live entertainment. Froggy Bottom's had also changed management, and whether it was the fault of the new managers or something else, the club was not as successful as it had been a year earlier. We did our gig, but it was a bummer because the audience was so small.

I was never especially fond of going to Dallas, anyway. It's a big city, easy to get lost in and hot as frying pan most of the time. We went to see Dallas guitarist Mike Morgan play on one of our nights off. He had ex-Johnny Winter drummer Uncle John Turner at the time, and Dave and I got on stage and jammed with Mike and Uncle John. It was a great moment in the middle of a few bad nights we had down in Texas.

Dave decided to do his laundry half an hour before we were supposed to leave Dallas, after we'd been in town, doing nothing, for three days. At eleven AM, the time I said we were supposed to leave, his wet clothes weren't even in the dryer yet.

I had to say something to show my pissed-off Hummel side.

"Why didn't you do your laundry the other three days we were here?" I snapped. "Why do your laundry now, when we are supposed to be leaving?"

"Well, man, I can't do my laundry, you know, until all my clothes are dirty, you know?" Dave said with apparent sincerity. "I'm not going to waste time washing clothes when all my clothes aren't dirty yet. I just ran out of clean clothes this morning, man.

I knew we were leaving at eleven, but I thought I could get it done by eleven, you know. It seemed like I had plenty of time. I mean, I didn't end up having time, but that was because I forgot to put the clothes in earlier, when I was supposed to, and didn't get them in until ten-thirty. That's where I went wrong."

I couldn't tell if it was just an outcome of taking a greenhorn out on the road, a lack of experience or if Dave was simply a numb-nut. Burt, on the other hand, was also a greenhorn, but he obviously could keep a schedule and didn't mess us up with his daily chores. We waited an extra hour or so to get on the road while Dave's clothes washed and dried.

While I sat in the lobby waiting for Dave's clothes to dry, my blood pressure started going up. I began thinking about all the things that pissed me off on the tour, like hanging around in crappy motels, wasting days and nights with no gigs. The feeling gets even worse, I've noticed, on drawn-out tours with goofball companions. I was pissed about being in Dallas, the heat, lost money and a new band that just wasn't as good as I wanted it to be.

I began thinking about Kirk, the new drummer. Kirk the Jerk, as I've come to call him, was really getting on my last nerve. He insisted on rushing every beat on every song we played and couldn't figure out how to slow down. I would tell him to slow it down, but he just didn't get it. It is easy to see why Muddy Waters was always so concerned about what he called "timing" in the music. I got fed up and decided to talk to Kirk about it.

"You're speeding up the beat," I said as nicely as I could. "Why don't you try slowing it down a bit? See if it sounds and feels a little better."

Kirk started screaming at me, saying that he was doing fine and that I wasn't getting into his groove! Kirk yelled at everyone. He spent his life yelling and being in a foul mood.

I got fed up quickly with those two, Dave and Kirk. At first, they couldn't stand each other, Dave being Jewish and Kirk being a German, but they seemed to overcome it as the days went by. By the end of the tour, they were best pals because nobody else could stand either one of them. I guess it was a minor victory for world diversity!

Dave was so late in getting his laundry loaded into the van that I finally blew my top. After we left town, he sat in the van, humming as he folded his clothes. He was happy. I was livid.

"So what took you so long this morning?" I asked in a voice almost trembling with rage.

"I had to give Mike Morgan a lesson," Dave replied, still folding his last sock or two.

"Mike Morgan a lesson?" I said sarcastically. "Mike's a better guitar player than you are. Why in the world would he want a lesson from you?"

I wasn't mincing words.

"No, he's not a better guitar player than I am," Dave snorted. "I was showing him all kinds of stuff. That's why he wanted a lesson."

"Really?" I said with even more sarcasm. "Well, that's odd, because I bet that Doug would also say that Mike's a better guitar player than you."

I knew that would get Dave, because Dave liked and respected Doug.

"No, he wouldn't," Dave jabbed back in his cocky style. "There's no way Doug would say Mike is a better guitar player than I am. No friggin' way!"

"Well, I'll tell you what," I said, letting my nasty Hummel side take over. "When we make our next gas stop, I'll make you a bet that Doug thinks that Mike's a better guitar player that you are. How 'bout that?"

"Okay," Dave replied. "I'll bet you five bucks on that one."

When we stopped at the gas station, I jumped out of my van to stretch my legs and walked over to Doug, who was in his own van with Dona.

"Doug," I said, "I need you to answer a question that's raging between Dave and me."

"What's that?" Doug asked, looking at me like I was a bit crazy.

"I told Dave that Mike Morgan is a much better guitar player than he is," I explained. "Dave bet me that you think he's a better guitar player that Mike. What do you think? Which one is the better guitar player?"

"Mike's better, for sure," Doug answered.

"Thank you," I said with conviction. "That's what I figured you'd say."

I went into the Kum & Go convenience store, got a few things that totaled about five bucks and went back to the van. Dave was still sitting there. He hadn't moved during the whole rest stop.

"Doug says that Mike's a better guitar player than you are," I said smugly while munching on some of my treats. "You owe me five bucks."

"Doug did not," Dave insisted. "You're making it up—or it's the way you asked."

"It wasn't the way I asked Doug," I said. "It's just what Doug thinks and what I think and what everybody thinks!"

Dave's face wrinkled up with insecurity. I felt good for the first time since Dave screwed me out of travel time with his laundry.

"I'm still not going to pay you the five bucks," Dave said.

A little further on down the road, we were listening to the radio and something came on like Aerosmith or REO Speedwagon. Dave started telling us they were a great blues band. He also said they were more of a blues band than ours ever could be. He kept it up, and I realized he was trying to get back at me over the guitar conversation by putting me and the band down in return.

I was starting to realize that he was just saying things to be contrary. It seemed to be his nature. It wasn't good that we were bugging each other since there was quite a bit of tour left. We went on to New Orleans—another long day, another short dollar and more jabbering between me and the two greenhorns.

The tour seemed to be getting longer and longer. By the last week of the trip, nobody could stand either one of those guys. By the last gig, Kirk was threatening me physically.

"Shut up, Hummel, or I'll kick your ass!" Kirk snarled during the gig when I told him to slow down the beat.

Doug, who was a weightlifter, overheard Kirk threatening me.

"Don't worry, buddy," Doug told me. "I'll back you up. He won't be doing anything physical to you or anybody!"

I fired Kirk for his bad timing on the last gig.

"I'm going to kick your ass," he said again, standing up this time.

"Go ahead," I said. "You've been kicking my ass the entire tour on those drums with that hyper beat of yours!"

"If you go after him," Doug shouted at Kirk, "you're gonna to have to go after me. You don't go after your bandleader while I'm around!"

Kirk backed down right away, but he gave me the death stare.

On the last gig of the tour, in Albuquerque, we were wailing on "Seven Nights to Rock." Dave went off on guitar like a madman, playing the entire theme from "Green Acres" in the middle of his guitar solo, even though it didn't fit the song's twelve-bar format at all. We were all looking at each other like, What the heck has gotten into this guitar fool now? It was the last Dave straw for me.

On our long drive home, after I fired both Dave and Kirk, I got out some infamous Buddy Rich tapes that my old bass player, Mike Judge, had given me. Buddy is heard telling off his musicians, saying he can "get an all-L.A. band tomorrow," that "there's no sound in flutes" and "off with those beards." "What do you guys think you are," he asks, "the Star of David Baseball Team?" When one of the band members tells him that "I'll Take Manhattan" is "one of my best charts," Buddy replies, "Well, then, take Manhattan and get off my bus!"

The tapes horrified me the first time I heard them. After firing Dave and Kirk, I realized that I was in it pretty thick as a bandleader. At that point in my life, I related more to Buddy Rich than to the musicians he was yelling at. I empathized more with the bandleader's problems than with the band members' issues. That's when I realized I was in deep trouble, because the jerks I dealt with in this band of mine were making me into the same kind of maniac Buddy Rich was on the day those tapes were recorded.

We finally got home, and I got rid of Dave and Kirk and on to another band, but I was tired of the leadership role. I hired June Core back for the rest of my 1988 tours, which resolved the "fast beat" issue. Later that year, I took Pat Chase as my guitar player on another tour. I was still touring, but I felt kind of burnt out and was looking for something else to do with myself for a while.

Then I met Sue Foley. I realized it might be better to just start playing with somebody else's band, instead of with my own. That's how I ended up traveling with Sue and her band.

Thinking about it in hindsight, it all flows together, but at the time it seemed like a rough patch for me. I learned a lot from those experiences, but it was more about what I didn't want to do, rather than what I did want to do. I'm glad for the time I spent touring with Sue, but I was glad to start up my own band again as well.

Dave was a real piece of work, and his bad vibes continued long after he left my band. I remember introducing him to my first wife at Slim's in San Francisco. "You married Hummel?" was the first thing out of his mouth. I had to laugh at that point. It was just Dave, although he eventually changed for the better. Back then, however, he had a habit of telling anyone willing to listen about all the blues bandleaders who'd fired him: "William Clarke, yeah, he fired me." "Hook Herrera, yep, he fired me." "Mark Hummel, never got along with him. He's an asshole! He fired me." Dave became known as the most-fired guitar player in blues. What an interesting identity. I thought it was funny.

CHAPTER SEVENTEEN

Sue Foley and the Band

I met Sue Foley and her band in 1988 when I was playing in Canada. I had gotten a tape a year or two before from her bass player, Jon Penner. He had wanted to play in my band in '87, before he played with Sue. Jon was sixteen or seventeen at the time.

"You've got to be at least eighteen to be able to get across the border," I told him.

"I'll sneak across," he responded.

"That won't really work," I explained.

I happened to be really, really impressed by the tape Jon sent a year later of him playing with this young girl guitar player and the band they'd put together. The other guitarist in the band was Shorty Lenoir, who went on to play with Gary Primich for quite awhile. Jon ended up playing with Junior Brown and many others in Austin when he later relocated there. Sue was eventually signed by Antone's Records in Austin and lived there for a while before moving back up to Canada. She continues making records.

Sue hails from Ottawa, and Jon and Shorty Lenoir from Manitoba. They happened to meet up in Vancouver and started touring all over Canada around 1988.

I had thrown together some old band members—June Core on drums, Pat Chase on guitar and Flaco Medina on bass—for a trip to Canada to play in Edmonton, Alberta, for my longtime buddy, writer and promoter Peter North. We had the night off when we arrived, and Peter asked if we wanted to go hear a band. He raved about the Sue Foley Band from Vancouver. I told him I had their tape and would love to check them out. We were all knocked out by what we heard. We sat in with them that night, became pals and jammed with them, at our gigs and at theirs, throughout our week in Edmonton.

At the end of the week of gigs, I offered to book a tour for Sue and the band.

"Yeah, sure you will," Sue responded.

She'd probably heard it all before, but I managed to book a three-week tour up and down the West Coast, from San Diego to Vancouver, without a stitch of promo materials. I had phoned all the different buyers I knew and was able to get them to go on my word that Sue and the band were really good. This happened in December 1988, and I wasn't working too many gigs with my own band then, so I did the tour with Sue. It turned into a smashing success. Everybody loved Sue and the band and thought they and I were a good pairing.

At the end of the tour, we decided to continue working together. They booked gigs across Canada, and I booked dates in the States. They snuck into the United States as visitors, and I snuck into Canada as a tourist. That's how we did it the first few months of working together. We traveled together throughout 1989 and were only home for maybe a total of a month and a half the entire year.

Sue booked the Canadian stuff, all the way from Vancouver to Toronto and Ottawa, and I booked U.S. gigs from coast to coast. The only region we didn't do was the East Coast, except for Florida. We also played Denmark. Things went well, although we did have quite a few mishaps, as is always the case with such heavy touring.

I remember a two-hour tow from The Dalles, Oregon, to Portland because Shorty's van had blown a rod. The Portland club owner said it was the first time he'd seen a van towed to a gig by start time. We ended up taking a train back to San Francisco with all our gear. Poor Shorty went through hell waiting around Portland an extra two weeks, only to have the van blow another rod right down the road from the garage.

At the end of that year, I was so disoriented that, after waking up one day in Missoula, Montana, I left the hotel and started walking around. I didn't know where I was, what day or time of the year it was. It was a real wake-up call to how much touring I really wanted to do. I think Sue and the band felt the same way.

I'm a good ten years older than Sue and her musicians. As a result, they had some different viewpoints about things than I did. They liked to wear jeans, tennis shoes and T-shirts on stage. I wore suits. Eventually, they started dressing up a little, and I dressed down a bit so I could meet them halfway, especially after Gatemouth Brown gave Sue a lecture in Atlanta about the importance of dressing up.

Early on, at border crossings, I got nervous when they would sneak in or I would sneak in. I found an immigration attorney and had some important people write stuff about Sue and the group and me, which made getting in and out of Canada easier.

One Sunday we were coming down from Vancouver to an upscale club in Seattle. My immigration attorney was supposed to have had immigration papers sent to the border, but the U.S. customs people said they didn't have the papers. I had to call the attorney and get her to take some action, which is hard to do on a Sunday. She lucked out and got hold of an immigration judge she knew in Los Angeles, and he faxed a letter to the Peace Arch border-crossing people. It took a good six hours, during which we were being grilled by the customs people, before the officials got the letter.

We finally got into the United States and made the gig literally thirty minutes before we were supposed to go on stage. We had no time to check in at the hotel. At that point, it relieved everybody to no longer have to sneak across the border on every trip to Canada.

Sue had signed with a supposedly big-time Canadian booking agency that kept stringing her along about a Canadian tour that would follow two weeks in Denmark where we played a big blues festival and a group of club dates. She found out while we were overseas that her booking agent had been fired, that the tour wasn't going to happen and that we would have an unexpected two weeks off when we got home. We ended up sitting on our thumbs in Ottawa most of the two weeks, although we did one gig at the famous Horseshoe Tavern in Toronto and a little blues festival in Kitchener, Ontario, that we booked at the last minute. The rest of the time, we sat around in a cabin in the woods, essentially starving.

We finally started working again in Wisconsin. I had an agent who got us some last-minute, very un-lucrative two-hundred-dollar gigs there. We even had to pay for our own hotel rooms. The dismal situation really got the whole band down. Everyone looked at me sideways because the gigs paid so poorly, seeming to have forgotten that Sue's agent had dropped the ball. Things got so bad at one point that five of us were sleeping in one Motel 6 room near the Milwaukee Airport. It took a good three weeks for us to really get back on our feet.

The band had an odd experience on a gig we played at Skipper's Smokehouse in Tampa, Florida with West Coast compadres Little Charlie and the Nightcats. We were performing an opening set when an audience member came running up to the stage and informed us that the Golden Gate Bridge had just collapsed into the SF Bay. It was the night of the Loma Prieta earthquake October 17, 1989. After we finished our set we watched TV footage of the raging fires and buildings reduced to rubble all over the bay. I couldn't help wonder what I'd be returning to, in a couple months, when I finally got home.

We would play gigs in Canada for a week at a stretch, five to seven nights at each club. All Sue would have to do was book six different clubs, and we could work for six weeks. This made it easy to stay on the road, but the gigs were sometimes the dregs. There was a horrible gig in Regina where we played to nothing but a handful of drunks the entire week.

Another odd gig was in Saskatoon, Saskatchewan, at Bud's On Broadway. There was a dust storm so awful that we couldn't see more than five feet in front of us. Everything ended up covered in red dust when the storm was over. After the gig, some friends of the band had a party at the band house where we were staying. I had quit drinking in 1984, but in 1989 I was still coming to grips with being sober. It's a real trip being around people who like to drink, and these kids were drinking to excess. I watched them falling down stairs and throwing up on each other, but we had a good time, considering that I was stone cold sober and Sue and the band were high as a kite. We had many laughs together.

We were in Memphis for the Handy Awards when famed club owner and label president Clifford Antone discovered Sue while we playing at the Rum Boogie Café. Robert Lockwood attended that gig as well with his wife in tow. Guitarist Duke Robillard played in the big room, and we were playing in Handy Hall. I think Clifford saw Sue sitting in with Duke after we'd finished.

After we split up, Sue Foley and her band moved to Austin right after she got signed to Antone's, but the band lasted only about another year. She and Jon stayed together quite a few years, but Shorty left the band not long after they moved to Texas. He then joined the late harp master Gary Primich. Bob, the drummer, left even earlier than Shorty. I ran into Bob at a health food store in Key West, Florida, in 2010, while Bob was playing on a cruise ship and in town on his lunch break. Talk about a small world!

I stayed in touch with Shorty over the years and would see him with Primich when we ran into each other on tour. Shorty's no longer playing music. I kept in touch with Jon for a while. I haven't seen Sue since I ran into her at a blues festival in Edmonton around 2002. Always a good guitar player, she's developed into a *great* guitar player.

CHAPTER EIGHTEEN
Missing Drummer in Memphis

I was on the road with Sue Foley in 1989. We crisscrossed the United States and Canada for about thirteen or fourteen months and did a tour of Europe. In September, toward the end of the tour, we went to the W.C. Handy Blues Awards in Memphis. We were playing in the Memphis area during that time, staying at a little motel in Horn Lake, Mississippi, because we couldn't get a room in Memphis. The Handy Awards attendees had all the hotels and motels in the area booked solid for a few days. The funky little motel we found was only about twenty miles away, and we felt grateful to get rooms that close to Memphis. We had at least three or four local gigs during that week.

At one point, we had finished a gig and were going back to the motel. While driving through downtown Memphis, someone in the van said something that set our drummer off. He was a bit on the nervous, sensitive, slightly over-reactive side. Before anyone could stop him, he jumped out of the van.

It was three o'clock in the morning, and he just disappeared into the Memphis night. I asked to Jon Penner, our bass player, if he had seen what I had just seen—our drummer jumping out of a moving van in the middle of the night.

"What are we going to do?" I asked.

"Don't worry about it," Jon said. "We'll see him tomorrow night."

I stopped the van and searched for him before we drove on to Mississippi. It was as though he had disappeared. I didn't see him anywhere, and I finally gave up searching. We went to our rooms to sleep, but I worried about the missing drummer most of that night.

We drove back to Memphis the next day, but we still hadn't heard a word from him. What are we going to do? I wondered. We had a gig to do, and he had blown us off. He might have gone back to Canada or gotten hurt in Memphis. Who knew?

I called a couple drummers I'd heard were in Memphis and did some pre-gig preparation just to be sure I was covered. My years on the road have taught me it's better to be safe than sorry. I don't believe in leaving things to chance or depending on people whose work habits are unknown to me. I found a couple drummers who were available if I needed them and asked them to put themselves on hold.

We were scheduled to be playing at Huey's Club on Madison, a cool little place on the outskirts of Memphis. We showed up early for the sound check, and there was the drummer, sitting at the bar, waiting for us. I phoned the drummers I had on hold and said, "Don't worry about it. He showed up."

The missing drummer was missing no more.

CHAPTER NINETEEN

Aldo House of Horror

It was the year of our Lord 1987. I went to Revenna, Italy, for a week as part of a San Francisco Blues Festival package put together by Tom Mazzolini. Tom is the legendary creator of the San Francisco Blues Festival which had an uninterrupted thirty-six-year run. It was one of the most famous blues festivals in the world and the longest running of them all. By 1987, the festival had been going for fourteen years in a row, and Tom was at his height as a blues producer. Along with myself and the Blues Survivors, Tom's European package featured the Paul de-Lay Band, Bill Tarsha and the Rocket 88s, Roy Gaines, Freddie Roulette, Johnny Heartsman, Earl "Good Rockin'" Brown, Big Jay McNeely and Sarah Levingston. Tom was excited about taking this terrific lineup overseas. The only wrinkle was our flight to New York, as we were supposed to make a stop at the JFK International Airport. The plane ended up circling the airport for more than two hours. We were all sitting there wondering what the hell was going on when an announcement they came on over the plane's intercom.

"Ladies and gentlemen, there, ah, seems to, ah, be, a p-possible p-p-problem with the landing, ah, gear. We have a red light saying the landing gear won't come down, and we're, ah, running out of fuel," the pilot said haltingly. It was easy to hear the fear in his voice in spite of his attempt to "man up" to the situation.

Everyone on board became visibly nervous and started to sweat. Freddie Roulette, the famous Chicago lap steel guitarist, was sitting in front of me. Freddie, a practicing Buddhist, began chanting his Nichiren Shoshu mantra. Tom, sitting next to me, white knuckled the arm rest.

"This doesn't look good," Tom said thinly.

The pilot came back on and told us we were going to make a run at the landing. I could hear the various blues players mumbling their own prayers. I was thinking about my family as we headed toward the tarmac.

As we finally set down at JFK, the runway was lined with emergency vehicles, ambulances and police cars with lights whirling away. When we felt the wheels catch and hold and a smooth landing ensue, everyone applauded furiously. Freddie stopped chanting, and I breathed a sigh of relief. I still remember thinking at the time, if the plane had gone down, it would have been a day of infamy, a never-forgotten fateful day for the blues. It made me think about Buddy Holly, Richie Valens and the Big Bopper. I would think about it again three years later when Stevie Ray Vaughan perished in a helicopter crash.

Luck was with us, and we arrived safely in Milan the next morning after the all-night flight. The Italian promoter, Aldo Fumagalli, was an old friend of Tom's. Aldo appeared to be everything you would want in a promoter, and the blues festival was very well organized. A bus picked us up at the airport and drove us to Revenna on the eastern coast of Italy. Revenna is famous for its beautiful early roman mosaics. We not only got to play the festival but were able to sightsee. We even squeezed in a day trip to Venice.

After the two-day festival was over, Aldo told me he was a big fan of mine and would like me to come over and do a tour by myself sometime. I loved Italy so far. Why say no?

Aldo called me three years later and invited me to Europe. It was the year of our Lord 1990. I agreed to do a solo tour with Italian musicians on some theater and club dates. I didn't have a band at the time and needed some work. I was excited about another trip to Italy. I flew out of San Francisco and on to Europe. I landed at the airport the next morning and walked off the plane.

There was no Aldo waiting for me. I walked down to baggage claim and got my bags. Still no Aldo. I sat around and waited an hour or two. I did not know how to use the phones or how to speak the language. I was near panic when I finally saw him.

He wasn't as together-looking as he had been three years before. He appeared nervous and somewhat less in control. When we finally got in his car, he took off like a mad man. He sped up, slowed down and wove between cars at alarming speeds. When we got near the city center, I noticed traffic becoming very heavy and very slow. It didn't take long before I saw why. A sheet covered a body in the middle of the road with a bent-up motorcycle nearby, crushed underneath a car. I had already been nervous, but now I was starting to get apprehensive. I felt like I had entered into a world gone mad and out of control.

I stayed at Aldo's home on the outskirts of Milan with his South American wife and their young son. My initial feeling about the food was that you can't eat badly in Italy. All the food is good, even gas-station food. Also, the warmth, generosity and history of the Italian people is amazing.

While in Italy, I struggled to communicate, picking up words here and there, with lots of sign language thrown in. Aldo spoke English in a broken dialect, and I could grasp what he was saying. He also had an amazing record collection, which I raided every day. I had him make me cassettes of different LPs I'd never seen or heard at home in the States. The cassettes included a Roy Gaines collection I still listen to regularly.

I rehearsed with the band the day after I arrived. It consisted of Marco the guitar player, Marcio the drummer and a bass player whose name escapes me. Marcio impressed me with his Fred Below-like chops. They were a solid band and very friendly guys. They had studied my tunes and did a good job. Although they were not as solid as the players back home, they were giving all they had and playing with emotion. After the rehearsal, we all went and looked at the Castillo in the middle of Milan. I ordered cappuccinos everywhere we went.

We played everything from small theaters to tiny clubs, band gigs to duo gigs with just me and Marco. The gigs were fun because the crowds were so enthusiastic. More often than not Aldo would drive us back to Milan after the gigs, even when it was a two-or three-hour trip. I assumed this was because the gigs were low-paying. It did start to make me nervous, though, when Aldo would look so tired and drive really fast in the middle of the night on the highways.

Soon, we were doing gigs farther away and spending the nights in hotels. Aldo was bringing his crazy girlfriend, not his wife. She would be drunk and either amorous or jealous, depending on Aldo's behavior at the time. It would be a loud night either way, as I always seemed to end up in the room next door to them. This

ALDO HOUSE OF HORROR

became pure torture after the fourth or fifth night. To make matters worse, Aldo's spouse seemed to be aware of the other woman. Rows would start up when we returned to Milan. These also were very loud and hard to ignore, since I was sleeping on the couch in the living room. Several times, Aldo left in the middle of the night, leaving me in the house with his wife and child the next morning. They didn't speak a lick of English. It was very awkward.

I recall doing a hilarious recording session with a dude named Victor who would do his entire act in the recording studio, jumping up on top of the piano while trying to sing the tune on tape. The emphasis seemed to be on his dance moves rather than on hitting notes on pitch. The session paid well, and the studio musicians got a good laugh out of it.

I also released a very short-lived LP on Aldo's label, Deluxe Records, titled *Sunny Day Blues*. It came and went in six months and is extremely hard to find. It was made up of different sessions I'd done over the prior couple years, all previously unreleased.

I made it through the tour and went again the following year, playing with the same rhythm section and a well-known Italian guitar player I'd met on the 1990 tour. In the first week we did a gig where the billing had guitar player's name as the headliner and me as opener. I was fine with that and told Aldo I thought we should play the gig with me opening and the guitar player closing, but he said I should close and that he knew best. I said that it would be awkward and embarrassing if I closed, but he would not listen. We were outside in the parking lot and, finally, I got really angry and said he needed to listen to me.

Aldo turned beet red and said, "Madkkkk, you no know what I use su be like? I cut you twenty years ago. You no walk away from me."

I kept on walking.

Aldo yelled, "Where you go?"

"Home!" I yelled back.

I meant it. I would catch a cab to the airport and use my credit card to fly home if necessary. After a standoff of twenty minutes, Aldo agreed to do the gig with me starting, but it hardly mattered, since most of the audience left after the disco music stopped. We played to fewer than two dozen patrons. I also recall the hotel we stayed at that night was so cheap the heat was turned off at nine p.m. When we returned from the gig, I practically froze in the room, it being a very cold Italian February.

One of the few high points of the tour was taking a solo train trip to Rome. I'd never been there, and it was beyond anything I had ever experienced. To be in the Forum, high on the hill, and see Roman ruins from two thousand years ago and realize how advanced a civilization it was, that there were real live families living there, was a revelation. I spent two days trekking around by myself.

When it was time to return to Milan, I asked at the station which track the train was leaving from and was given the track number. I got on the train, and as it left, it seemed like it was leaving fifteen minutes early. I asked the passenger next to me if this was the train to Milan, and he said, "No, Napoli." I'd gotten on the wrong train, not realizing the Milan train hadn't arrived yet at that track. I had to stay on till the next stop two hours down the track. I didn't make it back till five a.m. Live and learn and always check the train boards!

Three years later, after having forgotten all those nightmares, I agreed to another tour when Aldo called and offered more money and the opportunity to bring along guitarist Joel Foy to augment an Italian rhythm section. There were some good gigs, but the fiascos really stick in my mind. We did one in Bologna with some of Aldo's friends opening. It was held on a Tuesday night in a tent out in the country. All I know is that the opener was supposed to start at eight p.m. but didn't start till ten. There was a good crowd when they started. Aldo had made no effort to get the band started on time or get them off so we could start on schedule. Their opening set was supported to run thirty to forty minutes, but it went on for an hour and a half. The tent had no heat, and by the time we went on, there were only a handful of people left. It was so cold I held my boots over a heater in a very makeshift backstage. Otherwise, my toes might have frozen. As before, it was February in Italy.

Another gig was at a Communist function that Aldo booked in an airplane hangar-type building. The acoustics were so bad that the note you had just played would come bouncing back to you a second later. It was very distressing. Again, it was so cold that Joel wore his big winter overcoat. I'm really surprised that he didn't have to wear gloves as he played guitar. On second thought, maybe he did? There were trash cans with fires burning to keep the two or three hundred people who were huddling around them warm.

This happened on the last tour I did for Aldo, although I did do a blues festival for him in Luxembourg in 2008. He flew us in the day before and flew us out the next day. I could have done other dates in Europe or France, but he wouldn't allow it. After the fest, Aldo left the hotel with seventy-year-old Sonny Rhodes, Jumpin' Johnny Sansone and some others for a twenty-hour drive back to Milan for a gig the following night. I was so glad not to be part of it, but it sure brought all the memories back. Some things don't change, and Aldo is one of them.

CHAPTER TWENTY

The Italian Drummer

I first traveled to Italy in the early '90s to do gigs for Italian promoter Aldo Fumagalli. I met an Italian drummer named Marcio there who played a solid double shuffle, in the Fred Below style. At one point, he told me he'd like to come to the United States and work for free, just to be able to play with me in the States. I wasn't going to let him play without pay, but I figured that if he really wanted to do it that bad, I'd give him a shot.

Pretending to be a tourist, he came over and did two tours with me. The first thing I noticed when Marcio came over here was his curiosity about certain things and places. I guess mini-marts in Europe are a lot different from in the U.S. because Marcio would spend an eternity in them at our gas stops. He would look over every item he found there and seemed amazed at the variety of items stocked in those stores. We usually had to pry him out of there fifteen or twenty minutes after filling up.

The first tour was just in the United States, and we went to Canada on the second. It gets very tricky when someone tries to get into Canada as a tourist. We told the Canadian authorities that we would be coming into the country as a three-piece band and that we would hook up with a drummer in Calgary. Marcio would then cross the border on a bus as a tourist. The ploy worked fine getting into Canada, but on the way back into the U.S., he pretended he had just hitched a ride with us.

The customs people apparently had gotten wind that Marcio had played the gigs with us, and they grilled him when we got to the border. We got to the border at about nine at night and were detained for three hours. Marcio was sweating profusely as they asked him over and over if he played drums. He told them he played conga drums. They didn't really believe him, but they had no way of proving it and finally let us through.

The next time we crossed the border, about a year or two later, the customs folks asked me, "Didn't you have an Italian drummer with you?" It's the kind of thing they definitely do not forget or forgive.

Beatle wigged Hummel,
Los Angeles, 1964

Willie King, congas; Reggie Scanlon,
bass; Hummel, harmonica;
Boogie Jake, guitar.
The Odyssey, Berkeley, 1976

Cool Papa, Larry Blake's, Berkeley,
circa 1982 (Art Leberman)

Ron Thompson, San Francisco Blues Festival, 1978 (Jim Bukiet)

Hummel and Charles Houff, San Francisco Blues Festival, 1978 (Jim Bukiet)

Hummel, Sonny Lane, Bob Klein, and Mississippi Johnny Waters. Bluebird Café, Santa Barbara, California, 1977 (Ed Hummel)

Hummel, Francis Clay and Mississippi Johnny Waters. San Francisco Blues Festival, 1980 (Ed Hummel)

Mississippi Johnny Waters, circa 1980 (Janet Hoelzel)

Sonny Lane and Hummel, Oakland Museum of California, circa 1980 (Janet Hoelzel)

Tom Mazzolini and Sonny Lane, San Francisco, California, 1978

*Hummel and Brownie McGhee, The Barn,
Riverside, California, 1985 (Ed Hummel)*

*Lowell Fulson and Pat Chase,
San Jose, California, 1983 (Jerry Grossetti)*

Luther Tucker, Jimmy Rogers and Louis Myers,
San Francisco Blues Festival, 1979 (Jerry Hausler)

Mike Judge, Hummel and Anthony Paule, Kansas City 1987

Burning Van Fest, 1986

Bob Grant, Hummel, Sue Foley, Shorty Lenoir and unknown driver, Denmark, 1989

Rick Estrin, Hummel and Mitch Kashmar, Sacramento Blues Festival, 1989

*Hummel and
Shorty Lenoir,
Kitchener Blues Festival,
Ontario, 1989*

*Jon Penner and Hummel,
Kitchener Blues Festival,
Ontario, 1989*

*Roy Rogers,
Hummel and
Carroll Peery,
Larry Blake's,
Berkeley, 1986*

*Standing: unknown,
Charlie Musselwhite and
Hummel. Kneeling:
Tim Kaihatsu. Larry Blake's,
Berkeley, 1985*

*Bottom Photo:
DJ Fred Broekman,
Rusty Zinn and Hummel,
Amsterdam, 1991*

Jimmy Rogers and Hummel,
San Francisco Blues Festival, 1993 (Jerry Hausler)

Jimmy Rogers and Julia Hummel,
Sacramento Blues Festival, 1993 (David Horwitz)

Hummel and Rusty Zinn, Waterfront Blues Festival,
Portland, Oregon, 1995 (Glen Todd)

Harmonica Hipster Hummel, Kansas City,
2001 (Evie Quarles)

Hummel, James Cotton, Kaz Kajimura and Charlie Musselwhite,
Yoshi's, Oakland, 2001 (Jerry Hausler)

Little Sonny, Hummel and James Harman, King Biscuit Blues Festival,
Helena, Askansas, 2002

*Little Walter Jacobs-
(drawing By
Mark Hummel)*

*Steve Wolf,
Monterey Jazz Festival,
2001 (Ed Hummel)*

Joann and Ed Hummel (Mark's parents) with James Cotton,
Blue Café, Long Beach,California, 2003

Rusty Zinn and Hummel, Freight and Salvage Coffeehouse,
Berkeley, 2010

Magic Dick, Hummel, RW Grigsby, Dick Shurman, Billy Boy Arnold, Billy Branch and Rusty Zinn, Beverly Arts Center, Chicago, 2007

Alexis and Mark Hummel with Chicago guitar man Jody Williams, San Francisco Blues Festival, late nineties

CHAPTER TWENTY-ONE

Overton Hydroplaning and the Holland Island Meltdown

Jim Overton was a sweet, funny, talented drummer who played with me in the early '90s. He died of a heart attack several years back while walking his dog. It happened a few years after he had sobered up and was living a great life with his wife Robin. I wrote "Blue Jimmy" on my CD *Golden State Blues* for him.

Jim played drums for me when I had Marc Carino on bass and Curtis Smith on guitar. We were doing our usual heavy amount of touring, crisscrossing the country. We were driving up Interstate 55 one day, through Mississippi on our way from New Orleans to Memphis. Sheets of rain were blasting off the van like a fire hose was aimed at us. Jim was driving, doing about sixty-five or seventy. I sat next to him on the front seat.

"What's that sound?" I asked, turning to Jim.

Jim was somewhat high strung, and the downpour was making him nervous.

"What sound?" he blurted out. "I don't hear a thing."

"You don't hear that sound?" I said. "There's an ugly sound coming from the van."

We listened for a few seconds, trying to hear over the noises of the rain and the road.

"I don't hear it," Jim said again.

We kept driving for another five minutes or so. The sound I was hearing persisted.

"What are you hearing?" Jim asked.

"Take your foot of the gas for a minute and listen," I said.

He finally heard it.

We were hydroplaning on the I-55 pavement at sixty-five miles an hour, and we hadn't known it. It was very scary!

The night before had been rather eventful as well. Jim was drinking heavily. After a gig at Tipitina's with our friends the Iguanas, we decided to go to another New Orleans club called the Maple Leaf Bar where harp man Jumpin' Johnny Sansone was playing.

"Hey, Mark, you want to sit in?" Johnny asked.

"Sure," I told him.

The Maple Leaf stage was right in front of a window that opened out onto the street. It's usually hot during Jazz and Heritage Festival, and Jim was outside the open window talking to someone. When Johnny introduced me, Jim leaned inside the window and started talking to Johnny's drummer.

"Hey, I'm Mark's drummer," Jim slurred. "If Mark's sitting in, then I'm sitting in too!"

Johnny's drummer wasn't quite sure what to do. Jim told him again that he was my drummer and that he was going to sit in.

I'd just counted off a song with a Jimmy Reed beat. As we played, Johnny's drummer relented and motioned for Jim take over at the drums. I looked around and saw Jim climbing through the window and sitting at the drums. He was pulling off his coat while trying to maintain the beat. I quickly ended the song and got off of the stage. A minute later, Jumpin' Johnny kicked Jim off the drums. Jim crawled back out the window.

Later, at a club in Starkville, Mississippi, we opened for a band that impresario and manager Dick Waterman was booking. Some frat boys decided to give Curtis, my guitar player, some shit. One of them was especially nasty. He was drunk and belligerent, thick and tall, and looked like a rugby player.

"Quit looking at my girlfriend, dude!" he barked at Curtis.

"I wasn't looking at your girlfriend," Curtis responded.

"Yes, you were, you pretty little guitar boy!" the guy insisted.

Curtis wasn't quite sure what to do.

"I don't want any trouble," Curtis finally told the kid.

Marc Carino saw something was about to go down between Curtis and the frat boy. Marc and Curtis were best friends, and they looked out for each other on the road. Marc is one of those people who get a crazy look in his eyes when he gets mad at somebody. He had that look on his face as he ambled on over to the frat boy, grabbed his wrist and clamped down on it.

"Is there some kind of problem here, buddy?" Marc asked.

The drunken kid took a look at Marc's eyes and realized he wasn't kidding.

"No problem," the kid said, as he backed down to Marc and backed off Curtis, took his girlfriend by the arm and drifted on.

We did a tour of Europe with this same band, plus Rusty Zinn as our second guitarist, which make us a quintet. Toward the end of 1991, we went to Denmark, Holland, Belgium and Germany. The first gigs in Denmark were on an island that is considered part of Holland. We took a ferryboat to the island. Ferry rides in Europe across a bay or inlet are usually quite peaceful, but on this one, Jim freaked out, claiming that some guy kept giving him the evil eye. Jim was sure the guy was a serial killer.

We got to the island, checked into the hotel, went to the club and did a sound check. It was a strange gig that night because the youthful audience seemed more interested in the disco records being played over the house sound system during our breaks than the blues we were playing on our sets. Jim was kind of weirded out by it. He always played a long drum solo on our rendition of a Buddy Rich number called "Rotten Kid." Instead of doing his usual jazz drum solo, he knocked out a frenzied disco beat lasting ten minutes. The crowd didn't know quite what to make of it and fled the dance floor as he was played.

When we finished the set, the club owner came up to me with a dour look on his fat face.

"I didn't feel that was very professional, what you were doing up there," he shouted over the din of the disco music.

"What can I say?" I told him. "The set's over. We can't get it back. I'll talk to the drummer. He tried something that didn't work. I'll make sure we don't do it again."

Jim claimed afterward that he'd played the disco beat because he spotted the same strange guy out in the audience who'd been giving him the evil eye on the ferryboat. He proceeded to get fairly wrecked on booze that night and almost got into a tussle with some locals. Rusty ended up helping him get back to the hotel, away from the guys who were hassling him.

It was quite the wild and crazy tour. The promoter was the same guy that Sue Foley and I had played for at the Djurs Blues Festival in 1989. He brought me back to Europe two years later, this time with the Blues Survivors. He put us up at his home on our off nights. He had a big box of porno tapes, and Rusty continued to go through every one. *Gulden Drobba* was his favorite!

The promoter threw a party for us and his friends at a restaurant toward the end of the tour. He gave a speech, and opened his remarks with a kick in my teeth.

"Rod Piazza is one of the greatest acts that I have ever had play in Denmark, and he was so, so fun to work with," the promoter proclaimed, raising his glass to his friends. "Let's drink a toast to the great Rod Piazza!"

Rusty took the promoter's remarks to mean that we weren't shit. On the way back from that party, the driver was supposed to drop the promoter off at his house before dropping us off at our hotel. Rusty, not knowing how much English the promoter could understand, made a modest request.

"Let's just drop this fuck off here, could we?" Rusty said to the driver with a big smile on his face, pointing his finger at promoter.

The driver dropped him off right where Rusty told him to.

On the day before we were going to fly home to the U.S., we had about an hour to kill at the railroad station in Amsterdam. We had our luggage with us, and Jim also had his snare drum.

Marc had agreed to watch the luggage and the drum while the rest of us checked out the little shops at the station and bought snacks.

Some thief must have been keeping a close eye on Marc without us knowing. When he turned his head to stare at some girl's ass, Jim's snare was snatched. Jim freaked out when he returned and found the drum gone. It was a rare 1929 Ludwig snare drum that was worth a pile of money and would be very difficult to replace. He was depressed the entire day and drank himself out of his mind that night. At about two in the morning, he went up on the hotel roof and started howling at the moon. We all felt bad for Jim, especially Marc, but there was nothing he could do to get the drum back.

Sometimes musicians leave behind important things like instruments or suitcases while on tour. On one tour, Marc left his bass at a club fifty miles away, and we had to turn around and go back for it. A week later, I left a suit bag behind in La Crosse, Wisconsin, and we had to drive back for an hour and a half while we were supposed to be headed to St. Paul. Rusty left five hundred dollars on a nightstand near Kansas City, and a maintenance man brought it to the front desk thinking it was drug money. They almost called the cops. Drummer Mark Bohn left the rear door of the van open one time, and luckily we saw the suitcase that fell out in the rear view mirror while doing about fifty miles per hour in Missouri. It was pure luck that we saw it.

We also had some fun times, but maybe not the kind most people would think of as fun. We would stop at rest areas in the middle of Wyoming or Nebraska, and the guys would pop out with some lunch meat or chicken. We would sit under those big blue western skies, with huge white clouds billowing along in the breeze, in the middle of American nowhere, laughing and enjoying each other's company. We had time on our hands and enough dough to last a few days. We were playing the music we loved and getting paid.

I have many great memories of traveling around the country with the guys, even though we went on some brutal tours. Our tours often would be anywhere between eight and ten weeks at a stretch, with us yelling at each other and at club owners and so much shit going down I can only hint at it in these tales of the big road. It was hard traveling, but when I look back now, it's been my life. The guys became my brothers after those long hauls in the van together, through thick and thin.

The tours occasionally stretched for as long as twelve weeks, even longer when I was touring with Sue Foley. Plenty of people, including big stars like B.B. King and Willie Nelson, still do crazy long tours. John Mayall told me he still does tours that go for two months at a time.

I must admit that I don't think I'm built for that anymore, but I've got the memories of the times I did. I was there and did it. I've always tried to follow my dream and made plenty of good friends along the way. It was worth it all.

CHAPTER TWENTY-TWO

Starkville Night of Horror

We were going to be playing our second gig in Starkville, Mississippi, having already been there on a road tour a few years earlier. The town is in Oktibbeha County, right next to Mississippi State University. Ancestors of Choctaw Native Americans settled the land around Starkville over two thousand years ago. The town has become something of a passthrough, rather than a destination, for folks heading to Atlanta, New Orleans and the Mississippi Gulf Coast. Starkville prides itself on being the home of the first T-Ball game and believes in Southern family values. It's also famous because Johnny Cash was arrested there for drunkenness and wrote a song about it.

We were booked for two nights at a new club in the downtown area. The owner was hiring blues acts to play his venue to get the club some local attention. The owner and I negotiated our rooms for the night we arrived.

"I got a hotel that you guys can stay at," he told me. "You can have the run of the place. You're gonna love it."

"It hasn't been really refurbished yet," he added. "I just bought it a couple weeks ago."

He gave us directions to the hotel, which was out on a rural highway north of Starkville. It was so dark along the little road that we couldn't see a thing past the ditch. The trees in the forest were shaking and seemed to be leaning in on us when the wind blew. Thinking of movie classics like *Easy Rider* and *Deliverance* and given the total isolation of the surroundings, we were a little spooked. We ended up driving up and down the road about four times, huddled up against the windshield looking for the hotel. What we didn't know was that we couldn't see the hotel because there were no lights on at the place, not even a sign.

Suddenly, from out of nowhere, a deer jumped out in front of the van. I slammed on the breaks and skidded to a flat stop. All of us were thrown forward on top of each other.

"Are you sure you got the directions right?" Fingers Taylor asked me. "I'm no genius, but I'd say you're lost, and it's pitch black out here. Damn it! This isn't the greatest place to be lost. There isn't a damn thing but crickets out here!"

I ended up calling the club owner from a pay phone way down the road.

"Where the hell is this place?" I demanded. "We're coming back to town and getting rooms there."

"No, no!" he said. "You're on the right road. You just got to keep on looking for it. There probably aren't any lights on at the place. Look harder!"

On our fourth pass and with further directions from the club owner, I finally spotted the hotel. We could barely see it in the dark at the end of a long gravel driveway off the main road. It had all the winning charm of the Bates Motel. The two-story wooden structure had many windows across the front, some broken or cracked. It appeared to be completely abandoned. In the moonlight, I could see that the white paint was peeling off the wood sidings; even where it remained, the paint had turned a faded, dull grey.

"Home sweet home!" I said to the band as we got out of the van.

When I knocked on the front door of the hotel office, a light turned on and the clerk opened up and invited me in. He was tall and thin and seemed to be shivering, even though it was a warm night. He had greasy black hair and acne, and he asked me to stand behind the counter. The counter was an ancient cream-colored Formica tabletop with a makeshift wooden cabinet below that had been painted military green. The clerk acted as if he was either mentally challenged or upset by my presence. Questions I asked about the rooms caused him to squint and stutter.

"W-w-well," he said, "I-I-I don't have any s-s-sheets on the b-b-b-beds yet, but you can g-g-go ahead and put your suitcases in t-t-there. T-t-there's no t-t-t-towels yet, so I'll bring you some t-t-towels in."

He never looked me in the face and seemed content to speak to some spot on the floor around his feet.

We went into the rooms, and I took a look at the beds in the room I was splitting with Curtis Smith, the guitar player. There were large blood stains all over the mattresses. The clerk was right about there being no towels. He'd forgotten to mention that there were no functioning locks on the doors. The carpet, or what was left of it, must have had a red-and-green pattern at one time, but the colors had long since faded to black and dark grey. The hotel was a real hell hole, but I had stayed in worse and Curtis never gave a damn about rooms, anyway. The rest of the musicians were barely OK with their rooms.

Fingers Taylor, who we had invited to play with us at the club, had come along to see if he wanted to share one of the rooms. "I think I'll just buy my own room in town," he said after seeing the bloody mattress.

We played the gig that night with Fingers and had a good time with the folks of Starkville, but I worried the whole time about whether my suitcase was still going to be in that shabby hotel when I got back to the room. The club owner wasn't around during any of our breaks, so I didn't get a chance to complain about the broken locks or ask about the bloody mattress. We finished the gig and dropped Fingers off at the room he'd rented on his own dime. The guys in the band stared at the Holiday Inn sign where Fingers was staying as if it was a Hilton or a Westin. I drove back to the scary hotel as fast as I could without getting a ticket, worried about my clothes and shoes being stolen. I carry over fifteen vintage outfits on any given tour and didn't want to lose any of them.

The hotel clerk was standing in front of our room when we arrived. He had a large push cart, or TV stand, with sheets and towels on it. The door to the room was open. I ran past him, opened my trunk and checked my bags. Everything was there.

"Y-y-you d-d-don't have to worry, M-m-mister H-h-hummel," he said. "I-I-I kept m-m-my eye on your s-s-stuff!"

He squinted at the wrinkled dollar I tipped him.

"T-t-thanks," he said as he closed the door behind himself.

Curtis unpacked some night clothes from his bags and showered. I sat on a desk chair and began counting my money from the gig. I got absorbed in what I was doing when I thought I saw something move, out of the corner of my eye, by the bathroom door behind me. I turned my head, but there was nothing there. I thought it might have been steam coming out of the bathroom after Curtis' shower and didn't think anymore about it.

It had been a long day of driving and a long night of playing at the club. We were dog tired. After Curtis ate a bag of chips, he fell fast asleep on his bed. His head was on one pillow, and he had a second pillow covering his face. I got in the other bed, pulled the aged covers up over my shoulder and turned out the light. In a few minutes, I was fast asleep too.

I was awakened by Curtis snoring. At least that's what I thought it was at first. I delivered a quick heel to his calf and heard him roll over. The noise stopped, and it was very quiet in the room. I turned on my side, figuring that I'd resolved the issue of the snoring.

Then I heard it again, but I knew right away it wasn't Curtis snoring. The sound was more like a person whistling, softly but with a raspy, buzz-humming tone. It sounded like someone was whistling either right at the door of our room or on the cement deck just outside the door. I didn't move and cringed beneath the covers, but when I heard it again, I sat up and stared at the door where it seemed to be coming from. I couldn't see a thing in the darkness, so I turned on the light. There was a something there. Was it a whistling blonde in a faded wedding dress or was it a shadow? I wiped my eyes and looked again. There was nothing there.

Later that night I thought I heard the door to the vacant room next to ours open and close and someone flicking the bolt lock. I sat in bed, awake and wondering what the hell was going on. I don't know how long it was before I fell asleep again.

Curtis woke me a while later with a jab to my back.

"Are you whistling?" he asked. "If you're gonna practice, do it in the daytime!"

He fell back to sleep. I laid there for a long time. I decided I wouldn't go back to sleep but did at some point. I woke up before Curtis, and when I sat up in bed, the door to our room was open a crack.

I checked my stuff. Curtis checked his. Nothing was gone.

"I thought you closed the door," Curtis said.

"I did," I said. "I know I did!"

We packed our stuff and got the other guys and headed out of that hotel forever.

Later that morning, I called the club owner and insisted he put us in a nicer hotel in town. I didn't say a word about the whistling or the doors opening and closing or the ghost of the blonde in a wedding dress. I just said I wanted "nicer" accommodations.

He didn't argue, gave in and got us some decent rooms—right there with Fingers at the Holiday Inn!

CHAPTER TWENTY-THREE

Bohn Balcony Incident, Nicknames, Boston Inquiry, and Tranny Trouble

Mark Bohn played drums with the Blues Survivors off and on from about 1992 through '97. Pacemaker also played drums with the band during that period, but not as often, since he lived in L.A. Rusty Zinn held the guitar chair in the band in '92 and recruited Bohn for us in Santa Cruz when Jim Overton left. Bohn was a surfer, as were Rusty, Marty Dodson, Curtis Smith, Marc Carino and other guys who played in the band during that time. My band used to be a pack of Santa Cruz blues surfers.

"I think he might be a good possibility on drums," Rusty told me by phone. "He's got the right equipment and accessories to his drum set. He's really into learning the blues, so it might be worth giving him a try."

Bohn did a good job as far as the actual sound he created on the drums and working different drum sets into the mix. He happened to be very green around the gills, but I was used to that after so many years on the road. We worked with him the best we could. We all tried to teach him the art of blues drumming from the harp band perspective. He had a few tempo problems, but when he played well, he played great and I felt I could work with him on the rest. When he did not play well, his playing could be very timid and I wasn't as sure I'd made the right choice. Bohn could be kind of an idiot savant and a very humorous guy to play with, but I was never sure what I was going to get from him musically.

I had Ronnie James Weber on bass, Rusty on guitar and Bohn

on drums at one point. It happened to be a very hilarious band to hit the road with. Each guy had a wicked sense of humor, and they were great pranksters. They were always pulling off different stunts and tricks and "punking" each other, long before it was a TV show.

Bohn came up with some of the all-time greatest nicknames for members of the band and others. For a while, Ronnie James was "Leather Toughy" due to his bad attitude. Rusty became "Star Baby" when he was hired by Kim Wilson, who Bohn dubbed "Mr. Big." I was "The Great Baldini." Joel Foy was "The Grumpy Farmer." Mike McCurdy was "Beaner Froggy." Chris Masterson was "Banus." Flying J Truck Stops were aptly named "Flying J-nus."

Another amusing nickname that Bohn came up with was for a bass player we used on a tour named John. Jim Overton told me John would be an ideal replacement for Marc Carino, after Carino left to go with the Fabulous Thunderbirds. Bohn, Rusty and I had been playing together for quite some time, and we needed a good bass player for the band. We auditioned John. He was more of a modern jazz player than a blues player, which was not good for the Blues Survivors, mainly because he played in a style similar to that of Jaco Pastorius. John did have an upright bass, though, and so we took that into consideration. We gave John some clues on how to how to play blues bass and had him listen to Willie Dixon tapes as part of his schooling. Once we got John out on the road, we force-fed him blues bass examples during the long drives.

We were listening to Sonny Boy Williamson's "Don't Start Me to Talkin'" on the tape player at one point, and John pulled out his Zonn electric bass and began slapping the strings along with the tune. Slapping the strings is a gigantic no-no if you're playing blues bass the way we wanted him to. We yelled at him all at once about not slapping the strings, and, I can tell you, he never did that again. It also led to a nickname for John from Bohn.

Sometime after the slapping bass incident, Bohn called over to the bass player.

"Hey, John, give me a pillow," Bohn said, still smirking about the excessively harsh blues bass lesson.

"Get your own pillow," John retorted.

"No, give me yours," Bohn said, still mocking the bass player.

"Fuck you, Bohn!" John shouted over the hum of the van engine.

"No, fuck you, Zonn," Bohn lashed back at John, who was still holding his Zonn bass.

From that point on, John became known as "Zonn" to members of the band.

I think the final straw for Zonn came before our tour went to Boston, while I was visiting my in-laws in New Jersey. We were all at their house, and my then-mother-in-law asked Zonn a question.

"So, who do you like to listen to, John?"

"Well, I listen to Jaco Pastorius and Wilton Felder," he said before pausing and then adding somewhat sarcastically, "Oh, I also listen to my supposed mentor, Willie Dixon."

When I heard "supposed mentor," I got really pissed off. I held it inside until we got to Boston, and by then we were totally fed up with Zonn's playing and his condescending attitude.

Before we started the Boston gig, I pulled Zonn aside.

"Zonn," I said, "you're slowing down the beats too much, and I need you to get more on track with me and the tempos."

"I'm working on it," he said, but he wasn't getting it.

We sat down with Zonn in the motel room at one point. I took the lampshade off the light and I shined it right at him, like a KGB interrogator. I was progressively trying to get Zonn to pace tempos that I kept speeding up, faster and faster. I was trying to get him to hold the tempos tight through the process.

"Stay with it! Faster!" I kept shouting at him.

Ultimately, we were grilling him so hard that he practically started crying. Our interrogation became known as "the Boston Inquiry." In retrospect, I had been too cruel to the guy about learning correct tempos. At the same time, I was the bandleader, and Zonn did have real challenges playing our style of blues and keeping pace. I guess I was being a MOSF—a mean old stepfather.

Bohn also had trouble reading maps.

"How do we get to this next town," I once asked him while I was behind the wheel.

He couldn't figure it out. I looked over, and he was reading the map upside down.

There was another time when Bohn got completely drunk, and Rusty and Ronnie locked him out on the hotel balcony in his underwear on a freezing night in Nanaimo, British Columbia. We took some pictures and video of him stuck on the balcony. It was a pathetic scene, but it was humorous at the same time, the way much of what happens on long tours seems to be.

On another tour with Joey Foy in the Midwest, we let Bohn take a crack at the two o'clock in the morning driving shift. I told him what route to take and went back to sleep. At one point, we were all snoozing peacefully, feeling the miles rolling by underneath us. Then I woke up, and everything changed.

"Bohn, where the hell are we?" I asked as we drove past cornfields somewhere in Wisconsin.

"I don't know," he retorted. "I'm on the 16 somewhere."

"This isn't the 16," I told him. "We're in the middle of a damn cornfield. Turn around! You're lost!"

Bohn turned around, after a bit of an argument about him being right and me being wrong. We backtracked for many miles. It turned out that Bohn had missed the exit where we should have turned off to get to our next gig. After that fiasco, we really didn't let him drive without "adult" supervision.

Another time, when we were playing gigs with Ronnie and Bohn, the guys ran into some unexpected tranny trouble. Ronnie, Rusty and Bohn were outside the Yale Hotel on a street in Vancouver, B.C., checking out the sights while on a break from our gig. A really rough-looking he/she, with a big Adam's apple and a two-day stubble, came up to them from across the street.

"Which one of you boys has the twelve inches I'm looking for?" the he/she asked, propositioning them with a coy smile. Bohn replied,"Maybe if you put all three of us together?"

They turned and ran, slamming into each other as they entered the Yale Hotel door. After that, they stayed inside on their breaks.

CHAPTER TWENTY-FOUR

Little Elmo's in Atlanta

M ost acts sometimes have bum nights. Blues bands can have many such nights due to the non-commercial nature of the music. One was in 1992, when Ronnie, Bohn, Rusty and I did a gig at Little Elmo's that our agent, Tom Radai, had secured for us. Our three nights at the Atlanta club just happened to be the same three nights the Atlanta Braves were up against the Toronto Blue Jays in the World Series. Those were not great nights to be booked in Atlanta, and we ended up playing to about twenty staunch blues fans each evening, though we were guaranteed some decent coinage for the gigs.

The couple that owned the club were from Hollywood. They had relocated to Atlanta but really didn't know anything about the South. They knew even less about the nightclub business and honoring a deal. They claimed they knew everybody in Hollywood and had made huge money while working there in the movie business. They kept bragging about how they'd gotten "a great deal" on their house in Atlanta and that it had a multicar garage big enough for all their expensive cars.

They lost money the three nights we played Little Elmo's because of the World Series, and I felt bad about it. We sat on our thumbs most of the nights. I found myself watching the games on TV, but I keep my mouth shut because I was rooting for Toronto. The Blue Jays won the series, which was a bummer for the folks in Atlanta while we were there.

At the end of our third night, the woman came up to me with a sour look on her face.

"We're not going to be able to pay you," she said flatly.

"What do you mean you're not going to be able to pay us?" I replied flabbergasted. "I don't understand."

"We lost our ass," she explained. "The World Series killed us. You know that. We're not going to be able to pay you the money we agreed on. That's all there is to it."

She folded her arms across her chest and just stared at me.

"Okay." I said, not sure of how to respond. "I'm going to talk to the booking agent."

What else could I do? I couldn't make her pay us, and we had already finished our part of the agreement. I phoned Tom Radai and read him the riot act.

"What the hell kind of people are these?" I asked him. "They don't honor their agreements after we've already played?"

Tom called the owners up immediately and read them the riot act. He and the woman got into it.

"Look, I've got a signed contract," he told her. "I've got a case here if you decide to make me take it to court. You're going to have to pay these guys, regardless. You made a deal. It's too late to change the deal. They've already played the gig. You didn't cancel the shows beforehand, so we expect you to pay in full. What's right is right."

This went on for about two hours. The woman did not want to pay her bill. Tom finally won the argument, but she decided to pay us in one dollar bills and some pocket change. The club owed us over two thousand dollars, and the lady plastered all the dollar bills together to make the payment to me. It was a gigantic wad of money.

It was a lesson learned. Never play a gig during the World Series, especially in a city like Atlanta, which hadn't had the World Series in over twenty years, particularly if the home team is going to lose. Why couldn't I have become a fortune teller instead of a harmonica player?

CHAPTER TWENTY-FIVE

The Gay Porn Motel

Many times on the road, the cheapest motels are not the nicest motels. Club owners often pay for the rooms, and for some of them, the quality of the band's accommodations is not a top priority. On every tour through the South with the Blues Survivors, we'd play a little restaurant in Lafayette, Louisiana called Poet's. It was a medium sized venue with a small stage for the band. The owner never dumped enough cash into our rooms for the nights we were in town.

On one trip to Lafayette, the club owner put Ronnie James Weber, Mark Bohn, Rusty Zinn and me in a sleazy joint that we'd never stayed in before. The motel looked really funky on the outside, with a light orange paint job and pink trim on the doors and windows. The numbers on the room doors were done up in a large curlicue style I can best describe as western brothel effeminate. We got there very late that night, after our gig. We hadn't had time to stop and unpack earlier. We were looking forward to long, hot showers and decent beds.

When I went inside to register and get keys to the rooms, two strange men working in the office looked me up and down as I entered. They were both wearing lip gloss and thick mascara around their eyes. One had long hair, cut in the Farah Fawcett mode, and the other had a regular haircut and a mustache. Both were doing exaggerated imitations of women's hand gestures and postures. As they spoke to me and to each other, one guy was doing a Southern Valley girl routine. The other one might best be described as Dolly Parton without her "friends."

I first thought it was a comic gag or Halloween thing, but it turned the desk clerks were gay. I remained cool as I registered. They were OK by me, as long as they gave me my room keys so I could hit the shower and get some sleep.

We got our bags together and headed to the rooms, we immediately noticed that porn was playing on the television sets in both rooms. Motel guests normally have to sign up for porn and pay for it, yet the gay videos were being streamed into each of the rooms for free. The best was the actor that had sex with Cornish game hens prior to cooking them . He then served them up to his dinner guests who marveled at the delicious seasoning of their entrees. We were tired and, after a laugh, turned off the TVs and got ready for bed.

We were rooming together, two beds to a room, as the band members often do on the road. Club owners generally are not willing to pay for separate rooms, and we had to make do. The mascara-wearing clerks must have gotten the wrong impression when they saw the four of us divide up and go into just two rooms.

As Ronnie and Bohn were unpacking, the office-keepers knocked on their door and asked to come in. They probably were hoping to catch some lonely guys looking for some action.

Terrified, Ronnie and Bohn didn't answer at first, then finally told them to go away.

Ronnie phoned Rusty to tell us what was happening. Rusty laughed and hung up the phone. I went in the bathroom and jumped in the shower.

A few minutes later, the two desk managers knocked on our door. Rusty, who is quite a character, couldn't resist playing along.

"Who's there?" he asked in his best effeminate voice.

The clerks began knocking even harder.

"Let us in!" they shouted excitedly.

Rusty told me what was going on as I walked out of the bathroom dripping wet.

"Get the hell out of here!" I yelled. "We're straight!"

The two managers fled back to the office. I called down to the front desk and told them again to lay off, that we were not interested. They told me I misunderstood their intentions, but after that, they left us alone.

As we later figured out, the clerks were piping gay videos into all the rooms to test the reactions of the customers. It was kind of like fishing. If a tenant didn't phone the front desk to complain, the desk managers would go to the room to see if they could get something going. Being tired, we hadn't bothered to protest and thus became potential targets of their strange scheme.

Needless to say, we never again stayed at that sleazy place.

CHAPTER TWENTY-SIX

Jimmy Rogers and Billy Boy—1993

I phoned San Francisco Blues Festival organizer Tom Mazzolini in 1992 about hiring two Chicago blues legends, guitarist-singer Jimmy Rogers and harp blower-singer Billy Boy Arnold, to perform at the festival with my band, which included Rusty Zinn, Mark Bohn and Ronnie James Weber. Ronnie had just joined. He had started playing upright bass a month or two earlier and had already mastered the instrument. Rusty could play Jimmy and Billy's music perfectly and idolized Jimmy the same as I did. Jimmy and Brownie McGhee were my two favorite blues vocalists from my beginnings in the music business, due to their sophisticated country blues voices, which were urbane yet natural. Rogers had also been one of the founding members, along with Little Walter, of Muddy's most famous aggregation in Chicago in the early '50s that made some of my favorite records of all time.

I had the same agent as Jimmy, his longtime friend Tom Radai. I had called Billy ten years earlier, when I booked Eddie Taylor out in San Francisco, but his price was out of my range then. This time, though, I could pay both artists' asking prices. I lined up two fests and a series of club dates, so each artist would spend ten days in California. Jimmy also could fly to Portland and do a night between our dates.

Both Jimmy and Billy flew in a couple days early to rehearse the band. I asked if they'd mind staying at Rusty's parents' house in Santa Cruz.

"No way," Billy said.

"Take me to the liquor store," Jimmy requested.

I bought them rooms and dinner in Half Moon Bay.

Jimmy, for some reason, kept calling Billy "Bo," much to Billy's consternation. It must have been a reference to Billy's beginnings with the then-unknown Bo Diddley in the early '50s.

We rehearsed at the Zinn house. We covered Jimmy's material with no sweat. Billy's rehearsal was a different matter. When the drummer struggled with "Wish You Would," Billy's famous song, Billy shrugged and said, "That ain't it." Finally, the drummer exclaimed in frustration, "Maybe you should get June," referring to June Core, the Santa Cruz drummer who used to play with me. "Yeah, get June," Billy responded. We all were in shock. Finally, Billy said he'd try it with the drummer we had.

The first gig after rehearsal was at Moe's Alley in Santa Cruz on a Friday night. Jimmy was high as a kite but managed to do a smoking version of "Take a Walk with Me." We were up and out the door early the next morning to play the San Francisco Blues Festival and barreled up Highway 1 to make the twelve-thirty gig. The set came off good. Jimmy saw Mississippi guitarist Honeyboy Edwards backstage. I could barely understand Honeyboy's thick Southern drawl, but Jimmy understood him perfectly.

We played in San Jose at JJ's Downtown that night. The club had lost some money, and owner June Stanley asked if Jimmy and Billy would take a reduction in pay. I told her it was doubtful. We played a blues festival in Sacramento on Sunday. Randy Chortkoff asked me if he could drive Billy and Jimmy to the gig. I agreed. Unfortunately, that morning Jimmy was blasted by the time the limo pulled onto the site. Thanks, Randy! Billy's set came off so well that he told my wife he felt like Michael Jackson (I hope he meant in terms of adulation). Jimmy was so incapacitated that Rusty had to tune his guitar for him. Jimmy barely managed the intro to "That's Alright," and then proceeded to do "Got My Mojo Working" and "Ludella," followed by "Mojo" again. Fortunately, promoter Phil Gavant was used to such shenanigans. I did, however, get some wonderful photos of my six-month-old daughter Julia on Jimmy's lap that my friend Dave Horowitz had taken.

We drove Jimmy to the Oakland Airport after the fest. During the hour-and-a-half ride, while my wife and I sat up front, Jimmy laid on the van bench seat, mumbling "motherfucker" or "cocksucker" every time we hit a bump in the road. When we finally got there, Jimmy caught his flight to Portland. I worried about Jimmy's performances after the Sacramento debacle, so when we met Jimmy in at the airport in Reno the following Tuesday, I brought it up. He said it wouldn't happen again and that night played the best I'd heard him. He was playing like a kid again, especially on his song "Act Like You Love Me."

The last gig with Jimmy and Billy was at Slim's in San Francisco. We recorded with Billy the next day, with everyone agreeing to work on spec and Rusty and I paying for the studio time. We had Tom Mohan on piano, Ronnie James Weber on bass, Mark Bohn on drums and Rusty on guitar. I produced the session. Billy said it would be the last time he'd rerecord his old Vee-Jay material. He had sung kind of hard the night before at Slim's and had blown his voice a bit, but his conviction showed through, especially on his version of "I'm a Man." One of my faves is "Sonny Boy's Jump," with just Billy and Mahon. It was a fruitful session, the first Billy had done in many a year. I called Bruce Iglauer at Alligator Records and sent him a mixed tape. He said it was good but that some of the vocals needed to be fixed.

Unfortunately, Billy had signed an ill-fated management deal with Chortkoff couple months later. Chortkoff had recorded Billy immediately after our session, and sold the album to Alligator, thus cancelling out our recording. Billy reneged on his promise to not rerecord the Vee-Jay material and did many of the same songs he'd done on our session. Eighteen years later, our session was issued as *Consolidated Mojo* on Electro-Fi Records to rave reviews. Better late than never! Billy has continued to have a fruitful relationship with Electro-Fi. He still does my Blues Harmonica Blowouts and always has the youthful look and sharp memory of a man half his age. Jimmy died in 1997 at age 73. Some of his best performances from our tour are on my *Mark Hummel's Chicago Blues Party* CD.

CHAPTER TWENTY-SEVEN

Chrisickins and Left Hand Earl

I did a tour of the Northwest in 1993 with a couple of guys that I didn't gig with all the time but knew well enough to hire for the tour. Left Hand Earl was a drummer and friend of mine from New Orleans. Chris was a guitar player from Redondo Beach, and Curt was a bass player from San Diego. Chris and Curt were playing with me for the first time, as opposed to Left Hand Earl, who had done countless gigs with me on past tours. Chris did a couple Bay Area dates with me before leaving on the road. I noticed right away that he was a ladies' man.

Chris had a proclivity for picking up a different woman every night we played. At the first gig in Santa Cruz, we ran into a musician friend of mine, Mark Bohn, a drummer who had worked with me in the Blues Survivors. Mark told me a story about Chris and his ability with women. Mark had been playing a club, and there was a beautiful woman who would attend the gigs regularly. Mark had made several attempts to speak to her, but she always told him to take a powder. Chris came down and sat in one night at the gig where Mark was playing drums. Chris was able to pick up Mark's longtime crush in less than ten minutes with just a few words and a couple of smiles. Mark hadn't been able to get two kind words out of the woman in six months. Chris took her home that night. The closest Mark ever got to his fantasy chick was listening to Chris brag about the details of his conquest. By the way, did I mention that Chris, along with being a mean blues guitar player, was a successful a male model on TV commercials and in department store catalogs?

A week later, we all left in the van for our first gig in Walla Walla, Washington. It went well. Chris gave strong performances on guitar, and Left Hand Earl and Curt found a happening pocket and stayed in it. We also did a several wild, wild west gigs in Montana. On each gig Chris would pick up the prettiest available cowgirl at the show. You would think I was lying if I told you how easy it was for him. Chris barely had to look their way and the woman would come over. It was like they were hunting him. On van rides to the next gig, Chris would tell us the details of these strange encounters of the second kind. One of the cowgirls from Montana, a gorgeous woman with long chestnut hair, had Chris spank her like a bad little girl before they did the deed in the horse barn. A blonde jazzercise teacher took Chris home from our gig at the Silver Dollar in Butte and gave him a stretching lesson. Chris told the entire band the sordid story on the van ride the next day up to Canada.

We were on our way up to Edmonton, Alberta, to play a week at Blues on Whyte, a biker and student blues bar in the hippest part of the town. While we were there, Chris hooked up with a tough biker's girlfriend. He spent every night with her on sexual escapades that I don't dare to repeat. Let's just say that there was nothing that went unexplored and nothing she would not do to please Chris. She was furious at her boyfriend for some unknown indiscretion that had recently taken place, and Chris took sexual advantage of her insane desire to get even with him. He would tell us the stories of their trysts the next day before the gig while we laughed like hyenas. Chris had a contagious sense of humor and no heart when it came to the girls. He used to always say to us, after each lust-filled story, when we would tell him what an asshole he was, "Don't hate me just because I'm beautiful."

Chris spent each night of the Edmonton gig carefully avoiding the big, burly boyfriend, who would drop by occasionally to check up on his chick. I noticed Chris was very good at this part of his deceitful game. He would disappear at the start of the break and reappear only as we got back on stage to start a new set. I never could figure out where he went, but that's the point of good hiding technique, right? Anyway, the biker showed up occasionally to see what his supposedly loyal maiden was up to in the club. He had tats covering his entire body and wore a sleeveless Levi vest to show off his body art, his scars and his bulging muscles. He reminded me of Mickey Rourke without any of the humor. Chris was terrified of him, not that being terrified of the guy stopped Chris from having his way with the guy's girl every night.

As I recall, on the last night of our gig, the boyfriend came in looking for his main squeeze. He was wide-eyed, like a meth freak, and immediately started drinking. He walked into the club in frenzy, searching each corner. His presence was making Chris a nervous wreck. No doubt Chris was thinking of what this guy would do to him if he knew he was the guy his girlfriend had been seeing or, worse yet, if the tough biker had any inking of the things

Chris had been doing to his girlfriend on a nightly basis. I waited apprehensively for the proverbial shit to hit the fan. At the same time, the band sounded damn good, and we were setting the place on fire. Luckily, for all of us, the girlfriend never showed, and Chris disappeared again right after we packed up our equipment.

The next day, we drove all the way to Vancouver. On the fourteen-hour drive, Chris told us the tale of the night before. He and the wild woman were partying at her place in the middle of the night when they heard the sound of the boyfriend's motorcycle pulling up in front of her apartment. There was no way out. She had Chris hide in her closet, in which he stood terrified, without moving, while the amped-up biker and the girl partied and drank. A couple of hours later, he went to the john and the girlfriend ushered Chris out of the apartment without an even a goodbye. He had to walk about six miles back to the hotel. He told us that, after all he been through on this trip, he was swearing off chicks for a while. He slept for most of the long drive to Vancouver.

We arrived, fried and crispy, at the old four-story brick Cecil Hotel in the middle of the night. The now-defunct Cecil was a serious strip club and sleazy hotel. If you look it up online, it says, "For thirty-five years we bought the best in exotic entertainment to Granville Street, where we picked the sexiest, most fun-loving girls on the planet to..." It was a hellhole used by the Yale Hotel to house musicians who were playing the Yale. We were going to be at the Yale for the next week, so I asked for four rooms. The desk clerk at the Cecil told me that he only had two rooms and that the band had only been approved for two rooms, anyway. I was too tired to argue, so I roomed with Curt and Left Hand Earl and Chris shared a room. We got in at two a.m., and I fell asleep like a baby that had just driven for fourteen hours.

At four a.m., I was dragged out of a dead sleep by a banging on the door like the hotel was on fire. I groggily opened the door to find Chris standing there looking severely distressed. He was shaking and in his underwear.

"What happened?" I asked. "Did the biker show up?"

"Not that! How well do you know Left Hand Earl?" Chris asked.

"I've known him a long time," I responded.

"Left Hand Earl was in my bed," Chris announced.

"What?" I said, still half asleep and rubbing my tired, dry eyes.

"Left Hand Earl was in my bed, man! I dreamed I was home spooning with my girlfriend. The next thing I know I woke up and it was Left Hand Earl, man, right next to me!"

"Get outta here!" I said.

"No, really, he was in my bed, and then I pushed him out! I can prove it. Listen!"

Chris pulled out a small cassette recorder, and played a tape that went:

Chris: "What were you doing in my bed?"

Left Hand Earl: "Huh?"

Chris: "What were you doing in my bed, man?"

Left Hand Earl: "What are you talking about?"

At that point Chris said, "See what I mean? That proves it!"

"What are you saying?" I asked. "Are you telling me Left Hand Earl tried to have his way with you?"

"I don't know," Chris said.

"Is your ass sore?" I inquired.

Chris did seem dumbfounded, like a guy who had just been ass fucked for the first time.

"I'm kinda sore," he mumbled.

At that point I was too stunned to know what to think about any of it. Was this guy having a nervous breakdown or what? During the whole trip he had been hyper-sexed with women on every gig and talking it up in the van. Had Chris' tall tales gotten Left Hand Earl excited? I didn't know what to think.

I went downstairs to the front desk and got Chris his own room. For the next twenty-four hours, things deteriorated. Chris couldn't sleep and kept calling me on the hotel phone and weeping. I was certain Chris was not getting better, and it was obvious he wouldn't be able to play the night at the Yale. I hate to be pragmatic when a guy is falling apart at the seams, but I have a show to put on no matter what else is happening. The fact that Chris was breaking down gave me two problems. I needed to help him out, of course, but I also needed somebody to play guitar for the week at the Yale.

I called everyone I knew to help me hook up with a guitarist for the first night. There was literally nobody available, except for a dude named Muddy Kaiser. I was thinking that at least he'd know the catalog of Muddy Waters songs. No such luck. Kaiser showed up horribly drunk and didn't seem to know who Muddy Waters was or how to play like him. Even worse, Kaiser didn't know how to play blues guitar at all. He was a total sham, and I had to make it through the first set with just Left Hand Earl and Curt backing me up. Kaiser just stood there on the stage brushing his fingertips across the strings of his electric guitar. On the second set, however, he did do one thing like Muddy Waters was known to do at times. Our new Muddy sat down on a chair and barely touched his fingers to the strings and frets. He was too intoxicated to stand up or even move his fingers.

The next morning I felt I might have to fly somebody up from the States to play guitar on the Yale gig. Chris had not improved. If anything, he was worse than the day before. He stayed in his room, having nightmares all day. No doubt he was thinking that one those nasty acts he had performed on so many girls had been done to him. I called Joel Foy, a renowned blues guitarist from Los Angles, to see if he could fly up at the last minute. He said he could fly to Vancouver if needed him. That morning I checked to see if Chris had been committed to an insane asylum yet. The day before Chris had informed me he was going to visit a Vancouver proctologist to have himself examined. I checked on him at midday to see how he was and how the appointment had gone. I asked him flatly if he had been anally penetrated the night before last. He said the doctor told him there was nothing more than a little redness on his anus and that it did not appear be related to any kind of anal penetration. Chris was coming to grips with the fact that he may have been wrong about Left Hand Earl taking his cherry while he was sleeping. He begrudgingly said he'd give the show a shot that night and would try to finish the next two weeks of the tour. He told me I could forget calling Joel for the time being. Chris warned me, however, that he'd kill Left Hand Earl if Left Hand Earl said a word to him.

Everything was pins and needles at the Yale that night. Chris kept a poker face while he played, and Left Hand Earl managed to avoid saying one word. Everyone kept their mouths shut as the band worked its way through three strong sets. The night was a major improvement over the Muddy Kaiser fiasco. We finished out the last four nights without incident, but I noticed that Chris was not his usual self. He ignored advances from women that he would have moved on swiftly just the week before. He carried on only limited conversations, and did not spend time with any of us. It was a tense situation, but workable. I was careful to keep Left Hand Earl and Chris apart as much as I could.

I was glad to pack up and leave the sleazy Cecil Hotel adventure behind us. The strippers were just arriving as we left the hotel at the end of the week. We drove back down into the States and on to gigs in Idaho. I had thought the worst was behind us, but words were exchanged during the long ride. On our way over an icy mountain road, Chris and Left Hand Earl started screaming at each other. Chris claimed Left Hand Earl had winked at him. Left Hand Earl laughed and said he didn't wink at Chris and that Chris was a psycho. The war of words continued, and they demanded I stop the van. I had to stop in the middle of the icy highway since there was no place to pull over. They got out of the van and threatened to annihilate each other. They exchanged insults and challenges and feigned throwing punches, but it was all talk.

It was quiet in the still mountain air when they got back in the van. The rest of the ride to Idaho was uneventful, and the feelings in the van were closer to normal. The band members all were lost in their own thoughts as we circled slowly around and down the mountain roads toward Idaho.

We played our best show of the tour that night in Boise at a club called the Blues Bouquet. I guess a little tension really can get the creative juices flowing.

As the tour wore down, Chris and Left Hand Earl were increasingly at each other, but I didn't care as the number of days left was dwindling to nothing. I was almost free of this insane tour.

We were at the Central Saloon in Seattle on the last night. In 1888, the same year Washington became a state, there was a great fire that burned down a large part of the city. In 1892, the Pioneer Square section of Seattle was rebuilt. The Central Saloon was a featured part of the square. The club is billed at the oldest saloon in Seattle and is famous for its battered onion rings.

Chris and Left Hand Earl had been bickering and threatening each other all day long. At the final sound check, all bets were on for a wild boxing match between these two. They had been telling each other all day, and Curt and I as well, how they were each going to clean the other guy's clock. Chris was going to pound Left Hand Earl into the ground and teach him the lesson of his life. Left Hand Earl was going to beat Chris' psycho, little-girl ass and teach him how to be a man. There was a huge build up during the day, and I played the last set of the night full of excitement that these two guys would beat each other to a pulp. The tour was over, and I wanted to see it. I felt they deserved it. For all the problems they had caused me, all the bullshit from Chris and all the wasted effort I had to go through to keep the tour from falling apart, I wanted to see a long, drawn-out fistfight where each guy drew blood. I was hoping for fists banging off foreheads, with a knockout in the end. I didn't care who won, as long as they got a little punishment for the pain they had caused me. Instead, each of them disappeared after the gig. I didn't know where Chris went. Left Hand Earl got his pay and grabbed a cab to the Seattle train station. He bought a ticket to Chicago to visit his family.

On the entire ride back to San Francisco, I got an earful from Chris. I heard about all the male producers that had tried to seduce him in exchange for TV spots. He told me that on almost every job he interviewed for, some producer had demanded a sexual favor for the part. He told me that was why he quit working in TV and focused on the blues guitar. The conversation triggered a Left Hand Earl thought, and Chris told me again how he was still going to kick Left Hand Earl's pervert ass. I told him Left Hand Earl was gone now and it was time for him to shut up about Left Hand Earl.

We never played a gig together again. I would catch Chris around occasionally at a show, but he eventually disappeared from the blues scene. You see a lot of guys like that; they come in for a few years and then they are gone. It takes a ton of grit to stay on the scene and earn the handle "Blues Survivor."

CHAPTER TWENTY-EIGHT

Pacemaker

Rusty, Mark Bohn, Zonn and I did a double-bill gig in New York City in the early '90s. We performed first and were followed by William Clarke. I thought we had played a real good set, but when Clarke got up there, he ripped us a new one. It left me thinking about why. One of the reasons for his band's super set was that he had a tighter rhythm section. They really smoked, and Clarke's drummer, a guy known as Pacemaker, was the key to the pocket. I'd been hearing about Pacemaker for a while. He played a solid double shuffle and scorching slow blues. He played with a confident and deliberate style.

William Clarke was a very dynamic performer who would play songs for a short time before breaking into something else, and the guys in the band never knew what kind of cue he was going to give to switch from a slow blues to a shuffle. Clarke had worked out cool cues so he could modulate from one song to another. He would do a set that might have thirty songs. It might go from a swing to a slow blues to a shuffle to another slow blues to a boogaloo, then to a rumba, a swing, a slow blues, two shuffles, a rumba and a Bo Diddley beat. His band members would have to be totally on their toes and watch his every move. If they missed a cue, he would turn around and glare at them. Maybe he'd even beat them up later. He was an imposing fellow.

The guys in the Clarke's might have been scared of their boss, but they really played well behind him. They also wanted to do a good job to impress him. Pacemaker was doing an especially good job. We gave our drummer a hard time, asking him "How come you can't play more like that?"

A year later, I phoned Clarke after hearing that Pacemaker was no longer playing with him.

"What happened to Pacemaker?" I asked.

"Well," he said, "I just needed another drummer."

"What'd you think about Pacemaker?" I asked.

"He's a good blues drummer," Clarke replied. "He can sound just like Fred Below."

"How was he to travel with?" I asked.

"He's a pretty nice guy and a hell of a driver," he answered.

That was a darn good recommendation, so I phoned Pacemaker and asked him if he'd like to do a tour with the Blues Survivors. He told me he'd love to.

Pacemaker seemed like a decent bloke. We started rehearsing, and I noticed he had an odd tempo thing going on. Sometimes I'd count off a tempo, and he'd begin at a different pulse. Many times he'd speed up or slow down in the middle of a song. At least he hit the drums hard and played certain beats quite well.

We did our first gig with Pacemaker, guitarist Joel Foy and bassist Vance Elhers. I had also just started working with Joel. He and Pace had played together with Clarke, and Joel was a hell of a guitar player who also had worked with James Harman. Slow blues tended to slow down and the shuffles tended to speed up on the first gig. I usually do fairly long songs, as opposed to Clarke's short ones, which is probably why he didn't notice Pacemaker's tempo problems.

I hoped that things would improve as we headed out across the country. They didn't, really, so I began leaving songs Pacemaker was having trouble with out of our sets. I've learned from experience that you've got to find musicians' strong points and stay away from their weak spots. That's what I started doing with Pace. I just stuck with the things I knew he was going to do a good job on.

Pace would drive long, long hours in the van. The reason they called him Pacemaker was because he had had a heart attack in his early twenties and had a pacemaker put in. By the time I was working with him, he was probably his forties or fifties. He was definitely older than the rest of us. He was a Vietnam vet and liked to call everybody "little brother."

"Hey there, little brother," he'd say, "I'll show you how it's done."

He loved to talk about movies and seemed to know every little thing about every movie that was ever made. I consider myself something of a film freak, but there were very few movies I had seen that he hadn't. He knew all the little details about films, like who directed them, who starred in them, who all the character actors were, the plot lines and the endings. We had a good time talking about movies. He also read a maps well, which helped, and he was hugely valuable as a driver or as co-pilot while I was driving.

Joel, on the other hand, tended to like to find alternate routes and little byways that went way off the highway and might save miles. His shortcuts often didn't save time, however, especially if we hit a farm road with a slow speed limit.

We did a show on that tour at the Legion Hall in Baltimore for Baltimore Blues Society. Carey Bell also was on the bill.

"How'd you get the name Pacemaker?" I overheard Carey ask our drummer after the show.

"I had one of these pacemakers put in my heart," Pacemaker said. "Keeps my ticker on pace!"

"Oh, man, they shouldn't call you that," Carey said, shaking his head slowly from side to side and rolling his big eyes sadly. "That ain't right. That ain't right."

"I also play the drums," Pacemaker explained. "I call myself Pacemaker because I keep the pace for the band."

Pace would always want to go to Denny's after gigs and order biscuits and gravy. One night during breakfast, Vance said to Pace, "When I get a pacemaker, I want the one you got, Pace, 'cause all those biscuits and gravy are likely to kill anybody else. Whatever that pacemaker is doing, it keeps you going like the Energizer Bunny in spite of all that bad food you eat."

"No doubt, little brother," Pacemaker replied. "Now pass me some more of that maple syrup, the butter and the flapjacks."

CHAPTER TWENTY-NINE

Stanhope's—A Scream

While on a long East Coast tour in 1993, we played a club in Stanhope, New Jersey, called the Stanhope House. Joel Foy was on guitar with Mark Bohn on drums and Vance Elhers playing bass. I'd been hearing about the place, which bills itself as "the Last Great American Roadhouse," for years. Although it had a tiny stage, it was supposedly a really good-sounding room and had a rich blues history. Muddy Waters and Magic Slim had played there all the time. Roomful of Blues made Stanhope House a regular stop, as well.

I phoned the club's booker, who was the brother-in-law of the owners, and was able to secure a Friday gig for eight hundred dollars. Then, three weeks before the scheduled date, I got a call from the guy.

"Things have been tough lately," he said. "We're going to have to cancel the gig."

"We've had the gig booked for three months," I told him. "I can't cancel it. It's only three weeks out. I'm already out on the road. We've got to go through with the deal."

"I can't pay you eight hundred for the gig," he said.

"You can't cancel the gig now," I insisted. "It's too late for me to get anything else."

"The best I can do is four hundred bucks," he responded.

I hemmed and hawed and did my best to talk him into keeping the guarantee what it was, but he ended up beating me down to four hundred bucks. There was nothing else I could do.

Before we got to Stanhope, I called the manager to inquire about our lodging.

"There's a convention in town, and there are no rooms available," he told me. "The Howard Johnson's that we usually use is booked up. How would you feel about staying here at Stanhope House?"

"What are the rooms like?" I asked.

He assured me they were fine.

After arriving at the club, we went upstairs and checked out the rooms. Stanhope House was built around 1794, and the bedrooms were the size of very small bathrooms. Each one had a single bed, no phone and no television, just a bureau. The bathroom was downstairs. It seemed like a rat trap and was way, way funky.

"This really is not going to do," I told the manager. "This isn't what we talked about. We talked about an actual motel."

"I can't put you in a motel," he said. "They're all booked up."

"Could you at least try?" I asked.

He called around and found us a little mom-and-pop motel about twenty minutes away. It turned out to be just fine.

Before we played, the club served us spaghetti and garlic bread. Our gig was sparsely attended, but we had a fun time playing for the thirty or so people who came.

"Really nice-sounding room," I told the manager as were loading out. "The spaghetti and meatballs were great. Thanks for getting us the motel rooms, but before we leave I want to tell you that what you did about cutting the money in half was not right."

"You can see I didn't have any people in here," he stated.

"Still," I responded, "you shouldn't have booked us if you were going to cut the money."

The guy blew up and started screaming at me full throttle, calling me an asshole, telling me how musicians were worthless pieces of shit and how dare I insult him and his club.

"The music is what makes you guys famous, not the club," I screamed back him. I had a mike stand in my hand in case he took a swing at me.

The president of the Blues Society of New Jersey happened

to be standing on the sidewalk next to me. After witnessing the manager in action, he decided he'd never hold another event there.

I was still seething as we drove out of town. That was the end of Stanhope House as far as I was concerned, and the Blues Survivors would never play another gig there. I heard they let the booking brother-in-law go not long after that. I've outlasted many of these guys, and I'm still here, if I do say so myself.

CHAPTER THIRTY

Hell to Pay Rounder Revue

I did a European tour in 1997 that kept me away from the continent for the next few years. It really knocked the wind out of me. At the time, I was recording for Tone-Cool Records, which was distributed by Rounder Records. The head of Rounder Records Europe decided he wanted to sponsor a tour featuring Rounder artist Michelle Wilson, myself and a few other musicians. The Blues Survivors and I would do a set of our own, as well as back Michelle, her saxophonist Scott Shetler, and keyboardist Little Anthony Geraci, who had played with Sugar Ray Norcia for a long time and recorded with him for Tone-Cool. Also on the revue was a friend of the promoter, singer-guitarist Big Monty Amundson. Monty and my band were from the West Coast; the other three were from New England.

My band's tour began with three weeks' worth of dates across the U.S., from California to Florida, before going to Europe for five more. The European leg of the tour was booked by Tornado Productions, a now-defunct agency in Holland. I had worked for them several times before, but the longer they stayed in business, the flakier they became. They were great the first time I played for them. The second time wasn't so great, and so on.

For the American part of the tour, I used my own van for transportation. Tornado Productions had agreed to ship the van from Florida back to California via semi-truck so that we could fly to Europe straight out of Florida. We didn't receive our plane tickets until the day before were scheduled to leave.

We had almost no days off as we crisscrossed Europe, covering

Spain, Italy, Slovenia, Belgium, France, England, Scotland, Germany, Holland, Norway and Denmark. After a week or so, it became one big Euro-blur. The gigs and rooms seemed to roll into one never-ending bad dream. We toured mostly by van, although we did travel through the Chunnel from Paris to London by train.

The tour started off on the wrong foot. The day we flew into Spain, Michelle looked totally haggard.

"Oh, my God, why am I here?" she said.

Michelle liked the musicians I had working with me at the time: Randy Bermudes on bass, Mark Bohn on drums and Chris Masterson on guitar. So with the addition of Anthony on keys and Scott on saxophone, Michelle had a real good band. As the tour progressed, however, Michelle started noticing Bohn's tempo problems. It was a challenge for her, and she became increasingly irritated.

Many of the drives from gig to gig were long and at times horrendous. Added to that, the van was very uncomfortable. Our tour manager, who'd once been Englebert Humperdinck's road manager, had a horrible sense of direction and not even a decent map. We found ourselves driving around many a European town for an hour or more, lost and confused. Once we got to the city center, he often had to ask a passerby how to get to the hotel or venue. If you've ever been in Europe—or most of the U.S., for that matter—and asked for directions, every person will give you a different answer. When things got bad, the tour manager would say, "Humperdinck would never stand for this!"

All our free time was eaten up by the incompetence of our one-man road crew. What normally would have been a five-or six-hour drive ending up taking seven. There was little time left to shower, eat and do a sound check before shows. The burden of this schedule became increasingly intolerable, and we found it difficult to hold our tongues. The musicians became short with one another. There were increasingly sharp exchanges in the van, which is normal during long drives day after day, but having a person in charge who doesn't know what he's doing or where he's going turns it into a real mess.

Nerves eventually frayed as a result of the long drives and getting lost so often. We drove from Barcelona to Milan in one day and then had only half a day to get to Torino. We drove the next day from Torino to Slovenia, which is above northeastern Italy. We drove through the Alps through Switzerland to get to wherever the next gig was in Germany. The routing was insane, and the promoters didn't seem to give a damn about the schedule or about us.

While at a record shop in The Hague that was owned by the head of Rounder Europe, he bragged, "I have blues records from everywhere. I have everybody here." He did stock a whole lot of blues records by nearly everybody—except Mark Hummel, who supposedly recorded for the Rounder-distributed Tone-Cool label. He didn't have a single record of mine in his shop to sell while I was in Europe on a tour he was sponsoring. He did have some of Michelle's releases and Little Anthony's and even Big Monty's, but he didn't have one of mine. I was pissed.

I was exasperated by the end of the tour in Scotland. Michelle and I were getting along so terribly that at one point during a BBC broadcast there, all hell broke loose. While the guys in the band were being interviewed, she and I were outside having a horrible screaming match.

"How's everybody getting along on this five-week tour?" the interviewer asked Randy at one point. Randy was looking out the window and saw me and Michelle screaming our heads off at each just ten feet away. Fortunately they couldn't hear us through the window due to the music on the sound system indoors.

Giving the perfect and proper entertainers' answer, Randy replied, "Oh, everything's great. Everything's just going swell, like clockwork. We all love playing together."

The challenge of the road tour, the lack of sleep and the daily grind had driven us all nuts. By the end of the tour, everyone was just dying to go home. I swore off doing another European tour for a good four years. Down the road I did end up seeing Michelle at a few different shows, and we patched things up and got along fine after that.

It was a grueling tour, but Michelle and I both survived, even if it did cause my band to break up.

CHAPTER THIRTY-ONE

Band Houses

The band has to have a place to stay after the lights go down and show is over. It is one of the foundational tenets of booking a traveling band. In times of plenty or if the band is getting top dollar for the gig, the club owner puts us up in a comfortable hotel or motel and we spend a night or two in relative comfort before moving on to the next gig. That's how it should be. Unfortunately, that scenario is not common. Room quality for traveling musicians is generally somewhere on the lower end of the accommodation scale. Club owners are always looking to save money and the cheaper the rooms are, the more likely the hotel or motel will be located in an urban pocket with more drug activity and crime than where the club owner lives. We have come to expect crap or worse.

Occasionally club owners have vacant houses or furnished apartments that they offer to the band instead of hotels or motels. Such places of dubious reliability are known as "band houses." All I can tell you is that if you are a musician who is new to the road game, be careful when you receive this kind of offer. In general, the newer the club, the nicer the band house; the older the club— well, you can guess the rest.

One of the worst band houses I can remember was one we were offered in the late '90s when the Blues Survivors consisted of Charles Wheal on guitar, Steve Wolf on bass and Marty Dodson on drums. A club owner in Great Falls, Montana, told me he had a great place for the band to stay. It didn't look too bad on the outside, but with band houses, looks can be deceiving. The four of us trooped in and wandered around the house. The interior smelled like natural gas, like there was a serious leak in one of the main gas lines. The air hung heavy with a scent of danger.

"Don't light up!" I said to Wolf. "This place will blow to smithereens!"

The house was an empty dump. There was nothing inside but a few box springs with nothing on them—no mattresses, no sheets! Let me add, there were no towels, no soap, no shampoo and no chocolate under the non-existent pillows. It was lower than very funky low. The main thing that concerned us, however, was the gas smell. We immediately called the club owner.

"Hey, man," I told the guy," are you aware this place reeks of natural gas? You've got some kind of major leak here."

"Really?" he said, "I was just over there and didn't smell anything. Are you sure one of the guys didn't fart or something?"

"This is no fart," I told him. "You're gonna have to put us up at a motel. This house won't work. It's a damn death trap!"

"Oh, all right," he said. "Just make sure and leave the windows open when you leave."

The unconcerned way he answered my warning about the gas leak convinced me that he already knew there was a bad leak. Can you imagine? He was willing to risk all our lives just to save a few bucks on motel rooms.

He put us up that night in a real dump, but at least there was no leak.

We were in Pennsylvania on a fairly recent tour. I'd had a conversation with the club owner about our rooms, and even though it was part of the gig contract, he wasn't very happy about getting us motel rooms.

"I've got you guys some cheap motel rooms, but they aren't very comfortable," he said. "If you can deal with those, then fine. If you can't, you're on your own!"

"I'll check it out at least," I told him.

That's what I always say. What else am I supposed to do? I

can't say no without even looking at the rooms. Club owners are smart, if you think about it. It's twice as hard to leave a crappy motel you've already seen for an unknown one down the road that could be even worse. Once you're already in the motel and staring at the bed, you usually give in. You say to yourself, "What difference does it make? I'll be out of here in the morning. Why make a fuss?"

We took a look the rooms our employer had reserved. They were worse than we had expected, but you guessed it, we stayed anyway! A couple of our rooms had black mold, and the guys had to open their windows and put pillow cases over their noses and mouths just to breath. My room wasn't quite as bad, but the guys certainly let me know about the moldy smell in theirs. R.W. Grigsby, the bass player, had the worst room. The shower head blasted water straight up in the air to the bathroom ceiling, instead of down on top of his head. As a result, he had to stand right under the spot where the water bounced down from the ceiling. Not one of our TVs worked, most of the light bulbs were missing and the locks were broken off all the doors.

"What a palace," I sighed as the guys gathered in my room.

"The black mold was moving around in my room," Rusty said. "I could hear it crawling toward me."

"Can I use your shower tomorrow?" R.W. asked Rusty.

"You'll have to use Mark's," Rusty informed R.W. "There no hot water in mine."

What a place! None of the guys were too happy. At least we spent the following night at a Hampton Inn. It's a constant crapshoot, and sometimes you end up in the crap.

CHAPTER THIRTY-TWO

Bell's Palsy

It's hell to play harmonica with a mouth full of Novocain and even harder to play with Bell's palsy. This happened while dealing with fallout from my divorce back in 1996. At the time I was dating Alexis, my future wife and soulmate, and I was also going through a traumatic custody battle with my ex-wife over our beautiful daughter, Julia. Alexis saved the day for keeping me saner and more centered than I normally would have been on my own. I might have jumped off the Golden Gate Bridge if it weren't for her.

Right before I was leaving on a tour of the United States, I had gone through all kinds of court appearances with my lawyer and my ex-wife's lawyer about child custody. She had tried to get sole custody, but the judge ruled for me to share custody. Then, at the very last minute before I left town, she dropped the bomb on me.

"I'm moving to Los Angeles," she said. "Even though we have joint custody, unless you can figure out a way to watch Julia while you're on your tour, I'm taking her with me, and there's nothing you can do about it."

Alexis and I were supposed to be celebrating the court decision over dinner. I was in a state of shock during our dinner date, and Alexis also was very upset. I had to leave town for my tour in the middle of this legal dilemma and was emotionally fractured by the turn of events.

At the end of a week on the road, the Blues Survivors and I were in Indianapolis playing a club called the Slippery Noodle. Before the gig, I went for a walk to get a little exercise. It was fairly warm, about seventy degrees. During my forty-five-minute walk, dark clouds appeared in the sky, a wind whipped up and the temperature dropped about twenty-five degrees. I got back to the band house feeling OK and went on to play the gig.

We were at Memphis Smoke in Detroit the next night. I couldn't hear the monitors well during our first set, and the sound was really distorted.

"Why is it so distorted?" I asked the sound man.

"I've got them cranked," he answered.

Right before I got off the stage, some old guys from the Society for the Preservation and Advancement of the Harmonica (SPAH), an organization that does harmonica conventions on a yearly basis, showed up at the club. While closing the first set with "Hand Jive," I had a hard time hitting the high notes and blow bends I normally do during my solo. Between that and the distortion I was hearing, I realized something was seriously wrong.

The SPAH guys were mostly in their seventies, and one of them suggested to me that I might be having a stroke. I couldn't be having a stroke, could I? I thought to myself, realizing that my mouth wasn't working very well. What the hell is going on? I wondered.

As the gig continued on, my face started feeling numb, and my hearing on one side made the sound seem even more distorted. I then realized it wasn't the monitors. It was my ear!

When I woke up the next day, one side of my face felt paralyzed, but we all got in the van anyway and continued on to the next gig. The show, as they say, must go on.

By the time we got to Erie, Pennsylvania, I couldn't take it anymore. I freaked out. I went to an emergency room.

The doctor checked my blood pressure and told me it was fine.

"Well, what's going on?" I asked him.

"Sounds to me like you have Bell's palsy," he replied.

"What's that?" I asked.

"It's an airborne virus," he explained, adding, "or you can get it from stress. It can be caused by emotional stress or an airborne virus, brought on by extreme temperature differences."

When he said that, I realized the severe emotional stress I'd been under from the child custody issue. Perhaps that, combined with the sudden temperature drop during my walk in Indianapolis, had worn me down to the point where I got this strange illness.

I was only ten days out on a five-week tour. I could barely play the harmonica. I was not even able to smile out of one side of my face, and the sound seemed so distorted. I had to wear earplugs to hear myself properly. Singing was easier to do because my ear was plugged, but I had a hell of a time playing because I was not able to make my lips tight enough to cut off the air with the holes of the harmonica. I was, however, still able to tongue block. If I had been just a "lipper," I would have had to cancel the rest of the tour, but I was saved by my tongue.

This event made me realize how fragile health is and how important staying in good health is to making a living as a touring musician. It also made me realize that if I had not been able to tongue block, I would have been screwed.

Another thing the doctor told me about Bell's palsy scared the hell out of me.

"It normally lasts three weeks, but in some cases, there's about a thirty-to-forty-percent chance that your face will remain paralyzed on the one side and you may never be able to get that back," he explained.

If that happens, I thought, I might never again be able to play the harmonica the way I'm used to playing it. I might have to stop playing harmonica for a living. The thought was very disconcerting.

When we got to New York City, I met a harmonica player at the club we were playing at who told me that he'd once had Bell's palsy that left one side of his face permanently paralyzed. It took him twenty years before he was again able to bend a note. The conversation scared the hell out of me.

Also that night in New York, some great harmonica players came down to visit and play. They included Dennis Gruenling and

Adam Gussow, and there I was playing with half of my face para-lyzed and having to keep my solos super simple.

Fortunately, three weeks to the day, the paralysis in my face went completely away, and I was able to play exactly like I had prior to coming down with Bell's palsy. I had gone to an acupuncturist during the three weeks and tried all kinds of different things to bring my face back quicker, but nothing had worked. Then, I was completely recovered and no longer had to worry about the pos-sibility of half my face being paralyzed for twenty years. It seemed miraculous. I must be a lucky guy.

CHAPTER THIRTY-THREE

Another Horrible Rear End Story

I got my first Ford van in 2001. Before buying it, I had always purchased Dodge vans for my cross-country road touring. I paid more for the recent-model Ford than for any previous van I'd owned. We left California right after I picked up the Ford. Our first gig was at a theatre in Ponca City, Oklahoma.

Shortly before pulling into Ponca City, I started hearing suspicious sounds, like moaning coming from within the van itself. The van also kept pulling to the left while driving on the freeway. A mechanic at the repair shop there told me some very bad news. The van previously had been in a really bad accident, and the frame was severely bent. That wasn't all. He told me the bent frame would eventually crack, which would completely total the van. He informed me that there was nothing I could do to avert the inevitable.

I asked the mechanic to do a patch job for me, a temporary half-ass fix so I could make it to my next set of gigs. It almost worked. We made it as far as Florida. In a way, we won the battle but lost the war. Something else in the engine started making noise, and by the time we got to Fort Lauderdale, the van completely quit on me. We had it towed to Famous Frank's, a friend of a friend's shop there, and he found something else wrong with it.

"What the hell is wrong with this thing?" I asked him.

"You bought a pile of crap," Frank told me. "That's what's wrong with the thing."

"Can you fix it?" I asked. "How much will it cost? Is it worth fixing?"

"I don't know if it's worth fixing," he said, shrugging his shoulders and wiping some oil off his fingers with a pink shop rag. "That's up to you, but how else do you plan to get your band and your equipment back to California?"

Fortunately, all the van really needed was a new generator, which I had him install before we left town and completed the tour.

Two years later, I was in back in Florida with another Ford van. It was two-years old, with only fifty-thousand miles on it. It seemed like a good deal at fifteen thousand bucks.

Before a gig in Cocoa Beach, I took it in for an oil change. The mechanic called me about two hours later and said, "We've got a problem here with this van of yours, Mr. Hummel."

"What's that?" I asked.

"You need a new rear end," he said. "It's probably going to blow out if you don't get it done immediately. You'll never make it back to California the way the rear end is now."

My first piece-of-crap van had become just another bad memory, but there I was all over again. It was deja-Ford-van-vu!

I had no choice but to get the rear end repaired. The shop literally finished the work and got the van back to me twenty minutes before the gig start time, and the garage was about a thirty-minute drive from the Cocoa Beach club. I phoned the club owner and told him I was going to be a little bit late.

I showed up at the gig late and twenty-four hundred dollars light in my pocket book for the repairs. I had managed to have a new rear end installed and to complete a gig on the same day. That's how it goes sometimes on the road.

These van breakdowns have given me a special fear of Florida juju on my tours. I can't help feeling a bit jinxed every time I go to the state. At least I've helped make some Florida mechanics rich men.

CHAPTER THIRTY-FOUR

Niteclubmares or One Shot Deals

Sometimes you roll into town prepared for problems. Such was the case in Tacoma, Washington, in 2006. If you've been to Tacoma, you know the strange smell wafting from the paper mill on one end of town. The pulp stink adds special flavor to Tacoma's strip mall and fast food ambiance.

We were finishing a Blues Harmonica Blowout tour with James Harman and Paul deLay, driving south on Highway 101 from a gig in British Columbia. I had been trying for several weeks to reach the Tacoma club owner by phone to get my contract for hire returned. He wouldn't return any of my phone calls, nor did he return my contract, signed, as we had agreed when we set up the show. Finally, after playing the Upstage in Port Townsend, I was able to get his assistant on the phone. He told me, "Oh, don't worry about it. The date is on, and he's good for the money," and other stuff like that, which usually translates to, "You're heading into hell, and you'll be lucky to get out of this alive!"

"I still need to find out where we're staying the night of the gig, and I need to find out the other details that would be in the contract. *Please* have him call me," I explained.

The assistant got off the line promising he would do what he could, but the owner still didn't call me. I phoned the club repeatedly on the ride down but was still unable to get the owner on the phone. When we finally arrived at the club, I was miffed. The marquee read, "Paul deLay and Friends." There was no mention of James Harman or Mark Hummel. I had taken the time to forward posters for the show, but they weren't hanging anywhere in sight. It was clear that this owner's lack of follow-up was resulting in the mess I'd been worried about all along. The advance promotion for our show stunk, just like the smell from the paper mill. I made up my mind not to let this blowout get any further blown out.

The owner's failure to respond to my calls had ticked me off. That, combined with the marquee out front, absent our billing, put me over the top. I'd done everything I could to avoid it, but I couldn't help falling prey to the bad mood this club owner had placed me in. The Hummel-inator was in full swing when I parked the van and headed inside the club. I was not smiling.

There was a rawboned redheaded waitress, about two decades past the outfit she was wearing, working in bar as I entered. I asked her if Samson, the club owner, was in.

"No," she said, adjusting her blue moonstone necklace. "He's not here right now. Who are you?"

"I'm Mark Hummel, the bandleader, and we're supposed to be playing here tonight," I answered. "I would like to speak to him."

"He's not here, like I said," she told me again, lighting up a Capri cigarette.

"I don't know when he'll be in," she added, glancing quickly at a stairway leading to the second story of the club.

"I need to find out some details about the gig tonight," I stated. "I still don't have a signed contract, and I won't do this gig tonight unless we've got a contract."

"What are you worried about? We know you're here now," she said, exhaling a long draft of menthol smoke in my face.

"First of all, this guy hasn't called me back in four days; second my name, Mark Hummel, isn't even on the marquee, nor is James Harman's; and third, because I have never worked for him before and it's not looking good so far, I'm a little nervous about the gig," I replied, waving her plume of smoke out of my face.

"I'll try him, but I don't know where he is," she said as she wiped the scarred oak bar top with a washrag so dirty I wouldn't wipe the bugs off the window of my touring van with it.

I finally informed her we would wait right there until he arrived, and furthermore, we would need a signed contract before I would start setting up the instruments for the sound check. She gave me a look, the kind usually reserved by barmaids for the drunk and disorderly, and stalked away. I could see her on the phone talking animatedly with somebody for a couple of minutes. She came back and shrugged. Forty-five minutes or an hour later a large hairy man, reminding me of Big Foot, came ambling down the stairs from the second story of the club and said coldly, "My name's Samson. What do you want?"

I answered, just as coldly, "Well, I'm Mark Hummel. I need the signed contract I've been calling you about for tonight's show."

"I've heard about you" he responded. "I know all about your type. Look, all your friends play here. They don't need a contract. Why do you think you need a contract?"

"Because I've never played for you before and I don't see any advertising to speak of for my gig," I answered. "The advertising you have on the marquee doesn't mention anything about the show tonight being a harmonica blowout, and you don't even have James Harman's or my name on it. I understand there was an article in the paper, but I don't know what kind of turnout you're going to have because you have not advertised the gig the way we originally agreed you would."

"Look," Samson snorted, "if you aren't going to do this gig without a signed contract, you can just go home right now."

"Go home?" I countered. "We just drove twelve hours to get here. You're crazy if you think we're going to 'just go home.' We had a deal, and that's that. I expect a signed contract, and we expect to play and be paid!"

Samson pulled himself up to his full height and stared right down his nose at me, and saying flatly, "You know, you can leave right now."

At that point, James Harman jumped in and started jiving with the owner. James was playing good cop to my bad cop. He took over the conversation. He was schmoozing Big Foot, saying, "Hey, look, you know, Mark's an all right guy. Don't get him wrong. We just had a really long drive, and he's tired, you know. Hey, I'm James Harman, and we want to do this gig. It's not like we don't want to do the gig for you." James asked me to wait outside, and I followed his direction.

James is one of the great personalities in the blues and has been working in clubs and with club owners all his adult life. He knows how to play the good cop and schmooze when he needs to. The club owner was listening to James and falling under his spell. Paul deLay was just sitting there, his large mass on a stool, not wanting to lose the gig either. He wasn't saying a thing and chose to let James do all the talking. Paul was rolling his eyes, however, about what a mess this whole discussion had become, but he wasn't offering a whole lot of help to me or James. Since I was basically the bad guy, Paul became the neutral guy, and James was rapidly becoming the good guy.

James eventually saved the day with Samson, who, at the end of a long conversation, told him, "Look, I don't want to speak to that asshole anymore. That's all there is to it."

James came outside and told me, "If you can keep your mouth shut to the owner, we can do the gig. It's just that he thinks you're an asshole!"

"I'll do whatever to save the gig, since you and Paul want to do it, but I don't really want to deal with him anymore either," I said. This is an example of what happens occasionally on the road, and I'll be the first one to admit that it goes both ways. The communication breaks down somewhere, and you never know what you're going to find when you get to the club. I take the time to send out the promo packs, I negotiate on behalf of the band and then, along with the club owner, we set the expectations for the night of our gig. Sometimes after we've all agreed to the terms, club owners or producers forget about everything we'd discussed. They don't return my calls, and the gig promo goes to hell. If I say anything about the poor treatment, the guy usually calls me an asshole and everyone else kind of agrees with him. Road justice!

"The guy's going to pay me," James explained. "I'll pay you, and you can pay everybody. That's the way we'll have to do it. He's all pissed off."

"I'm ready to blow the whole thing off at this point," I told him. I wanted to tell them all to go to hell, but what was I going to do after I did that? I had a hungry band with a gig six hundred miles from home. My good sense ruled the day, and we decided that, since we'd driven all the way there, we would do the gig. I had to be the asshole and the bigger man at the same time. Welcome to the exciting life of the touring bandleader!

We all rushed back to the hotel, changed in fifteen minutes and returned quickly to the venue to eat our dinner. I didn't see the owner again, and the red-headed waitress tried to ignore me when I wanted to get a bottle of water after my meal. Trust me, I wasn't surprised. Later, we went on stage and played a great show in front of about forty people. After the show I went outside, and James left the bandstand to get the night's pay from Big Foot. James ambled out of the club a few minutes later and handed me the money. I took the bills from his hand and passed most of them out to the band. We packed up, got in the van with our instruments and amps and drove on down the road. I found the freeway quickly and headed south. That was the end of it. That was the first and last time I played that club in Tacoma. I never returned to smell the sweet stink of the paper mill again. At least I can say, when I think about it now, that I came face to face with Big Foot up in the great northwest and lived to tell the tale!

CHAPTER THIRTY-FIVE

Florida Sunshine

One must beware the many dangers in traveling the mean roads of Florida. You've got to worry about hurricanes, highway bandits who rob European tourists, alligators sleeping in ditches and, for touring harmonica players, the outdoor biker bars. We were heading to a Florida juke joint that had tropical landscaping in the outdoor area, complete with palm fronds over the top of the bandstand for shading the musicians from the burning sun. I was already prepared for disaster as we drove down the freeway leading up to the gig. The woman I was dealing with was a bleach-blonde, biker sea-hag "crankster" (as in meth-head). That doesn't sound kind, but there is no other way to put it. She had far too many decades of the sun frying her skin and far too many tokes on a crank pipe that was burning up her brain cells. She was smoking a cigarillo as I approached. Her halter top did not even come close to covering her large beer belly. Her rotund gut hung over her Levis like a double scoop of vanilla ice cream sagging down over a waffle cone. The waistband was about four inches too small for her hips and appeared to cut her nearly in half. A small but frightening green snake tattoo, with two large fangs dripping venom and a forked red tongue, slithered up to her alabaster navel from between her front pockets. All indications were that the rest of the snake's scaly green body was hidden down there somewhere, maybe coiled around her private parts.

I was already aware the club owner was a nut case because her strange e-mails had arrived on my computer in giant letters that were way too big for the page. It's kind of weird how we get a feeling from e-mails about people we haven't met. In her case the large letters and belligerent writing style gave an impression of cunning, extreme frugality and an unfocused IQ all at the same time. I do a portion of my preliminary setup work for my touring gigs online with folks I haven't yet met face to face. I'm exposed to bizarre behavior in e-mails all the time, but the Florida Crankster was a standout. It's gotten to where I can tell a great deal about a person's mental status and personality from their e-mail. From e-mail to e-mail, she would forget half of our financial discussion and ask the same questions over and over. She continually wrote back lowering the fee for the gig, and I would gently remind her of our agreement. I decided to ride it out with her, just in case it might become a regular gig for the band, but in my heart something told me this one was destined for disaster. I tried to work out the show logistics with her, but she was forgetful about our band's requirements, yet very nit-picky and exact about start times, the time we were to play and time limits for the breaks.

I could tell this gig was going to be a tough one. The way she interacted with me was a combo of hypersensitivity and flipped-out mania about the whole production. For a few of the folks I work with, when I'm arranging a gig with them online, they have no idea how to do their part, especially around the setup and advertising for a successful show. I'm constantly educating some of my clients as I work with them, since many of them ask for or need instruction. The problem with clients like this one is they are club owners who are sure they know best, even when they don't. Already suspecting I might have a problem with the Crankster, I promised myself I'd keep cool.

On the day we were finally driving down to her neck of the swamp, it was looking like it was going to rain. I knew it was an outdoor venue, so I called and asked, "Are we still on for today? It looks like it's going to rain."

"It won't rain here," she responded in her gravely whiskey-and-cigarillo voice. "It never rains here. It rains everywhere else in Florida but not here."

How would you have responded to her answer? I was on my cell phone, a few miles from her club, looking out my windshield at a sky so dark and threatening I thought a tornado would drop down on my van at any second. What if she was mistaken? What if it poured so hard that it shut down the gig? I was thousands of miles from home and under stormy skies. I had a band that was expecting work and expecting to be paid. I had two harmonica stars in the van who were looking to me for professional leadership on the gig. I had to trust that the Crankster was right, as she was my only contact in the area. I kept going forward since that's what a road tour is all about: moving from club date to club date and giving our fans a hot show every time we're on stage. I had to take her word for the weather; after all, she was the one that lived here, and it was her club.

I had Curtis Salgado and Rick Estrin with me on this traveling harmonica blowout. They are two of the top harmonica players and singing troubadours on the planet. Rick and Curtis are also experienced road warriors and very smart guys. They peered out of the van windshield at the ominous sky, shook their heads and then stared back at me like I was crazy.

"Sure looks like it's gonna rain, Marx," Rick said, shaking his head and still surveying the grey, foreboding sky with his "Are you kidding me; we're gonna play in this?" face.

Rick always calls me "Marx." I call him "Rix."

"It is gonna rain," added Curtis without even looking up at the sky. "It's gonna rain hard."

We got to the club and pulled to a stop under the threatening skies. There were all kinds of different Harley fat boys, Harley pan heads and Harley lookalike motorcycles in front of the club and jam-packing into the parking lot. Each motorcycle appeared to have more chrome parts than the chopper next to it. I've never seen more flames etched on cycle gas tanks or ape hanger handle-bars in my life. I felt like I was on the set for the Clint Eastwood's movie *Every Which Way but Loose.* There were so many bushy white beards, bushy white goatees, bushy white eyebrows, bushy white lamb chop sideburns and bushy white mustaches on the wrinkled tanned faces, so many bad tattoos on the arms, chests, hands and necks and so many shaved-bald dome-heads that it was like we had died and found ourselves in geriatric biker heaven. In reality, we were just at a typical biker bar in Florida.

There were still heavy rain clouds lurking right over our heads, and the humidity was at about ninety-nine-and-one-half percent. It wasn't raining, though, and for a minute I thought the Crankster might be right about her weather forecast. We carried our amps to the stage and began plugging in all the electric cords for the band equip-ment. The two sound guys that she hired for the show were typical rock 'n' roll gear heads. Their hair was way longer then their attention span, and they were both already high on beer and who knows what else. They had a PA that was large enough for a sold-out rock concert by Miley Cyrus at the Epcot Center. The huge square unit was at least four times the size of the PA that we needed for the gig. While the band was setting everything up, Crankster was telling me where to set our equipment and what time she expected us to start. She de-cided to put the huge PA right in the middle of the stage.

"By the way," she said with a rasp, "this is the bar manager. She is also the promoter of the show. She'll keep track of the time and the breaks we discussed. Her name is Sunshine."

The bar manager and I waved at each other. She was short, with small features, henna-colored hair and fingernails and lips painted black. There wasn't one thing about her that made me think of sunshine.

"Okay, no problem," I said, keeping my promise to myself to be cool. "We'll go ahead and fire it all up and we'll start right on time." I nodded to the two ladies, excused myself and walked back up to the stage.

We tried to complete our sound check but it was a no-go. The rock 'n' roll sound men ended up getting horrendous feedback. They couldn't seem to navigate the sound correctly or get any kind of good modulation out of the monitors or the mains. They kept blasting the biker audience and the band members with ear-shattering feedback. The old bikers screamed and shook fists at the two gear heads and then went back to drinking and endless prattle about their bikes. Rick, Curtis and I tried to assist the soundmen by turning down the volume on the feedback and helping with the coordination of the sound. We finally got the sound a little bit closer to a tone we could live with. However, that extra work to complete the sound setup took even more time, and it began to sprinkle.

"Don't worry; it won't rain," Crankster said. "Time to get started!"

Sunshine mimed the club owner's orders: "Time to get started. You heard the boss! Don't worry; it won't rain!"

"It already is raining!" Rick said. He gave me a sideways look and a not-so-happy bluesman grin as the raindrops from the darkening sky splattered against his flowered shirt. Curtis turned up his collar against the wind and covered his harp case with a hand towel.

We went ahead and began playing. I spotted the mom of one of my old girlfriends. She had driven down from a nearby town to see me play. I had hoped to visit with her on our first break, but she only stayed for two songs. As it began raining harder and harder, she covered her head with her purse and left. The electric wires were buzzing and snapping fiercely as the rain steadily increased. The huge PA was smoking and making an unnerving "whirrr" noise. Rick and Curtis and the rest of the band had backed up to be under the palm fronds. They were all crammed together around the drummer like sardines, trying to keep out of the rain. I was left up front with the rain pouring down on me. I was lucky that wearing a hat is part of my Hummel onstage fashion statement. The water poured off my hat like rain off a slanted roof. I tilted it backwards so the water drained down my back instead of on my face while I was singing.

We managed to finish the gig just before a raging downpour. We played the exact minutes according to the contract, plus a half hour more, and we gave them a damn-good harmonica blowout. Curtis had captured the audience with the fire of his vocals, and Rick had charmed bikers with his comic tunes and cryptic stories. As we finished saying goodnight, the sky opened up and the downpour became a deluge. We started to run to get the instruments and amps unplugged before they blew up or got completely ruined. At that moment Sunshine went up on stage, hid under the palm fronds and, while standing in a deepening puddle, started chanting, "Encore! Encore! Encore! More! More! More!"

The band had already packed most of our gear into the van. As the musicians huddled under the overhang, wiping water off their clothes with paper towels, Sunshine came up to me and snarled, "How come you're not playing more music? The boss wants you to play longer. Listen to the crowd. They want an encore. They love you guys."

No one, however, was asking for an encore except Sunshine.

"We've already played a half hour past our contract time, and it's pouring rain, if you hadn't noticed," I answered. "We're not willing to die up there! The gig's over! That's why."

"Well, the boss wants you to play another set," she responded.

"That should have been something that we discussed way ahead of time," I said. "We're already done. Have you noticed the damn hurricane out there?" As I shouted to her over the sound of the wind, the palm fronds above the stage were whipping back and forth in the torrent. "This gig is done, and that's it," I added with conviction.

"You'll never play here again" she said. "You're an asshole."

We didn't talk to Sunshine anymore after that. Crankster paid us but complained that we'd cut the show short. I politely disagreed as she put wet bills in my hand. Instead of sitting out the storm at the unfriendly club, we left and headed out into one of the worst rainstorms I've ever driven in. I couldn't see past my front windshield from the force of the drops being blown sideways against it.

About a month later, Crankster returned the promo package I'd mailed her before the gig. She mailed it at her own expense. It was unopened and contained posters that had been intended to help promote the show. I guess that was her way of saying, "I'll never work with you again."

CHAPTER THIRTY-SIX

Harp For Claw

I first heard about Flavio Guimaraes from his ex-wife in '96, when they were still married but apparently on the verge of separating. She linked up with us on a blowout tour with Paul deLay and Johnny Dyer. I'd been told by Charlie Musselwhite that she wanted to attend the shows, was a very friendly person and that her husband, Flavio, happened to be one of the most famous harp players in Brazil.

"She's pretty, too," Charlie added.

She showed up at Ashkanaz in Berkeley on the first night of the blowout and seemed mighty impressed with all the harp playing. She asked for a ride to North Berkeley, and I obliged, wanting to look out for Charlie's friend. She asked me to check the place out and showed me her room. I felt a little uncomfortable and said goodbye. She asked if she could tag along to the gig the next day in Chico. I said, "Sure, why not."

Flavio's wife, Paul, Johnny, Rusty Zinn, Vance Elhers, Jim Overton and I all left for Chico the next day in my van and had fun laughing at Paul's corny jokes and trading blues stories. When we arrived at the cheesy motel, everyone got their rooms.

Mrs. Flavio came up to me and said she didn't have enough money for a room. I was a little shocked. What's she expecting? I tried to be polite and said I'd see if I could get a room with two beds, but they only had one queen bedroom. What the hell, I thought, we'll sleep with our clothes on. At this point, I was freshly divorced and dating my future wife. The last thing I was going to do was sleep with another man's wife, especially a fellow harp player, and possibly cause a divorce in an already shaky marriage. So nothing happened that night in the queen bed. We said our goodbyes when we returned to Berkeley and said we would write and stay in touch.

What a surprise when four months later I got a package from Brazil. Along with some beads, there was a letter talking about how she'd left Flavio and had told him about how we made this strong connection and slept together. I was pissed! I wrote a letter back to her immediately, and told her I didn't appreciate her using me to make her husband jealous and thanks for nothing!

Ten years later I got an e-mail from Flavio asking if I'd come to Brazil. At first, I wondered if it was just to fly me down to drop me in a flavela, but after talking with Flavio, I realized he wasn't sore about anything including his ex-wife. Flavio flew me down in February of '05. I worked with his band on a ten-day tour.

It turned out to be an awesome tour, except for one incident. Claw was also on those gigs. I'd known Claw since '87, when we met in Denver. He's from San Jose but had moved to San Diego, then Texas and now Spain. He'd talked his way onto the tour after hosting Flavio in Spain. Flavio explained to me that Claw had been a great host in Spain, but that he couldn't understand why Claw was being such a pain on this tour. I didn't get it either. Flavio put us in his almost beachfront apartment in Rio, fed us, got us great gigs and took us sightseeing. I remember one gig in a town called San Jose where I felt like a star, as I got five encores from five hundred people. After the gig, a line of eighty to a hundred folks bought CDs and had me sign autographs. I felt like Paul McCartney, but on a much, much, much smaller scale.

Meanwhile, Claw had opened up to me like we were close friends. Finally, we talked about everything together—life, sobriety, music, gossip. I thought we were becoming buddies.

I did, however, notice a tinge of jealousy emanating from him around the gigs. Claw complained increasingly about Flavio's drinking, which wasn't that bad at the time. Everything became a problem for Claw as the tour progressed.

The last gig we did before Claw flew home was a trio performance in a small club for a very generous couple who fed us a home-cooked meal and took very good care of us. The wife was very attractive, and Claw kept making eyes at her and little asides under his breath. As we traded songs, I could feel Claw getting more competitive. After the last song, he beat it out of there, but we got an encore after he left. So the guitarist and I had to go it alone. I looked for my G harp, but it was nowhere to be found. I looked on the floor to no avail. Finally, I checked Claw's harp belt, and lo and behold, there was my Marine Band harp sticking out among all Claw's Golden Melodie harmonicas. Hmm, I thought, this looks bad. If he had asked to borrow one, no problem, but to STEAL MY HARP? I was so livid I had to leave the club. I did not want to see him. I went back to the hotel, slept fitfully, wondering why he would do something like that to me. At eight the next morning, there was a knocking on my door. I heard Claw asking if I was awake and telling me how he had a good time hangin' with me. I was too pissed off to go to the door. When I finally got out of bed a couple hours later, there was a small Alcoholics Anonymous *Big Book* under the door with an apologetic note in it. It seemed obvious Claw felt remorseful and knew he had made a mistake. I've forgiven him since then, realizing he had attempted to make amends for his transgressions, but I doubt we'll work together again. Flavio and I, however, remain good friends and still work together.

CHAPTER THIRTY-SEVEN

Frozen Canadian Goose

Here's a doozy that happened up in the snowy north. We did a tour to Edmonton, Canada, in December 1991, right before Christmas. As you may be able to guess, December in Alberta can be icy and very, very cold. The inclement weather just adds one more element of danger while traveling in the northern states and Canada in the winter months. As a touring musician and self-promoter, I've tended to overlook the elements and the seasons in my travel plans for many years, so it was not unusual that I would plan a tour to Canada in the middle of winter.

I secured several gigs up in Canada that winter. Although I didn't bother to think about the weather, I did negotiate our nightly accommodations with the club owners. On this particular night, the club owner put the Blues Survivors up in a band house that we had never been to before. I thought I'd memorized the address, which I also had written down. As we drove through downtown Edmonton in a blizzard of snowflakes, we found the right street but couldn't locate the right house. We were driving on very icy, slick streets in a sleet storm, and the van was sliding all over the road. I did my best to control the steering, but the conditions were very dangerous. I drove very slowly, but even at five miles an hour, I could barely control the van.

After finding what we thought was the right house, I parked the van and we walked up to the house. The door was unlocked. It was dark inside. I held the door wide open as the guys carried in their suitcases. While climbing the stairs with my suitcase, I saw toys sitting on the stairway and suddenly realized that we were in somebody's home. I'd memorized the address incorrectly, and we had walked into someone's house while they were sleeping. I could hear snoring in the bedroom at the end of the hall. I quickly turned to the guys as they were bringing their stuff in.

"Shhh," I whispered. "We're in the wrong house! There are people in here asleep!"

If this had happened in America, somebody probably would have come out with a shotgun and filled our butts with buckshot. Or worse! Luckily we were in Canada and nobody even woke up. I hurried the guys out of the house, and we got back in the van.

"You know," Marc Carino our bass player said, "in Canada many people leave their doors unlocked. The Canadians don't have the same paranoia or fear about strangers that Americans do."

"They should have locked their door," I said. "They got a group of musicians walking right into their house while they were sleeping."

I looked at my note and finally found the right house a couple doors down the block. After checking the place out carefully, we started bringing our stuff in. After I brought in all my suitcases, I went back outside to get my harmonica case that I wanted to keep with me in the house. I also wanted to check out our equipment status before I went to bed. I decided to rearrange some of the band equipment for the ride the next morning. I pulled some guitar cases out of the van to begin the process of making more sitting space for the guys. I had the van doors wide open and was standing on the street side of the van. It was so quiet you could have heard a pin drop on the flakes of snow around my feet.

I was moving an amp when I heard a skidding sound, like something big sliding on ice coming towards me. I saw two headlights spinning and then a car twisting around on the street. It was coming at me sideways at about thirty miles an hour!

I was petrified. We've all heard of "the deer in the headlights." Well, I'm here to tell you it's true!

I was standing next to the open doors of the van, but I couldn't make myself move. I watched the car coming at me as if I was hypnotized. I couldn't lift my legs. I just stood there and stared, waiting for the inevitable.

At the very last second, the front end of the car lurched past me and continued spinning out of control. I braced for the impact. The side of the car hit the tip of first van door that was open toward the road, then the second door. The two open doors kept the car from smashing flat into the back of the van. They created a little protective pocket for me. The car could have easily pinned me to the van, but instead its momentum caused it to career off the doors. The doors crumpled but didn't give.

I was amazed that the car hadn't slammed right into my lower body, crushed me against the van's frame. I could have been crippled me for life. It could have taken one or both of my legs off or, worse yet for a harmonica player, pulverized my hands.

It was over in two-seconds. I was still standing in the same spot, unharmed, but the van doors were badly bent. Snowflakes were falling gently. The only sound was the quiet rumbling of the engine of the errant vehicle that had stopped just past me in the middle of the street. It sounded as if the car was panting.

I ran over to the car and pulled open the car door, ready to scream at the driver. He was seemed dazed as he sat there.

"You could have killed me!" I shouted.

"Sorry" was all the guy said. He kept both hands on the steering wheel. I slammed his car door shut.

I had my guys call the police from the band house. Two Canadian Mounties showed up and gave the driver a sobriety test. He was staggering around like a drunken clown and couldn't find his nose with his finger. He couldn't walk in a straight line and couldn't say the alphabet backwards. After the Mounties administered the tests and the guy failed them all, they let their Canadian brother go. I couldn't believe it! The weather conditions obviously had been a factor in the accident, but the guy was clearly going too fast and was out of control due to his drinking.

It was one of the hairiest moments I've ever experienced on the big road. I sometimes think of how different my life could have been if those two van doors hadn't protected me on the icy street that night. It was a miracle!

Between going into the wrong house and almost getting killed by a drunk driver, I vowed to never to go to Edmonton or anywhere in Canada again in the wintertime.

I broke that vow in February of this year. We flew into Edmonton for four days of gigs there and in Red Deer and Calgary. When we arrived at the airport, we discovered that Canadian customs had cleared us for our shows at cultural centers in Red Deer and Calgary but not for Rusty Reed's House of Blues in Edmonton, which is a bar. My old friend Rusty hadn't filed the proper immigration papers. His business partner Al runs the club. Rusty works on an oil rig in Fort McMurray, north of Edmonton, and can only be reached by phone. The officer told us we could do the first two dates but not the one in Edmonton unless the paper work was filed in the next two days. I called my agent Greg and asked him to deal with Rusty and Al.

In the meantime, we rented a car, drove to Red Deer and played at a Moose Hall. It was twenty below zero outside but warm inside. We next played a fun gig at the Calgary Midwinter Bluesfest. As we drove through a four-hour blizzard on our way back to Edmonton, we passed dozens of upside-down cars littering the side of the highway.

Al's daughter Bella filled out the immigration papers in time for the gig at Rusty's, and we had to run to the airport to complete the documentation. Greg had been on the phone with the customs officer the previous day and buttered her up to do paperwork she really didn't have to do. We returned the rental car to a lot near the club in the north of town, and Rusty's friend Ron came and took us to the club. A jam session was going on when we got there, and no one seemed to know where we were supposed to stay for the two-night gig. I normally don't go for band houses these days, but

235

Rusty had assured me these were quality condos. Nobody could find keys to open them, however, so I phoned Rusty and asked him to put us up in a hotel down the road. Trying to save him some dough, I told him we'd split two room between the four of us. The food at the club was good, and the servers were friendly. The early evening jam session was hilariously bad. We rocked a full house afterward.

It was twenty degrees below again the next day, too cold to do anything at all outside. R.W. Grigsby and I stayed in and read books. Marty Dodson and Rusty Zinn watched movies all day in their room. Unlike the previous night, only one paying customer turned out to see us at Rusty's on the second night. We played anyway and quit early. Cam and Carol Hayden, our friends from the Edmonton blues fest, showed up with two of their friends right after we finished. I thought I'd be able to watch the Academy Awards, but the ABC network wasn't on cable in Alberta, at least not at my hotel.

Bella was supposed to take us to the airport the next morning, but she didn't show. I phoned the club, and the cook told me she'd left a message for us to take a taxi. The fare turned out to be a hundred dollars.

"Did she leave us money at the bar?" I asked.

She hadn't, so I called a cab and we got to the airport on time. We checked in for our Alaska Air flight. We boarded a flight to Seattle at one p.m. At one thirty, the pilot announced that the door latch was broken and that passengers would have to deplane and wait for the next flight out. I had checked a bag and had to go through customs to get it back, then walk back to the upstairs ticket counter to check in again. The other band members had checked their luggage at the gate. I figured they'd get on a flight sooner than me, but when I returned from rebooking myself, I saw the band was slated to take the same flight to Seattle as me. We read, ate expensive bad food and twiddled our thumbs. When they announced pre-boards for the six o'clock flight, we got ready, but ten minutes in, the counter agent announced that someone had pulled a lever in the aircraft and maintenance had to be called to solve the problem. After an hour, it was announced that the flight had been cancelled and that passengers would have to stay the night.

"Don't worry," we were told. "We'll give you hotel vouchers, and you can reschedule for the first flights out."

I immediately worked on getting a direct flight to San Francisco instead of one to Seattle that connected with one to Oakland. The Alaska agent booked us on United instead of Alaska. I was relieved to have a direct flight. I'd just have to pick up my vehicle in Oakland.

After standing in line an hour and a half, we were informed that there would be no hotel vouchers after all because it had been determined that the problem with the plane was weather-related rather than mechanical. We instead were offered airline credits. I told them that I had no interest in again flying Alaska Air after what had happened.

I booked a Super 8 Hotel for the four of us at five hundred and eighteen dollars. When we tried to catch a shuttle to the hotel, we were bumped by the flight crew and told the driver would return in ten minutes. We had comfortable rooms, and I slept well—until the phone rang at three thirty, an hour before my scheduled four thirty wakeup call. It was Pike, my travel agent, calling to inform me that she discovered we'd been booked on an April 1 fight out of Edmonton instead of one that March 1 morning. She'd been up all night getting us on the eight o'clock Alaska flight to Seattle that connected with one to Oakland.

We arrived at the airport to find many of the same agents we'd dealt with the night before. They couldn't have gotten the four hours sleep we got. The flight we were supposed to be on was being created as we stood in line at the ticket counter. When we went through security, they couldn't find our flight on the computer and made us wait until they found it. When we finally got to the gate, the crew was just arriving at the time the plane was supposed to be taking off. I wondered if we ever would get to leave Edmonton. We also had a ten a.m. Oakland flight to catch in Seattle. Would we make it on time? After we boarded, the crew apologized and said that in fifteen years of flying, it was the worst fiasco they'd heard of on Alaska Air. The seat belt sign remained on until the final twenty minutes of the turbulent hour-and-a-half flight. My bladder almost burst!

We got to Seattle with fifteen minutes to spare before our flight to Oakland was scheduled to depart. We were told that the plane was being held at the next gate, but when we got there, the agent said the gate had been closed and we couldn't board. It was back to the drawing board. I steamed over to the Alaska Air customer-care counter loaded for bear. The woman took one look at me and, before I could even say a word, said, "Sir, please calm down." I asked to see her supervisor, and he did a great job of getting us on a United flight to San Francisco that left at noon. We made it back by three thirty. I hired my friend Eric to drive us in his limo to Oakland. I picked up my car and made it home by four thirty in the afternoon. The temperature was seventy degrees. My goose was thoroughly cooked, but what a relief it was to be home!

CHAPTER THIRTY-EIGHT

Hefty Handed—One/Two Punch

I first heard about Hefty's Pizzeria from the late Paul deLay. Paul was a large man who loved life, music and pizza. He called me out of the blue when I was on the road in the Northwest in the early part of the millennium to tell me that there was a brand-new club in Springfield, Oregon, where I might get some work.

"You just play your blues Bubba," Paul told me. "The people are great. It's a happening new place. You need to check it out."

"By the way," deLay added, "the pizza there is great. Thick and meaty!"

I didn't really think any more about it. I was sure I would eventually contact the club, but you know how that goes. I was preoccupied with the day-to-day obligations to the clubs on my tour at the time. I thought maybe I'd get around to contacting new opportunities in a couple of months, when, lo and behold, I got an email from a woman named Jacklyn Hoff informing me that she and her husband John owned a place called Hefty's Pizzeria. She went on to explain that Gary Primich and Paul deLay (two of the greatest harmonica players of my generation, both now sadly deceased) and me, Mark Hummel, were all highly regarded by her husband. She said she'd love to get me and the Blues Survivors up to Springfield to play her club.

It's fairly rare when a blues musician gets an e-mail from a club owner, especially a brand-new club owner who has some money to spend, is looking forward to having the musician in the club and is going to treat him well. We struck a deal, and I went up to rock the pizzeria. We did a harmonica blowout with James Harman, Paul deLay and John Nemeth. The following night, it was just me and the Blues Survivors.

John Nemeth is a harmonica player and singer from Idaho who hit the scene a few years back and now lives in Oakland. He's a crowd-pleaser whose career is really taking off.

James Harman is a longtime friend who started singing the blues during the '60s. He began playing when he was only fifteen, just as another great harp player, Rick Estrin, had. Working with a fake mustache in black clubs in Panama City, Florida, James was promoted as "that boy who sings like a man." He has a Southern flair to his blues and really can rock a blues show plus be wickedly entertaining!

Paul deLay was a giant of the Northwest, bigger than Paul Bunyan and twice as wide! He was one of my absolute favorite harp players, singers and songwriters of all time. He was known and loved in the Northwest and was my contact with Jacklyn and John's pizza joint. We gave them a great show, they treated us like rock stars and we left town. I had a good feeling about Hefty's.

I was a bit surprised when about a year later I got a call from Gary Primich warning me about Hefty's. He told me that he'd travelled to the Northwest play at Hefty's and that Jacklyn and John had completely taken him for a ride. I kept hearing more of this kind of bad intel from different people, that the club wasn't doing so well, that it was losing money. If that wasn't bad enough, the word on the street was that Hefty's was booking name acts for big, big money but did not know how to properly promote their shows. When I got Gary's call, I felt sorry that he was so distressed about his experience in Oregon. Gary was completely undone by the fact that Hefty's had treated him so shabbily after they had called him and asked him to travel there. They'd told Gary how great they thought he was and that they really wanted him. As they say, "If it sounds too good to be true, it probably is!" That's certainly how it worked out for Gary at Hefty's. Gary played a couple of his scheduled shows, and then they tried to cancel his already booked third night.

Instead of letting them cancel a night in the middle of his tour, Primich ended up letting them cut his money in half so he could keep the date. After the show, when Gary went to get paid for the gig, they only paid him a portion of what they had already cut in half. Gary went over the top and got into a huge screaming match with Jacklyn. I suspected, from having dealt with her when I was in her town, that she might have trouble dealing with the pressures of club ownership. It wasn't anything you could put your finger on, but you could tell she didn't have the kind of experience she needed for the demands of the business she was trying to run. It was clear, from talking to Gary, that she was unraveling quickly. I got the feeling that John, her husband, was under her thumb. He was playing the good guy most of the time, while she'd be the hard ass, but it didn't sound like the good-cop bad-cop system was working.

In spite of what I had been hearing on the street, Hefty's had been good to me, so I went ahead and booked another date with them. We were going up to the Northwest on a long tour anyway, so I afforded Hefty's the benefit of the doubt. I was wary of them, though, especially after what Gary had related to me. I booked a blowout show at Hefty's featuring Johnny Dyer and Lee Oskar. Lee is a renaissance man, from his work with the band War in the '70s to building Lee Oskar Harmonicas into a worldwide corporation. I'm not even going to start talking about his paintings and his band the Lowriders (the real War, since four of them are original members). Let's just leave it that Lee is a force of the universe. Johnny goes back to the early days of Chicago blues in Los Angeles when he hung around with legends like Shakey Jake, George "Harmonica" Smith, William Clarke and Rod Piazza and was an integral part of the L.A. blues scene for forty years. Lee flew in for the gig; Johnny was already traveling with us. For this Hefty's date, I had a very difficult time contacting Jacklyn. She would never answer my phone calls or my e-mails. I did, however, get a contract and a deposit, after much haranguing, so the gig was on.

Everything was clear on what we were to be paid and how

many motel rooms we would have, but I could never get her to answer any calls regarding promotion or the name of the motel or what time we needed to be there for sound check. The devil is in the details, and I was getting increasingly frustrated, so we stopped by the club on our way up to another gig in Seattle. It seemed like a good idea at the time. Charles Wheal, my guitar player, said, "Why don't we stop in for a slab of pizza." Big mistake.

We went to their club, and I saw a poster hanging on the wall. It let me know right away what I was in for. Our names— Mark Hummel, Lee Oskar, Johnny Dyer—were in very small print next to a drawing of a cross-eyed squirrel playing a harmonica. There were no photographs. I was in utter shock and disbelief. What are they trying to do, I thought, promote the show or kill the show? I knew, from many years of experience, that photos of the players, some bio and a few quotes from raving critics are the best way to build a crowd. The promotion needs to inform the public and create a desire to attend the event. The goofy cross-eyed squirrel poster was a show-killer. I told John Hoff how I felt, but he disagreed and said he thought it was the greatest. Jacklyn must have designed the poster herself, probably to get back at me!

We got our slices of pizza and got back on the road to our gig in Seattle. I thought everything was on schedule, but when we came back to play Hefty's a week or so later, I could not get in touch with Jacklyn. I wanted to find out the time of the sound check and information about band accommodations. I had asked John the week before, but he didn't seem to know.

The first thing I wanted to do when we got to the pizzeria and loaded in our equipment was to get Jacklyn on the phone. The bartender called Jacklyn—she wouldn't even speak to me on the phone—and we were told we'd be staying in a motel down the street. It was a different motel from the one we'd stayed at on our previous visit and was nowhere near as comfortable. We also found out the club had only registered the band for three rooms instead of the six we required.

I had to double up the musicians, whereas the first time we had separate rooms for each player. Lowered standards for hotel accommodations are nothing unusual, though, and are a fairly common pattern with some nightclubs. The longer the clubs stay in business and the more road acts they have coming in, the cheaper and cheaper the rooms they provide become. Once club owners find out that running a club is not the cinch they thought it was going to be, they start cutting corners. It's understandable from the economic point of view.

I called Jacklyn, but, of course, all I got was a voicemail. I got the band checked in and waited in the foyer for the phone to ring. Finally, forty-five minutes later, Jacklyn called back. She was irate and in a very bad mood. I asked her about the number of rooms, and she informed me that I had a room down the road at the motel where we had stayed before.

I wasn't real pleased about having to be at two different motels, but I said OK and went down the road and got my room. A short while later, I rounded up the guys at the other motel, and we went to Hefty's to eat. When we tried to order, the waiter said, "John's not buying your meals today." The band's meals had been negotiated in our contract. It was a pizza place, after all, and it couldn't have cost the club a fortune to make a pizza or two for us.

"Can you call John?" I asked.

"No," the waiter said. "He won't talk to you."

We ordered pizza anyway, figuring we'd get the money back from John or Jacklyn at the end of the night. Our pies arrived after a short wait but didn't seem as good as they were the first time— not as thick and not as meaty. We finished our meal and set up our equipment as patrons started to walk in. I went back stage to change, and as I was coming out, I saw John.

"John, what's the story on dinner? I asked. "Don't we get pizza?"

"Don't talk to me, you asshole," he blurted out. "You've been treating my wife like shit. I don't have anything to say to you."

He said this in front of a table full of customers, about seven people that had shown up to watch our performance. These were patrons who knew John and knew I was the bandleader and had come to see me play. I turned on my heels and went back toward the dressing room, steam coming out of my ears. I saw Lee Oskar back there, and he noticed I was hot.

"What happened, buddy?" Lee asked me.

"I just saw John Hoff, and he cussed me out in front of a table full of customers," I explained. "You guys can play the show. I'm not playing tonight. You guys can go on without me. Go ahead and do the show. I'll just go back to the motel. You guys can get paid, hopefully."

"You can't do that," Lee said. "You can't let him beat you. Go ahead and play your heart out. I'll take care of the rest."

Lee was right. I went ahead and played my ass off. I did the best I could do and got over well with the crowd.

Meanwhile, Lee was in the back talking to John.

"Nice place you've got here, John," Lee told him.

"Well, thank you," John said. "I wish all the performers were as cool as you are, Lee."

"What are you talking about?" Lee asked.

"That guy up on stage," John responded, "he's a real asshole. He sure pissed my wife off."

"Pissed your wife off? What do you mean?" Lee asked.

"Well, yeah," John responded. "He was supposed to promote this gig, and he didn't do a damn thing."

"Didn't do a thing, huh?" Lee said. "Well, tell me, where does he live?"

"I don't know. San Francisco, I think," John responded.

"Where are we right now?" Lee asked.

"Springfield, Oregon," John answered.

Lee responded, and not so nicely, "What do you expect him to do? Come up here and poster your town? He lives in San Francisco. How's he supposed to promote it? Look, you're the promoter. He's the musician. It's your job to promote the gig at your own club. How long have you been in the business?"

"About two and a half years," John answered.

"How long do you think I've been in the business?" Lee continued.

"I don't know. How long?" John asked.

"I've been in it for forty," Lee said. "Who do you think knows more about the business, me or you?"

"I guess you, Mr. Oskar," John replied sheepishly.

"Well, then I guess your job is to promote the gig and his job is to play the gig, right?" Lee told John, who turned around, shook his head and walked away.

I never said another word to John Hoff. I played the gig, we did the blowout and we left town. Hefty's went out of business about six months later. God bless them, and may they rest in peace, or in pieces, whichever.

CHAPTER THIRTY-NINE

Oregon Coast Psycho

I was getting ready to play a gig with the Blues Survivors in Newport, Oregon, a coastal town alongside Highway 101. Newport is quiet and pristine and has a small group of folks living there who love the blues. It's a peaceful, friendly town, one of the last places in the world where I would expect to be attacked by a psycho!

Our engagement was at the Uptown Pub, a little bar where we'd played a number of times over the years. We'd been driving for hours, and I knew we were close after we crossed over the Yaquina Bay Bridge that spans the entrance of Newport Harbor. I pulled off 101 at around four in the afternoon, found the club, parked and cut the engine. After the band members jumped out of the van to stretch their legs, we began unloading and setting up our equipment. I asked them to please be careful with my original 1959 Tweed Fender Bassman, the holy grail of tube amps.

"Whatever you do, don't drop my Fender Bassman or set it down hard," I pleaded. "Treat it like you would a newborn baby, only better!"

There were only ten people in the bar. These were the early birds looking for the worm. I noticed, after we'd set up our equipment, this non de script guy with long straggly brown hair and no shoes on his feet, asking the band members many questions about their instruments. They were polite to the man, but they each excused themselves and returned to their normal preshow activities, such as making phone calls to spouses, having a smoke, getting a bite to eat or locating some bottled water to drink during the gig. Meanwhile, the shaggy-haired guy meandered up on the stage and started tapping away on Marty's drums.

Marty rushed over and politely but firmly asked him to stop playing with the drums. The guy ignored him and kept tapping away and mumbling to himself, like a drunk. Marty looked over at me with a perplexed expression and held out his palms, as if to say, "What do you want me to do here?" At the same time, our un-invited guest was getting more into his playing, tossing his head as he played, as if imitating Gene Krupa. Marty ordered him to stop again, but the guy began bashing away on the snare drum and cymbals. Marty turned and walked off the stage.

"Get security, or do something," Marty said to me, "before this psycho wrecks my drums!"

I figured I could handle it, so I climbed the stairs to the stage, crossed the bandstand and stood in front of the uninvited guest.

"Hey, the drummer doesn't want you playing," I said forcefully. "Leave his drums alone. He set them up for the gig tonight, and he has them just the way he wants them. He doesn't want you playing them. They are not toys!"

The guy stopped playing and asked, "Who are you?"

"I'm the boss," I informed him. "Stop goofing around and get out from behind those drums!"

"Make me!" he said with a sneer.

I grabbed a mike stand that was close to me and ordered him off the stage.

"Get the hell off the stage! Now!" I shouted, waving the mike stand like a golf club. "I mean it!"

"What are you going to do with that mike stand?" the psycho asked. He put down the drumsticks and leaned forward.

I stared at his face and could tell from his crazed eyes that he was diseased mentally. I'm no doctor, but I would say this guy was a paranoid schizophrenic with several voices speaking to him at the same time. He was most likely off his medication.

"I might just hit you with it if you don't get off the stage," I said, but I was lying.

Sensing his off-balanced nature, I then urged him politely, "Now get up on out from behind those drums and get off the stage, and we can all return to being friends."

The guy moved so fast I didn't have time to respond or even raise my hands to protect myself. He leapt over the drum set like a wounded tiger, shouting obscenities and dove at me with the fingers of both hands outstretched at my face. I dropped the stand and raised my arms to protect myself. The psycho landed right on top of me. I lost my balance and tumbled backward. The force of his body weight knocked me head over heels and right over the top of my Fender Bassman amp. I tumbled off of the edge of the stage and fell a full five feet from the bandstand to the concrete floor below, landing on my side.

The psycho drummer boy landed beside me, with my eight-thousand-dollar, one-of-a-kind original 1959 Tweed Fender Bassman amp toppling off the stage behind him. I'd fallen from the stage first and was looking up as I fell. I could see the guy and my amp in midair above me, both falling toward the concrete floor. It seemed to be happening in slow motion, so I put my hand on the side of his shoulder and pushed him slightly to the left. That small movement, made to keep him from landing directly on top of me, also placed his body under the falling amp. I could see the psycho's left shoulder blade directly beneath the amp a split second before impact. The folks in the front rows jumped out of their seats to get out of the way.

I heard something crunch in his shoulder blade when the corner of the amp hit. It sounded like a stalk of celery being broken in half. The psycho grunted like a stuck pig. I rolled over and grabbed the amp as it continued its slow plummet off his back. I was able to get my arms around the tweed sides and break the fall before it hit the floor. I heard glass breaking as it landed, my heart breaking as I heard it!

I was ready to kill the guy. Wreck my car, my life and my marriage, take my dog, but do not mess with my 1959 original Tweed Fender Bassman tube amp!

The psycho was sane enough to realize he had gone too far and ran out of the club, his left arm dangling limply at his side. I chased after him to the entrance door, my adrenalin pumping, but he was long gone. The staff at the club told me they didn't know the guy, and none of the patrons seemed to know him either. I sensed that they did, but it seemed as if nobody really wanted to 'fess up to knowing him.

At least the jackass had been good for something. He may have been a lousy drummer, but he proved to be a damn good human cushion.

I examined the amp, and, fortunately, there was only one broken tube. That says a lot for Fender's workmanship in the old days. They just don't make 'em like that anymore!

I can't say the same for the psycho and me. I'd heard that snap from his shoulder when the amp hit him, and I'd seen his arm dangling as he ran out the door. He'd paid a price for his stupidity, and I'd paid one for mine. My backside hurt for a week, but the lesson I learned has lasted to this day.

Hummel and his Fender Bassman aren't made to fly! From now on, I will let security handle psychos, and I'll stick to the harmonica!

CHAPTER FORTY

Sitting In and Falling Down

Reverend Timothy was a solo acoustic guitarist who opened for us in Eugene and Newport, Oregon. He was a real respectable guy, and the band liked him. We first got together with him for dinner at the Rogue Brewery in Newport. He was obviously gassed to be opening for Mark Hummel and the Blues Survivors. He really enjoyed playing for our crowd that night and did a good job with his spot.

One night, though, he came up and asked me a common question we often get on the road.

"Can I sit in, man?" Reverend Timothy asked.

"Sure, of course. Not a problem," I responded. "Did you bring an electric guitar?

He hadn't.

"Well, that's OK,' I said. "I'm sure Charles will let you use his."

Reverend Timothy suddenly got very nervous about sitting in and continued to drink too much Rogue beer to calm down. I guess he'd expected me to turn him down. I called him up to the stage, and he strapped on Charles Wheal's 330 guitar. Charles walked off the stage to let the Reverend sit in for a song or two. I counted off a shuffle, and he started playing just fine, strumming some good chords. I felt comfortable with what he was doing and gave him the lead.

"OK, take it, Reverend," I shouted above the band.

When I encouraged him, I heard this flurry of strange and random notes coming from the guitar he was playing. I glanced over, and out of my peripheral vision, I saw him starting to spin on stage. As I turned to face him, he did a kind of whirling dervish off the back of the stage. The good Reverend toppled over, upside down and backwards off the platform. All I could see of him were shoes and legs sticking up in the air and kicking. The drummer, looking at Reverend Timothy's bottom side with shock, didn't know what to do except to keep on playing. We also were being blasted with colossal feedback from Charles' guitar that the Reverend had been playing when he toppled off the stage.

I ran back to help him up. His body was tangled in the cords of the guitar, and his fingers were caught in the strings. It was a complete fiasco. Steve Wolf, the bass player, was still keeping time with the drummer. Steve had a look of pure amusement on his face and a quizzical smile. "What next?" his smile seemed to say. "Will the good Reverend fly back up on the stage and keep playing? Will the show go on?"

I used to have a cat that had seizures. When the cat had a bad one, he would just spin around the house at what seemed like million miles an hour. When he stopped, he appeared almost embarrassed and would disappear for a while. One time, after a bad episode, the cat disappeared completely. Jon Penner, Sue Foley's bass player, was visiting, and we looked for the poor cat but couldn't find him. We eventually located him under the stove in a space that seemed too tight for him to have fit into.

The same as my cat, Reverend Timothy appeared embarrassed after spinning off the stage and disappeared from the club immediately. I couldn't find him to see if he was all right or if he had injured anything other than his pride. He was just gone.

Charles Wheal stumbled across the Reverend later, outside the club, in the dark. He was huddled in a doorway down the street, shaking and very embarrassed.

"Are you all right, Reverend?" Charles asked.

"I'm really sorry," he replied. "I hope I didn't break anything."

The Reverend kept repeating that over and over, apologizing and apologizing again.

"I hope I didn't wreck your guitar," he added.

"No, the guitar is fine," Charles told him.

So much for Reverend Timothy's one time sitting in with the Blues Survivors. And just like that cat of mine, he never came out of his crawl space.

CHAPTER FORTY-ONE

Hotel Hell Stories

One of the worst places we ever stayed at was the King Eddie Hotel in Calgary, Alberta. It was a transient hotel that had a night club and a strip club on the ground floor. The strippers were funky, although I did meet one very nice-looking young woman there. The dinner menu consisted of little more than hot dogs and Asian noodles. Several winos lived in the second—and third-floor rooms. The building has since been torn down.

Charles Wheal was the only Blues Survivor who had the stomach to stay there when we last played the place. I'd stayed there many times in the late '80s and early '90s. We made the club owner put the rest of us up at another hotel, although we had to split rooms. Charles would make his room at the King Eddie habitable by taking blankets off beds in vacant rooms and putting them on his floor so he didn't have to step on blood, glass from broken bottles, used syringes and whatever else. There were no curtains or blinds on the windows, so Charles would stick a blanket over them to be able to sleep in relative dark in the morning. I think maybe Charles willingness to stay there had something to do with the Canadian strippers downstairs.

Another sleazy place was the Twin Cities Motel in St. Paul, Minnesota, where the Blues Saloon had booked us. As we drove into the motel parking lot, we saw a group of men who looked like ex-cons barbecuing meat for their dinners on portable hibachis that lined the walkway in front of the rooms. Obviously, they were permanent guests.

The rooms themselves literally had "turds in the punch bowls."

Not a single toilet had been flushed. There were holes in the ceilings and syringes in the hallway. We ended up staying at a Days Inn across the street.

HoJo's in Richmond, Virginia, was another hellhole. The first time we stayed at the place, there were holes in the ceilings and cigarette burns on the bedspreads and carpets. On a return visit to Richmond, we noticed bulletproof glass in the lobby—a sure sign of potential trouble.

I phoned the club owner and told him it looked dangerous. He got us a better motel down the road. After the gig, we had to drive past HoJo's. Trash cans in the parking lot were ablaze, with a group of hollow-eyed, scabby-faced crack heads standing around keeping warm and smoking glass pipes. We were all very glad we hadn't stayed there on our second visit to Richmond.

Just the name of the Crystal Inn in Ashbsury Park, New Jersey, should have been enough to keep us away. It was definitely the

"Crystal Meth Inn," and most of its clientele were crack and crank heads. It was a grim place to have to spend the night.

Once, we almost stayed at the Ambassador Motel in Fresno, California. We were doing a sold-out Blues Harmonica Blowout show at a theater in town with Huey Lewis, James Cotton, Paul de-Lay and James Harman. As we were pulling into the Ambassador parking lot, we saw Cotton smoking a cigarette and waving to us from the balcony. Having been accustomed to staying at even worse places early in his career, he didn't seem to mind this one.

"Ah, you must be Mr. Huey Lewis," the Pakistani innkeeper said as I walked into the lobby.

"No. I'm not Huey Lewis, but he'll be here soon," I said.

"Ah, you make sure we have big picture, please, of Mr. Huey Lewis," he told me.

"Can we look at the rooms first?" I asked.

"Ah, certainly," he replied and handed me a key to what was probably the nicest room in the place.

James Harman went in, checked it out and told us we had to come in and see for ourselves. It was the honeymoon suite, with a mammoth mirror on the ceiling over the bed. It also had what looked like a kiddy whirlpool, about one-foot deep and three-feet wide, with built-in jets. It smelled like there was a dead raccoon under the bed.

I phoned the theater owner and said, "This place is not going to fly with Huey Lewis. I think he's used to something way classier than this."

"In that case," the owner responded, "we'll put you guys in the Hilton down the road."

"Wow," I told him. "That sounds like a major improvement on this."

As we headed back to the van, I told Cotton we were checking out. Before we could pull out of the parking lot, a skinny, spaced-out crack head approached Junior Watson, who also was on the show, and asked, "Is Huey Lewis in that van?"

Watson thought he'd pull a prank on her and said, pointing to the noticeably rotund deLay in the back of the van, "Yeah. Huey Lewis is in there. Take a look. He's Baby Huey Lewis now. You can call him Baby Huey if you want. He's gained a little weight, but yeah, it's him."

She took a look and saw Paul. She probably thought she'd been slipped some LSD.

Major drug dealing was going on at a Motel 6 in Lansing, Michigan, when we were there to play at an old railroad station and for the local blues society. A guy who looked kind of like Snoop Dogg kept knocking on Mark Bohn and Charles Wheal's door, trying to sell them crack. They told him he had the wrong room, but he kept returning. At another Motel 6, in Pomona, California, people were working on cars, smoking crack and shooting meth in the parking lot. It was one of those places where you worry about leaving your suitcases in your room while you're away playing the gig.

Another regular stop along the big blues road used to be the Smiley Face Inn, a budget motel somewhere in the middle of Kansas. The rate was twenty-five dollars a night, and, being the cheapskate that I am, it made for an inexpensive rest stop after an all-night drive from California. A big face grinned down on drivers from a billboard a few miles before the actual place came into view. The rooms were done up '70s porn style, with mirrors on the ceilings and on every wall. At least the place was relatively clean, and no dope fiends roamed the walkways.

CHAPTER FORTY-TWO

Queen for a Day

Here's one that's right out of a Larry David episode. In 2009 we drove all day from Tallahassee to Boca Raton with a blow-out tour consisting of famed J. Geils Band harp man Magic Dick, Watermelon Slim and R.J. Mischo. Dick's mom had just had a mild heart attack, and Dick wanted to visit her in Ft. Lauderdale before our gig, so we planned to drop off luggage at the local Motel 6 the club owner has reserved. We made good time that day and arrived just ahead of schedule.

When I walked into the office, I noticed several scruffy characters and a very effeminate and impatient desk clerk trying to manage several equally impatient customers. It took ten or fifteen minutes before he finally waited on me. I gave him the reservation name and told him we needed all seven rooms quickly. He responded that it would take some time, since the reservations had been made separately instead of under one name. As this was going on, three different residents entered. One requested a new room due to a puke aroma, another a new room due to a loud toilet and the third a set of towels, as there were none. The queen clerk then asked if I would wait for him to wait on the other customers behind me. I explained that we were in a hurry, since we had to unhook the trailer at the club so Dick could go and visit his mom in the hospital before the gig, while we set up and ate dinner. The clerk again said it would be a while, to which I asked, "How long will 'awhile' be?" He then asked if it would be cash or credit. I said credit and entered my number. Then I asked if I could pay cash, since I got cold feet about my credit card. He said it was too late, that it had already gone through and he couldn't change it.

The lobby began filling up with even more disgruntled residents. When I asked him again for a time, he exploded.

"I'm canceling your reservation," he barked at me. "You don't have to be a dick about it!"

"I'm not leaving till I get my rooms," I insisted, to which he haughtily announced he was calling the cops.

All this happened just as Watermelon Slim was walking into the lobby. At this point, after having been in the lobby for twenty-five minutes, I promptly left. Fortunately, Slim saved the day and charmed the panties off the desk clerk. Twenty minutes later, we were finally able to get in our horrid little hotel rooms with broken latches, broken deadbolts, smelly shower water, cigarette burns on sheets and sink counters and toilets that didn't flush. I wrote an Internet complaint to Motel 6 spokesperson Tom Bodett, but nothing was resolved by it, much to my chagrin. As the desk clerk had earlier said to the customer in front of me, "We are a budget motel. Otherwise you can go to the Hilton up the road, sir!"

CHAPTER FORTY-THREE
The Fanny Pack Story

A few years ago we were doing a harmonica blowout with Kenny Neal and a harp player named Rich. We were playing a festival in upstate New York, and a fan brought his Harp King amplifier for Rich and I to use because we'd flown in for the gig and didn't bring out own amps. Rich and I played through the Harp King, and Kenny played through the house mike. The show went well, and at the end of the gig when the stage was being cleared, I set my harp case by the monitor sound booth.

"Keep an eye on this, would you?" I asked the sound guys.

Rich, I would come to find out, also left his harp case on the stage. Soon after the crew had cleared the stage, Rich came up to me with a perplexed look on his face.

"Have you seen my harmonicas?" he asked.

"I haven't seen them," I said. "Did you look up by the amp?"

"The amp's already gone," he said in an agitated tone. "Where the hell are they?"

"I don't know, Rich," I said. "I told you I haven't seen them."

"I've got to find my harps!" he shouted, "You've got to help me. Now!"

I walked around the stage looking for the harps to appease Rich, but I didn't see them.

"Have you seen Rich's harmonicas?" I asked the sound guys.

"No," they answered.

My case was still where I'd left it. I walked over to the crew who were loading a semi-trailer with equipment from the stage.

"Have you guys seen a briefcase filled with harmonicas?" I asked.

"Naw," the crew chief said, scratching his belly while a couple other crewmen looked on. "I haven't seen anything like that on the stage." The other guys shook their heads, too.

"Well, you've got to help me find them," I begged. "One of the guys that's been clearing the stage may have accidentally put them away or maybe put them in this big semi-trailer you guys are loading all the stuff into over there."

They followed my thumb with their eyes as I pointed to the large trailer that the rest of the cleanup crew was loading the equipment.

"This guy's harmonicas are gone," I said, pointing to Rich. "I think your guys picked them up."

As Rich was freaking out, one of crew came up to me and Rich holding a fanny pack.

"Is this them?" he asked.

Rich looked at it, and then shocked everybody by drop kicking it with his foot. It went flying about twenty feet out into field where the festival was being held.

"No, you dumb fuck," Rich shouted at the crewman. "That ain't it!"

"Settle down, man," the crewman said. "We don't know where your harps are."

"I'm going to kill somebody if they don't find my fucking harmonicas!" Rich hollered, clutching his fists to his side.

I'd never seen my friend so upset before. I tried to calm him down the best I could and told him not to worry, that we would find his harmonicas. I went back to the semi-trailer and told the crew that they had to unpack all the gear they'd put in their anvil cases until they found Rich's harmonicas.

"They're not here, man," I was told. "You and your friend don't think we know what we're doing, but we do. We don't load stuff that's not ours."

"You guys are just going to have to look," I demanded. "The harmonicas are missing, and this man makes his living playing them."

The guys didn't move. They didn't even look at me. They instead stared into the back of the trailer they'd just loaded. I didn't budge from where I was standing. The air was thick with tension.

"OK," the lead guy sighed. "Start unloading the shit."

"Thanks," I said, but not one of the crew acknowledged me. They hated my guts.

They began heaving the anvil cases to the ground in a very pissed-off manner. I went back to the stage and tried to keep Rich from blowing his top and killing somebody. He looked as if he might murder somebody soon.

As I looked around the stage some more, I spotted the fan who'd provided the amplifier. He was standing next to his Harp King.

"Rich's harmonicas are missing," I said.

"They're not missing," he said. "I took them off the stage along with my amplifier."

"You did, and you didn't tell anybody?" I exclaimed.

"I was just trying to do you guys a favor," he answered, totally oblivious to the problems he'd created by moving the harmonicas without telling anyone.

I found Rich and told him what had happened.

"Oh, God, I feel like such an asshole," he said and ran over to the crew to stop them from unloading any more equipment.

I thought the crew leader might punch Rich, but instead he calmly told the guys to pack it all back up.

"I'm glad you found your harps," the crew leader told Rich.

"Sorry I shot my mouth off over there," he responded as the crew reloaded the trailer.

Happy to have that problem resolved, I went a backstage trailer that everyone was using for dressing and hanging out. I took a seat to gather my thoughts and relax.

All of a sudden Rusty came storming in. He was fuming.

"Those assholes lost my fanny pack!" he shouted. "Those fuckin' assholes lost my fanny pack! I had everything in there, my money, my ID, my passport! All my shit is in there!"

I let Rusty know what had happened to it. He ran out to the field and found the fanny pack right where I said it would be.

"I found it!" Rusty shouted, holding it up in the air.

Everything was in the fanny pack, except for six hundred dollars. The thief had left everything else. Rusty was out his money because Rich, in his rage, had overreacted. Rich agreed he had to come up with six hundred dollars, which was probably more than his harmonicas were worth.

I went by Rich's room the next day before I left town.

"I feel like I'm still a sixteen-year-old kid," he told me. "You'd think I would have acted a little more grown up."

"Don't be so hard on yourself," I said. "The amplifier guy didn't tell us about moving the harmonicas. One thing just seemed to lead to another."

We just stood there for a minute and thought about it. So ends the saga of the missing harmonicas and the flying fanny pack.

CHAPTER FORTY-FOUR

The Bermuda Triangle of Harmonica Touring

The Pensacola Coast offers some interesting gigs for a traveling bluesman, but there was one that was a definite mistake by even the lowest standards. It was 2005, and we played at a place called Paradise Isle on the gulf coast of Florida. Paradise Isle is a sleepy little ocean community with houses built right on the sand and an elevation below sea level. The streets have names like Canal Drive and Barrier Reef Road, and the air is heavy with the scent of saltwater.

The guy that booked the gig seemed friendly enough, but looks can be deceiving, especially in promoters. I didn't quite realize what we were in for down there on the outer edge of the Bermuda Triangle. We had arranged to play a day gig at Paradise Isle, and then that evening we were going to drive all the way to Key West and stay the night at the Green Parrot band house. It was going to be a bit hectic getting from place to place, but nothing that unusual for a Mark Hummel and the Blues Survivors road trip.

We got to Paradise Isle in the early afternoon, unloaded our equipment and put it on the stage. We finished the sound check early, and all was in good order. The bar fed us oysters and coconut shrimp dinners, and the food was good. We even splurged and had a dessert. At show time we were ready for bear and raring to go. They opened the door to the club at seven o'clock. Not one person showed up during the first twenty minutes. After half an hour, only five people had strolled in. After another forty-five minutes, the promoter, who had originally been a friendly guy, stalked over and snarled, "Where the hell are all your fans?"

"Like did you advertise the gig?" I asked. It was obvious he hadn't. The place was dead. Again the over-optimistic promoter had convinced himself that he could spare the advertising dollars and still folks would somehow show up. We ended up playing the gig to about ten people.

The weather added to the misery, as often happens along the gulf coast, when an ocean storm blew in. During our first set, it started pouring rain like it only does in Florida. There was an open hole in the middle of the bamboo ceiling, and all the downpour falling on the roof came washing in through the hole. Rainwater collected in the middle of the dance floor. There was a huge puddle right in front of the bandstand. Our ten fans made the best of it, situating themselves in pairs circling the little pond. Oddly enough, the band was really in a monstrous groove that night. We were really kicking it. Charles was channeling Robert Jr. Lockwood on the hollow-body guitar, and Marty and Wolf were right in the pocket on bass and drums. This got me going on harp, and we did one of the best sets of the tour for that tiny crowd. By the time we finished the last song of the first set, the crowd was clapping, hollering and dancing around the puddle. Everybody seemed happy, and we were doing our job of making the most of the night for the bar and the promoter. While we were talking a break, the rain stopped.

An older woman in her late sixties or early seventies got really excited by the energy of the first set. She stayed out on the dance floor, shaking her ancient booty in a chartreuse-and-yellow bikini she should never have been wearing. She seemed to be alone, but that didn't inhibit her and she couldn't stop dancing. The bartender began playing "Smooth," the hit song that Carlos Santana recorded. You'd know it if you heard it. Whoever was controlling the music at the bar kept repeating the song over and over during our breaks. The snow-top bikini woman got into it and kept dancing and singing along. "A little bit of this...a little bit of that," she sang along with the record, clicking her fingers and swaying her emaciated hip replacements. She appeared unaware that she had moved into the middle of the puddle on the dance floor, and kept dancing and waving her arms around above her head with increasingly enthusiasm. I wish I could say it was a bright moment, full of the passion of dance overcoming the inhibitions of old age, but for some reason it didn't feel like that. Actually, it was really depressing, like a scary ghost shaman doing a tribal dance from the nether world. One couple left, then another.

"She's death warmed over," the promoter hissed at me. "You better get your ass back up there and start playing before the whole crowd leaves!"

I wanted to say, "What whole crowd?" and, "Who are you telling to move his ass?" but I was trying to be more polite and understanding than I once had been. It's part of my ongoing growth and maturity as a performing artist and a human being. I felt sorry for the guy, in spite of his bad manners. He hadn't advertised the show like I'd asked him to do, and he was paying the price. I understood the anxiety because I've been there and done that. I didn't mind going ahead and doing what he asked, and I understood his foul mood. I just wanted to help if I could.

I called the fellows back up to the stage. As we prepared to begin the second set, the bartender stopped playing "Smooth." The not-quite-ready-for-primetime bikini dancer kept spinning around the floor, raising her arms over her head and twitching them at the few remaining folks in the club. "A little bit of this...a little bit of that," she rasped frantically after the music stopped playing over the speakers. She was on her own, singing without the record behind her. Another couple from our first set audience drifted out.

The old dancer ultimately hollered at us, "Why don't you guys play this song? Play this one: 'A little bit of this...a little bit of that.' Play the one they were just playing!"

At that moment, her little white tennis shoes slipped out from under her due to the slippery floor. Her feet shot up in the air, and her fragile thighs gave out, probably from all that dancing. She twisted in the air and slammed face down into the puddle. I gasped in horror thinking the old woman had killed herself right there in front of me. The two or three remaining customers from our first set audience quickly deserted the club.

The bartender and the promoter ran to the woman and rolled her over. She was still breathing but completely disoriented from the blow to her forehead. They half dragged and half carried her out of the standing water and put her on a chair next to the bar. The promoter hollered for me to start playing, waving his finger in a circle in the air.

"Maybe it will bring in some folks off the esplanade," he said hopefully. I have to say there is nothing in the world so strong as the "optimism and hope" of a struggling promoter!

As I got back up on the stage and started playing the second set, the place was empty. The staff and the promoter were our only audience, except for the bikini dancer who was slumped over a table with her head in her hands. A little while later, two guys in stiff white shirts arrived with an ambulance to pick her up. They stayed to listen to me sing and the band play for a few minutes. I thought she must be all right, because the ambulance crew didn't seem to be in any rush. Later, after the show, I asked the bartender what happened to the old woman in the bikini.

"What old woman in a bikini?" he responded with a straight, bored face.

That's when I knew I was in the Bermuda Triangle of Harmonica Touring!

We packed up our gear to head toward the next town. It was back down the blues highway to the Florida Keys to spend the night at the Green Parrot. That night, after we checked into the band house, I passed out after driving for half the night. I had a nightmare about an older woman in a bikini feeding me oysters and coconut shrimp. I woke up in a cold sweat and didn't quite know where I was for a few seconds. And that was the last time I played Paradise Isle.

CHAPTER FORTY-FIVE

The Blues Harmonica Blowouts/ Rolling Fork Revisited

I started my Blues Harmonica Blowouts in Berkeley, California, in 1991 at Ashkenaz Music and Dance Center. Ashkenaz was founded in 1973 by David Nadel, a local human-rights activist and folk dancer. Rick Estrin, Dave Wellhausen (now know as Dave Earl), Doug Jay and I were featured. It was on Martin Luther King Jr.'s birthday holiday, and about 150 people attended, which was a good turnout for a Sunday night.

David approached me after the show and said, "Let's do it again. Let's make this a regular thing." So it became an annual January event at Ashkenaz on the Sunday closest to the MLK holiday. By the late '90s, the blowouts had become so successful that I was able to bring in bigger names like Carey Bell, Kim Wilson, Billy Boy Arnold and Norton Buffalo in 1997 and '98. (Carey's passing in 2007 and Norton's in 2009 were great losses to the music world.)

After David Nadel's murder in 1996 by a drunk he'd ejected from the club, I moved the blowouts to a different venue. I had them at Kimball's East in Emeryville in 1997 and '98. When Kimball's was sold in '99, we moved to Yoshi's, the internationally renowned jazz club in Oakland, and have been doing them there every year since 2000. The first one at Yoshi's featured quite a lineup: Rod Piazza, Kim Wilson, Billy Branch, James Harman, Rick Estrin and guitarist Junior Watson. Every year I have expanded the blowouts to several more nightclubs and theaters. There would usually be shows in Berkeley, Santa Cruz, Sacramento and Chico. Eventually they became little tours, anywhere from five to twelve dates. That's what it has been ever since, all around California and sometimes Reno or Lake Tahoe in January or February. I have taken these shows out nationally and internationally since 2002 to even bigger ventures.

Some of the bigger names I've had on the blowouts over the years have been James Cotton, John Hammond, Huey Lewis, John Mayall and Charlie Musselwhite, along with, in alphabetical order, Billy Boy Arnold, Carey Bell, Big Al Blake, Billy Branch, Norton Buffalo, George "Mojo" Buford, William Clarke, Little Sammy Davis, Paul deLay, Carlos del Junco, Mark DuFresne, Keith Dunn, Johnny Dyer, Rick Estrin, Dennis Gruenling, Steve Guyger, James Harman, Doug Jay, Andy Just, Lazy Lester, Little Sonny, Lynwood Slim, Magic Dick, R.J. Mischo, James Montgomery, Sam Myers, Kenny Neal, Sugar Ray Norcia, Paul Oscher, Lee Oskar, Rod Piazza, Jerry Portnoy, Gary Primich, Snooky Pryor, Annie Raines, Jason Ricci, Curtis Salgado, Jumpin' Johnny Sansone, Andy Santana, Gary Smith, Willie "Big Eyes" Smith, Sugar Blue, Fingers Taylor, Watermelon Slim, Mark Wenner, Kim Wilson, Phil Wiggins and maybe a few others I've left out unintentionally.

The blowouts we did with Huey Lewis were big, sold-out shows. The ones with Cotton, Mayall, Musselwhite, and Kim Wilson also did really well. I try to vary the shows and have different combinations of musicians instead of repeating myself, but many people have returned over and over. I always try to find at least one ringer with a really unique take on the harp, hence Oskar, del Junco, Ricci, Wiggins, Lester, Buffalo, deLay and Blue.

I was really blown away that Huey Lewis and John Mayall wanted to do my shows. I had phoned Angela Strehli on a long shot to see if she could interest Huey in getting involved, and two weeks later I got a call from him saying he'd glad to do it. He said he knew who I was and that he was a big fan of many of the harp players I'd been having on the shows, many of whom were major harmonica icons when he started playing in '68. I approached Mayall at the Blues Awards in Memphis a few years back and said I'd been trying to contact him through his agent but heard nothing back. Mayall handed me his personal phone number and said he'd love to be on some shows. He was extremely easygoing to work with and a true gentleman to deal with. Anytime someone I was listening to as a kid signed on, I was gassed about it and felt like a major success had taken place.

Presenting older generation harp blowers like Cotton, Carey Bell, Little Sonny, Snooky Pryor, Sam Myers, Billy Boy Arnold, Mojo Buford and Lazy Lester on my blowouts has been the greatest reward for me. Cotton is a real icon to me because he's the last of the big influences on me and has had a major effect on the way blues harmonica is played today. The others—Little Walter, Big Walter Horton, Junior Wells, George "Harmonica" Smith, Jimmy Reed and the two Sonny Boy Williamsons—are, unfortunately, no longer with us. Huey was game to be part of the blowouts because it gave him an opportunity to work with Cotton.

There was a camaraderie that developed between the musicians on the blowouts. The 2002 show with Snooky Pryor, Sam Myers and Anson Funderburgh comes especially to mind. It was just the four of us in my van as we rode from gig to gig, the members of the Blues Survivors having taken their own vehicles. Snooky, Sam and Anson told some really classic stories to each other during the long hours in the van. Sam did probably the worst imitation of Charlie Musselwhite's drawl I've ever heard. Snooky and Sam had lived in Chicago back in the 1950s and knew many of the same characters. They came up with names of musicians I'd never even heard of, and I know who most of the Chicago blues guys in the '50s were. Many of musicians Snooky and Sam talked about probably never recorded and therefore are unknown to most of us.

The same thing happened in 2010 when Cotton, Buford, Paul Oscher and Willie "Big Eyes" Smith were together and reminisced about their days with Muddy Waters. The kinds of hotels they would stay in make my stories pale in comparison to some of their tales about life on the road in the '50s and '60s. They stayed at some funky places and had to pay for their own rooms out of the meager wages they made with Muddy. Many times there was no heat and windows were broken. People would try to break into their rooms because the locks wouldn't work or were missing altogether. They cooked their meals on hot plates in the rooms. Such tenacious perseverance made them true blues survivors.

We did a show in 2009 in Los Angeles near John Mayall's house. It was the second year in a row he'd done the blowout. I had been pumping him for information on Peter Green because I'm such an early Fleetwood Mac nut. John brought along a guitar he'd had made from a piece of driftwood that he played in the late '60s on albums like *Blues from Laurel Canyon*. Not only is John a talented musician who plays many instruments, but he's also quite an artist in other respects, such as writing and painting. He has illustrated many of his album covers, including the painting on the cover of *A Hard Road*. John brought along a group of photos of Peter Green, Mick Fleetwood and John McVie taken during the recording of that album. They're really awesome historical snapshots, and we were impressed that he would share them with us.

The shows with Magic Dick, Lee Oskar and Jerry Portnoy in 2006 were very important to me because Magic and Lee were both guys whose licks I learned note-for-note when I was a teenager in Los Angeles. I learned everything off the J. Geils and War albums back then. The fact that I was able to book Magic and Lee was an amazing thing, and playing next to them on stage has been quite an experience. The same goes for Cotton and Musselwhite. Those are two other guys that I really look up to. I've known Charlie for years now and am proud to call him a friend.

One the most gratifying things about doing these shows are the bonds and friendships I've been able to have with the many musicians. Some of them I'd just met, but most I've known for years. Either way, it's been hugely rewarding. Another major factor that inspires me to continue producing the blowouts is the response I get from the public. It's life-affirming to have people tell me that a particular show was one of the best musical programs they'd ever attended. I get that all the time.

Another great project we were able to create was the 2004 Muddy Waters tribute CD *Rolling Fork Revisited* released on Mountaintop Records. It was something that Johnny Dyer and I had talked about for a number of years before we were able to go into the studio and record it for Charles Putris's MountainTop Productions label. We recruited our old friends Francis Clay and Paul Oscher. Clay had played drums with Muddy on and off in the '50s and '60s, and Oscher was with Muddy from about '66 to '70. They knew Muddy's music backwards and forwards. It was one of Clay's last sessions before he passed away in 2008 at age 84.

We recorded sixteen Muddy songs and were stoked to have them come out so close to the originals especially the sound of the instruments and the way the music is layered. Johnny's voice is so dead-on to Muddy' style. It really blew everyone's mind to get the feel of those old records. We had Muddy's original recordings with us in the studio and listened to them before cutting our own versions. When we listened to the playbacks in the control booth, it was hard to tell the difference between his recordings and ours. "Is that the original or is that the take we just did?" we asked ourselves. That's how close everyone felt we had gotten to Muddy's sound. It was particularly gratifying that the musicians who'd worked with Muddy felt that way. *Rolling Fork Revisited* is an album that all the players involved—Rusty Zinn, Charles Wheal, Bob Welsh, Marty Dodson, Steve Wolf, Clay, Paul, Johnny and I—felt was one of the most musically rewarding projects we'd ever done.

CHAPTER FORTY-SIX

Why I Blow

This is where I explain to you why I would endure the life I've lived on the road to make a living as a blues harp player. My life is first and foremost music. I'm a blues evangelist, and it's like a religion to me. Playing music on a great night is like flying or really great sex; once you go there you want to go back for more. It's really an indescribable sensation when the music takes hold of you. I think that's what folks outside of music see and envy, that sheer joy we get when everything is right and we're firing on all cylinders.

Even the road is like that when you've been home for too long. It starts to call your name and you've got to go. My life since I started in music has been devoted to blues and harmonica. That's what I live for, and it's almost all I talk about. Ask anyone. My wife Alexis has to be a patient and tolerant person to put up with the likes of me.

When I was starting out on harmonica, I played along with LPs by Little Walter, Sonny Boy Williamson, Big Walter, James Cotton, Junior Wells, George Smith, Buster Brown, Sam Myers, Jimmy Reed, Junior Parker, Jerry McCain and others. I learned songs note-for-note until I had them down. That's how I developed a large arsenal of licks—by recreating the sounds, tones and chops that all those legends had. If it wasn't for those harp players, I don't think I could have developed the kind of dexterity I have. Whatever prowess I have on harmonica is really due to the old masters I copied. Little Walter is at the top of the list, and I still listen to his records over and over, trying to figure out what he was doing. Every time I listen to those records, I hear something I missed the first time, and I've been doing it now for over forty years.

I practiced playing along with records for hours at a time in my early days. I think my devotion to practicing when I was in my teens and early twenties made it possible for me to become a solid harmonica player who could play well with other musicians. It took a while to get my timing down as a player with other musicians. It's different from playing along with LPs. Once I had that down, I moved on to playing with more musicians.

I think when we're young we're more aggressive about seeking out playing situations with other musicians. We have the nerve to approach people that we really shouldn't be talking to because we're really not good enough. I notice that today. Many young musicians come up to me and ask to sit in. Are you really good enough sit in? I think to myself. With many them, the answer is no.

I didn't have the courage to go up to James Cotton, Paul Butterfield or Muddy Waters and ask to sit in. I'm kind of glad I never asked those guys to let me sit in. It just didn't seem appropriate. Famous bluesmen back then were always getting hit up by harmonica players wanting to sit in.

After I'd been playing for a while and built up an arsenal of licks, I grew tired of copying things note-for-note. I began learning to improvise. Seeing the Fabulous Thunderbirds for the first time back in 1978 and hearing Kim Wilson improvise as he did really made me to realize that I didn't have to do everything note-for-note off records. I noticed that, especially in California, most of us young harmonica players were copying their solos from old records. Hearing the T-Birds was a real revelation to me that I could improvise my solos.

Nowadays, I get kind of bored with trying to do something note-for-note. I get a kick out of inventing my own licks and solos. I'm always trying to top myself. It's important to make mistakes on stage when you're improvising, not purposely, but to try something different and just go for it. If you make a mistake, so be it.

All the greats have made mistakes. I've heard Little Walter get off time on some material, and I doubt he could remember half of what he played on record.

Another thing in my early years that was very exciting—and remains so—was playing with older musicians in blues clubs. I'd grown up playing music around my little white friends. Playing with guys like Cool Papa, Charles Houff, Sonny Rhodes, Johnny Waters, Sonny Lane, Jimmy McCracklin and Lowell Fulson after I moved to the Bay Area was such a blast. I got to play with many of the Chicago blues guys later on, including Luther Tucker, Eddie Taylor and Jimmy Rogers, as well as open shows for some of the people I'd been listening to for a long, long time, such as Paul Butterfield, Canned Heat, Elvin Bishop, Bonnie Raitt, Buddy Guy and Junior Wells and Albert King.

The first time I opened for Butterfield in 1981, he came up and complimented me. I was in shock. It was sad later on when I did another show with him and found out that he'd gone back to using drugs. He was a totally different person from the first time I'd played with him when he was clean and sober. Ironically, I wasn't sober the first time I played with him. I offered him cocaine and felt bad when he called it the most insidious drug on the planet. I'd call that a warning. I was sober the second time we played together but unfortunately he was not. Butterfield overdosed on heroin a year later.

One time I did a gig with Lowell Fulson at the VIS Club, a long gone ghetto club on Divisadero Street in San Francisco. The first three nights were very, very dead. Few people came to see him. Then, on the fourth night, a Saturday, the fans came out of the woodwork. Most of them were in their forties, fifties and sixties. Lowell was probably in his early sixties at that point. It was so cool to be on stage and watch him perform for many people who'd been following him since the 1940s and '50s. His singing and playing were great, and the audience responded to every lyric. It was a gig I will remember all my life. It was almost like being in a time machine, as Lowell and the audience went back to their younger selves.

Another especially memorable gig was the one with Jimmy Rogers in Reno after he'd screwed up in Sacramento a few days earlier. He was as sober as a judge in Reno and played just brilliantly, almost as if he was twenty-five again. Everybody was hitting the groove, and it was just one of those moments that you remember forever.

Those are the kind of moments that really, really stick with me, especially now that most of those guys are no longer with us. That's something the younger generation of musicians will never have the opportunity to do, because these blues giants are gone and can't be replaced. I and other musicians of my generation were so fortunate.

There are particular venues that we usually play at that really bring out the best vibe. There are certain towns and certain bars that have it. Chicago is always an awesome place to play. It's always fun because we are playing in the city that has a defined musical history. New Orleans is the same way, with such deep history, and New York, as well. There really is something about the musical ghosts of the past. Some musicians take it for granted. You get used to playing these places and don't give it any thought, but there's a vibe, a certain sound or an atmosphere of the rooms that had the older bluesmen played in regularly. You can feel it when you're in those places.

I played a place called Roadhouse Blues in Wichita, Kansas, a lot in the 1980s and '90s. Many of old big bands like Count Basie's and Jimmie Lunceford's once played the room, and Charlie Parker even made some live recordings there. Bonnie and Clyde apparently stayed at the old motel in back. These older venues with such rich histories inspire me as I'm performing.

Same deal when I played B.L.U.E.S. in Chicago. I always felt the spirits of the older bluesmen who had graced that tiny, dumpy stage and sang through the terrible PA system. It is one of those small clubs where the audience is right in your face, which I've always loved!

That's something about a small, intimate club that's really special. I love playing festivals, too, but the intimacy of a smaller, appreciative crowd is very rewarding.

WHY I BLOW

There are a few people who have made me nervous. The first several times I played in front of James Cotton really got to me. He'd be sitting there nonchalantly checking me out during the sound check, and I'd be thinking about all the guys that he had seen and worked with, like Muddy, Wolf, Little Walter and Big Walter and Sonny Boy. That's who I've got to measure up to, I'd be thinking onstage. That's a nerve-wracking feeling to have on a sound check, let alone on a gig. James probably wasn't giving it a thought, since he'd heard them all.

I opened for Junior Wells and Buddy Guy once. It was the same kind of intimidating feeling, but Junior was so special to me after our set. He came up and complimented me and did one of the coolest things that I've ever seen a performer do.

"How much is your record?" Junior asked.

"Its ten dollars," I said.

Junior snapped his fingers and got the promoter to come over.

"Give me ten dollars," he said.

It was priceless how Junior got ten bucks from the promoter to buy my album. In retrospect, I should have just given him one for all the licks I'd stolen off him.

It's such compliment when one of the old guys says he likes what you do. I do not take such things lightly. Working with so many of the great blues musicians I'd listened to as a teenager has been one of the biggest thrills of my life.

I have received great response from people about the Blowout and Meltdown CDs we've done. They usually buy all four: the three on Mountain Top and the last one on Electo-Fi. All those CDs are great examples of how wide the stylistic spectrum is on blues harmonica. Everybody who plays harmonica on those records has their own sound. Nobody sounds the same as another guy. You do get your own sound when you've played for thirty or forty years. Even if you've tried to copy guy's note-for-note, eventually you'll end up getting a sound that can be called your own. That's the miracle of making music, writing, acting or painting;

you find your own groove in what you do. Johnnie Taylor sounded identical to Sam Cooke early in his career but eventually developed his own sound. Ray Charles sounded like Charles Brown and Nat Cole in the beginning but sure came up with his own successful style. It's just something that's going to happen, because you can't be anybody else but yourself. That's the beauty of it. Hopefully, I've found my own sound.

Discography

Mark Hummel & the Blues Survivors 45 RPM Single

"Gotta Make a Change"/"Sugar Sweet" (Rockinitus R-101), 1981

Hummel, harmonica and vocals; Johnny Knox & Randy Rattray, guitars; Gary Rosen, bass; Pat O'Brian, drums

Produced by Mark Hummel at John Altman Recorders, San Francisco, CA

Mark Hummel & the Blues Survivors LPs

Playin' in Your Town (Rockinitus LP R-101), 1985

Hummel, harmonica & vocals; Brownie McGhee (as "Poor Walter"), guitar & harmony vocals; Pat Chase & Bill Kirchen, guitars; Tim Wagar, bass; Norman Winkler, drums, Kevin Zuffi, piano; Nancy Wright, saxophone; Brownie McGhee & Ronni Raines, background vocals

Produced by Mark Hummel, Carroll Peery & Steve O'Hara at John Altman Recorders, San Francisco, CA

High Steppin' (Double Trouble DT-3018), Dutch, 1987

Hummel, harmonica & vocals; Pat Chase, Frank Goldwasser, Anthony Paule, Randy Rattray & Ron Thompson, guitars; Gary Rosen, Karl Sevaried & Tim Wagar, bass; Jimi Bott, June Core, Linda

Gieger, Kenny Dale Johnson & Norman Winkler, drums; Jim Pugh & Kevin Zuffi, pianos; John Firmin & Nancy Wright, saxophones

Produced by Mark Hummel, Carroll Peery and Steve O'Hara at Dave Wellhausen Studios, San Francisco, CA

Up & Jumpin' (Rockinitus LP R-103), 1989

Hummel, harmonica & vocals; Sue Foley-guitar & vocals; Frank Goldwasser, Shorty Lenior, Buddy Reed & Ron Thompson, guitars; Mike Judge, Jon Penner & Tim Wagar, bass; Jimi Bott, Bob Grant, Kenny Dale Johnson & Mark Lignell, drums; Charles Brown (piano & vocals); Jim Pugh, Doug Rynak & Kevin Zuffi, pianos; John Firmin & Nancy Wright, saxophones

Produced by Mark Hummel & Gary Mankin at Dave Wellhausen Studios, San Francisco, CA

Sunny Day Blues (Deluxe Records D-8001), Italian, 1990

Hummel, harmonica & vocals ; Sue Foley, Frank Goldwasser, Randy Rattray, & Buddy Reed, guitars; Mike Judge, Jon Penner & Tim Wagar, bass; Bob Grant, Mark Lignell & Walter Shufflesworth, drums; Jim Pugh & Doug Rynak, pianos; Dona McGee, vocals

Produced by Mark Hummel, Gary Mankin & Tano Ro at Dave Wellhausen Studios, San Francisco, CA

Mark Hummel & the Blues Survivors CDs

Harmonica Party (Double Trouble DTCD-3021), Dutch, 1988

Hummel, harmonica & vocals; Pat Chase, Frank Goldwasser, Anthony Paule & Ron Thompson, guitars; Mike Judge, Gary Rosen, Karl Sevaried & Tim Wagar, bass; Jimi Bott, June Core, Linda Geiger, Kenny Dale Johnson & Norman Winkler, drums; Jim Pugh & Kevin Zuffi, pianos; John Firmin & Nancy Wright, saxophones; Nancy Wenstrom, background vocals

Produced by Mark Hummel & Gary Mankin at Dave Wellhausen Studios,, San Francisco, CA

Hard Lovin' 1990's (Double Trouble DTCD-3029), Dutch, 1991

Hummel, harmonica & vocals ; Frank Goldwasser, Rick Olivarez & Junior Watson, guitars; Mike Judge, Karl Sevaried, Tim Wagar & Burt Winn, bass; Jimi Bott, Kenny Dale Johnson & Willie Panker, drums; Jim Pugh &,Doug Rynak, pianos; John Firmin, saxophone; Dona McGee, vocals

Produced by Mark Hummel & Gary Mankin at Dave Wellhausen Studios, San Francisco, CA

Feel Like Rockin' (Flying Fish FF-70634), 1994

Hummel, harmonica & vocals; Sue Foley, Shorty Lenior, Brownie McGhee & Rusty Zinn, guitars; Marc Carino, Jon Penner &Ronnie James Weber, bass; Mark Bohn, Jimi Bott & Bob Grant, drums; Charles Brown, piano & vocal; Jim Monroe and Jim Pugh, piano; Oscar Meyer, trumpet; Gino Landry, saxophone; Rick Estrin, harmonica

Produced by Rick Estrin at Dave Wellhausen Studios, San Francisco, CA

Married to the Blues (Flying Fish FF—70647), 1995

Hummel, harmonica & vocals ; Duke Robillard & Rusty Zinn, guitars; Vance Elhers, bass; Lance Dickerson & Jim Overton, drums; Steve Lucky & Jim Pugh, pianos; John Firmin & Rob Sudduth, saxophones; Charlie Musselwhite, harmonica

Produced by Mark Hummel, Rusty Zinn & Gary Mankin at Dave Wellhausen Studios, San Francisco, CA

Heart of Chicago (Tone Cool TC-1158), 1997

Hummel, harmonica & vocals ; Billy Flynn, Steve Freund & Dave

Myers, guitars; Bob Stroger, bass; Willie "Big Eyes" Smith, drums; Barrelhouse Chuck, piano

Produced by Steve Freund at Riverside Studios, Chicago, IL

Low Down To Uptown (Tone Cool TC-1169), 1998

Hummel, harmonica & vocals; Junior Watson, Monster Mike Welch & Charles Wheal, guitars; Mike McCurdy & Ronnie James Weber, bass; Mark Bohn & June Core, drums; Charles Brown, Steve Lucky & David Maxwell, pianos; Terry Hanck & Robb Sudduth, saxophones; Brenda Boykin, vocals

Produced by Richard Rosenblatt at Tone Cool Studios, Boston, MA, and by Mark Hummel at Dave Wellhausen Studios, San Francisco, CA, and Bay Records, Berkeley, CA

Harmonica Party—Vintage Mark Hummel (Mountain Top IV), 1999

Hummel, harmonica & vocals; Pat Chase, Rick Oliverez, Anthony Paule, Curtis Smith & Rusty Zinn, guitars; Marc Carino, Karl Sevaried, Tim Wagar & Ronnie James Weber, bass; Jimi Bott, Mark Bohn, June Core, Kenny Dale Johnson, Willie Panker & Norman Winkler, drums; Jim Monroe, Jim Pugh, Doug Rynak & Kevin Zuffi, pianos; John Firmin & Nancy Wright, saxophones

Produced by Mark Hummel & Gary Mankin at Dave Wellhausen Studios, San Francisco, CA

Blues Harp Meltdown (Mountain Top CDMT101), 2001

Mark Hummel, Billy Branch, Rick Estrin, James Harman, R.J. Mischo, Gary Smith & Kim Wilson, harmonica & vocals; Kirk "Eli" Fletcher, Junior Watson & Charles Wheal, guitars; Marc Carino & Steve Wolf, bass; June Core, Marty Dodson & Jimmy Milleniux, drums

Produced by Mark Hummel at Moe's Alley, Santa Cruz, CA

Golden State Blues (Electro-Fi E-fi 3375), 2002

Hummel, harmonica & vocals; Anson Funderburgh, Charles Wheal & Rusty Zinn, guitars; Randy Bermudes & Steve Wolf, bass; Marty Dodson & Paul Revelli, drums; Steve Lucky, keyboards; John Firmin & Robb Sudduth, saxophones

Produced By Mark Hummel, Jim Day & Charles Wheal at Jim Day Studios, Pacifica, CA.

Blues Harp Meltdown, Vol. 2: East Meets West (Mountain Top MT-102), 2003

Mark Hummel, Johnny Dyer, R.J. Mischo, Annie Raines, Gary Primich & Gary Smith, harmonica & vocals; Frank "Paris Slim" Goldwasser, harmonica, guitar & vocals; Paul Richell, guitar & vocals; Charles Wheal, guitar; Steve Wolf, bass; June Core & Marty Dodson, drums

Produced by Mark Hummel at Moe's Alley, Santa Cruz, CA

Blowin' My Horn—Mark Hummel Live (Electro-Fi E-fi 3386), 2004

Hummel, harmonica & vocals; Charles Wheal, guitar; Steve Wolf, bass; Marty Dodson, drums; Mel Brown, keyboards

Recorded at the Silver Dollar, Toronto, ON, and the Slye Fox, Burlington, ON

Ain't Easy No More (Electro-Fi E-fi 3398), 2006

Hummel, harmonica & vocals; Charles Wheal, guitar; Steve Wolf, bass; Marty Dodson, drums; Bob Welsh,keyboards; Mike Rinta, trombone; Scott Peterson, saxophone

Produced by Mark Hummel & Jim Day at Jim Day Studios, Pacifica,CA

Legends: Blues Harp Meltdown, Vol. 3 (Mountain Top MT103), 2006

Hummel, Carey Bell, Lazy Lester & Phil Wiggins, harmonica & vocals; Willie "Big Eyes" Smith, harmonica, drums & vocals; John Cephas & Steve Freund, guitar & vocals; Charles Wheal, guitar; Bob Welsh, guitar & piano; Steve Wolf, bass; Marty Dodson, drums

Produced by Mark Hummel at Moe's Alley, Santa Cruz, CA

Odds & Ends (Rockinitus RR-1004), 2009

Hummel, harmonica & vocals; Sue Foley, guitar & vocals; Kid Anderson, Pat Chase, Frank Goldwaser, Ronnie Jacobsen, Randy Rattray, Buddy Reed & Ron Thompson, guitars; Mike Judge, Gary Rosen, Kedar Roy, Karl Sevaried & Tim Wagar, bass; Jimi Bott, June Core, Marty Dodson, Kenny Dale Johnson, Mark Lignell & Bill Zelinski, drums; Charles Brown, Sid Morris, Jim Pugh, Doug Rynak & Kevin Zuffi, pianos; John Firmin & Nancy Wright, saxophones

Recorded in San Francisco & Santa Cruz, CA, 1982-2006

Mark Hummel's Chicago Blues Party (Mountain Top MTP-0013), 2009

Hummel, harmonica & vocals; Jimmy Rogers, Eddie Taylor, Luther Tucker & Mississippi Johnny Waters, guitar & vocals; Sonny Lane, Randy Rattray & Rusty Zinn, guitars; Gary Rosen, John Schmitt, Lex Silva & Tim Wager, bass; Mark Bohn, Jimi Bott, Jim Carrington, Francis Clay & Bill Zelinski, drums; Tom Mahon, piano

Recorded in San Francisco & Berkeley, CA, 1980-1992

Mark Hummel's Blues Harmonica Blowout: Still Here and Gone (ElectroFi-E-fi 3410), 2009

Hummel, James Harman, Billy Boy Arnold, Carey Bell, William Clarke, Paul deLay, Johnny Dyer, Rick Estrin, Lazy Lester, Magic Dick & Sam Myers, harmonica & vocals; Lee Oskar, harmonica; Steve

Freund, Anson Funderburgh, Junior Watson, Charles Wheal & Rusty Zinn, guitars; Bob Welsh, guitar & piano; Vance Ehlers & Steve Wolf, bass; Jim Overton, Marty Dodson & Willie "Big Eyes" Smith, drums

Produced by Mark Hummel in Berkeley, Oakland, Chico & Santa Cruz, CA, 1993-2007

Retro-Active (Electro-Fi E-fi 3417), 2010

Hummel, harmonica & vocals; Steve Freund, Charlie Musselwhite, Charles Wheal & Rusty Zinn, guitars; Vance Elhers, R.W. Grigsby, Burt Winn & Steve Wolf, bass; Lance Dickerson, Marty Dodson, Willie Panker & Paul Revelli, drums; Chris Burns, Steve Lucky & Bob Welsh, keyboards; Lech Wierzynski, trumpet; Johnny Bones, saxophone; Kid Anderson, mandolin & kick drum

Produced by Mark Hummel & Kid Anderson at Jim Day Studios, Pacifica, CA, and by Mark Hummel at Dave Wellhausen Studios, San Francisco, CA

Back Porch Music—Mark Hummel Unplugged (Mountain Top), 2011

Hummel, harmonica & vocals; Rusty Zinn, guitar; Bob Welsh, guitar & piano; R.W. Grigsby, bass

Produced by Mark Hummel, Kid Anderson & Charles Putris at Greaseland Studios, San Jose, CA

Mark Hummel as sideman, playing harmonica on
45 RPM Singles

Boogie Jake: "Automobile Blues"/"The Boogie Train" (Blues Connoisseur 1014), 1976

Boogie Jake, guitar & vocals; Eddie Ray, guitar; Reggie Scanlon, bass; Jerry Robinson, drums

Produced by Schoolboy Cleve in San Francisco, CA

Bob Kelton: "Grandpa Said"/"Race Track Blues" (Rhodes-Way 3902), 1979

Robert Kelton, guitar & vocals; Sonny Lane, guitar; Lex Silva, bass; Gary Hines, drums

Produced by Sonny Rhodes in Albany, CA

Mississippi Johnny Waters & the Blues Survivors: "I'm Wondering Woman"/"You Can Look for Me Woman" (Rhodes-Way 3903), 1979

Waters, guitar & vocals; Sonny Lane, guitar; Lex Silva, bass; Gary Hines, drums

Produced by Sonny Rhodes in Albany, CA

45 RPM EP

Mississippi Johnny Waters & the Blues Survivors: "I Can't Hang"/"Living with the Blues"/"I Left My Home"/"I Just Keep Loving Her"(Tree Of Hope Records TH-101), 1981

Waters, guitar (vocals on "I Can't Hang" & "Left My Home"); Hummel, harmonica (vocals on ("Living with the Blues"& "Just Keep Loving Her"); Sonny Lane, guitar; Lex Silva, bass; Walter Shufflesworth, Gary Hines, drums

Produced by Barry Broadbent at Sierra Sound Labs, Berkeley, CA

LPs

Charles Houff: "Sooner or Later" on *San Francisco Blues Festival. Vol. 2* (Solid Smoke SS-8010), 1981

Houff, vocals; Ron Thompson, guitar; Gary Rosen, bass; Gary Hines, drums

Recorded in Golden Gate Park, San Francisco, CA, 1978

Brownie McGhee: *Facts of Life* (Blue Rock'it BRLP-104), 1985

McGhee, vocals & guitar; Robben Ford, guitar; Steve Erhman, bass; Patrick Ford, drums; Clay Cotton, piano; Mark Ford, harmonica

Produced by Patrick Ford at Oasis Studios, San Francisco, CA

CDs

Robert Plunkett: four tracks on *Blues Across America: The Chicago Scene* (Cannonball-CBD 29204), 1997

Produced by Twist Turner at Twist Turner Studios, Chicago, IL

Too Slim and the Taildraggers: Three tracks on *King Size Trouble* (Burnside BCD 0041-2), 2000

Produced by Too Slim & the Taildraggers at VU Music Studios, Spokane, WA

Kid Anderson: Three tracks on *Rock Awhile* (Blue Soul MBA2312), 2003

Produced by Kid Anderson at Magic Sound Studios, Santa Cruz, CA

Dave Specter & Steve Freund: One track on *What It Is* (Delmark DE-779)

Produced by Dave Specter at Riverside Studios, Chicago, IL

Johnny Dyer & Mark Hummel: *Rolling Fork Revisited* (Mountain Top MTPCD-201). 2004

Dyer, vocals & harmonica; Paul Oscher, harmonica & guitar; Charles Wheal & Rusty Zinn, guitars; Bob Welsh, guitar & piano; Vance Elhers & Steve Wolf, bass; Francis Clay & Marty Dodson, drums

Produced by Mark Hummel at Headless Budda Studio, Oakland, CA

Jimi Bott: "Peter Gunn" on *Cheap Thrills* (Roseleaf RL001), 2005

Pat Chase & Luther Tucker, guitars; Tim Wagar, bass; Bott, drums

Recorded at the Chi Chi Club, San Francisco, CA, 1985

Canned Fish (AKA Canned Heat): "The Dance of the Inhabitants of the Palace of King Phillip XIV of Spain" on *The Revenge of Blind Joe Death: The John Fahey Tribute Album* (Takoma TAKCD-30048-25), 2006

Produced by Jon Monday at Fantasy Studios, Berkeley, CA

Anthologies

Blooze & Boogie: Blues Dance Party (Wax Museum CD-9302), 1990, two tracks

Got Harp if You Want It (Blue Rock'it BRCD-111), 1991, one track

Texas Harmonica Rumble,Vol. 2 (New Rose FCD 103), French, 1992, two tracks

Blues Harp Greats (Easydisc EDCD 7023), 1997, one track

Mean Street Blues (Biscuits & Blues MSCD0001), 1997, one track

Live at the Boston Blues Festival (Blues Trust BTP-101), 2001, one track

San Francisco Bay's Best Blues, Vol.1 (Raw Records 673843040429), 2002, one track

This Is Blues Harmonica,Vol. 2 (Delmark DE-780), 2004, one track

Blues Survivors from 1976-2011

GUITAR

Mississippi Johnny Waters
Sonny Lane
J.J. Jones
Johnny Knox
Randy Rattray
Pat Chase
Anthony Paule
Buddy Reed
Rusty Zinn
Curtis Smith
Joel Foy
Chris Masterson
Charles Wheal
Bob Welsh

BASS

Bob Klien
Lex Silva
Frank DeRose
Tim Wagar
Gary Rosen
Mike Judge
Burt Wynn

Marc Carino
Ronnie James Weber
Flaco Medina
Vance Elhers
Randy Bermudes
Steve Wolf
Richard Grigsby

PIANO

Bob Welsh
Doug Rynack

DRUMS

Gary Hines
Linda Gieger
Bill Zelinski
Norman Winkler
Jimi Bott
June Core
Willie Panker
Jim Overton
Mark Bohn
Pacemaker Bob Newham
Marty Dodson
Lance Dickerson
Jimmy Mullenuix

HONORARY members(plenty of gigs/recordings)

Kenny Dale Johnson
Chris Burns
Wes Starr

BLUES SURVIVORS FROM 1976-2011

Josh Fulero
Frank Goldwasser
Walter Shufflesworth
Paul Revelli
Kedar Roy
Robbie Bean
Junior Watson
Bill Campbell
Ron Thompson
Kevin Zuffi
Jim Pugh
Karl Sevareid
Lee Hildebrand
Steve Freund
Sue Foley
Jon Penner
Shorty Lenior
Mick Kilgos
Bob Grant
Steve Lucky
Mark Thiace
Little Charlie Baty

Thank-You's

My wonderful wife Alexis Hummel(for her being there for me and giving much needed advice on this first effort!)

Beth Grigsby(for her time consuming transcriptions and early editing that was so valuable to this book!)

My parents,Ed & Joann, for guiding me thru life & being wonderful examples

My loving brothers,Kirk & Peter

My beautiful funny,smart daughter,Julia

Lisa Butler(for her editing suggestions)

Betz Girourard(for being a first rate webmaster & loyal support)

Greg Baert(a hard working and honest as he can be booking agent)

Andrew Galloway(for unwavering support)

My kids,Daina and Carly and grandkids, Bailey and Aiden ,you too Chad!

The Horton family, Gene, Val, Bob, Jim and everyone else

Mark Overman

Greg Huemann at Blows Me Away productions

Dave Earl and Janet Wellhausen

Marty Dodson

RW Grigsby

Steve Malerbi (best Chromatic tech around)

Dave Barrett (getting me in on www.bluesharmonica.com)

Rupert Oysler (for Seydel Harps)

Sonny Junior. aka Gary Onofrio (best new old amp maker)

Karen Leipziger(for pushing my name out there as a first class publicist!)

Paul Benjamin

Ted Todd

Marley Walker

Tom Mazzolini

Chef Deni

Cholo Willsin

Brad Stewart/Dynamic Artists

Michael Morris at Rosebud

David Bernsten

Debra Ragar

Bill Wax

Carroll Perry

Yoshi's

Bob Littel

THANK-YOU'S

Bobby Ray Bishop

John and Starr Peterson

Larry the Iceman

Barbara Dane

Mike Fernald

Steve Brundies

Larry Boemer

Raoul Bhaneja

Dale Akins

Brian Phillips

Dave Walker & Rick Nicotra

Bob Welsh

Rusty Zinn

Magic Dick

Rick Estrin

Lee Oskar

John Mayall

Huey Lewis

The Musselwhites

Billy Boy Arnold

The Cottons

James Harman

Pike & Lazy Lester

Billy Branch

Anson Funderburgh

Wes Starr

Mike Morgan

Chuck Gurney

Aki Kumar

Lee Hildebrand

Dennis Gruendling

John Hammond

Regina Charboneau

Roger Nebar

Pete Waters

Gil Anthony

Gary Antone

Dan Bringman

Steve Freund

Dick Shurman

Sean Carney

Al Chessis

THANK-YOU'S

John Clifton

Frank Goldwasser

Susan Collier

James Day

Bernie Clarke

Jeannette & Joe Lodovici

Joe Filisko

Cam & Carol Hayden

Peter North

Ray Helshir

Jim Flynn

Flavio Guitimares

Fingers Taylor

Rune Myrhen

Mark DuFresne

Kim Field

Kid Anderson

Good Rockin' Derral

Friends of Bill

Bread & Roses Org.

Jim Johnson

BIG ROAD BLUES-12 BARS ON I-80

Kurt Huget-

Adrian Costa

Curtis Salgado

Scott Cramer

Sugar Ray Norcia

Ingram Content Group UK Ltd.
Milton Keynes UK
UKHW040710080323
418175UK00001B/31